The Air War in the Dardanelles

John Oliver

Copyright © 2017 John Oliver
All rights reserved.
ISBN-13: 978-1978001640
ISBN-10: 1978001649

Email author: john.oliver65@aol.co.uk

This book is copyright. No part of it may be reproduced, stored in a retrieval system or transmitted in any form or by any means without the prior written permission of the publisher.

All photographs are from the author's collection

By the same author:

Samson and the Dunkirk Circus: 3 Squadron Royal Naval Air Service, 1914 - 15

Contents

Map of area of operations Facing page	1
Introduction: The air war in the Dardanelles	1
Chapter one: The move to Tenedos, February-March 1915	6
Chapter two: Tenedos, April 1915	28
Chapter three: May 1915	58
Chapter four: June and July 1915	82
Chapter five: August 1915	112
Chapter six: September 1915	134
Chapter seven: October to December 1915	155
Conclusion	183
Appendix one: Description of portable buildings required by squadrons in the Dardanelles	188
Appendix two: Extracts from 3 Wing Standing Orders, December 1915	190
Appendix three: Ranks of officers in the RNAS in the Dardanelles, 1915	194
Bibliography	195
Index	198

Illustrations

Between pages 154-155

1. Commander Charles Rumney Samson on his horse, 'Nigger', in Tenedos village
2. Flight Commander C H Collet in a DFW Mars, c1914
3. Flight Commanders Marix and Thompson on Tenedos, Gallipoli, July 1915
4. Squadron Commander R Bell Davies
5. HMS Ark Royal
6. Ark Royal and Short seaplane Type 166 with Union flag national insignia
7. Deck view of crane at work with Sopwith Schneider seaplane, Ark Royal
8. Short Type 184 torpedo bomber seaplane
9. Unloading a Maurice Farman aeroplane
10. Unloading aeroplanes at Tenedos.
11. Taking aircraft up to the airfield from the beach on Tenedos
12. Reggie Marix with his Farman
13. Samson with his Nieuport
14. Samson enjoying a quiet moment
15. Building gun pits for anti-aircraft guns
16. HMS Manica with her balloon emerging from the hold
17. HMS Hector
18. Balloon aloft, showing observers' basket
19. HMS Ben-my-Chree, showing the large hangar-space aft
20. Short Type 184 with roundel insignia alongside Ben-my-Chree
21. No 856, Type 860, taxiing away from Ben-my-Chree
22. Sir Ian Hamilton's HQ on Imbros
23. 3 Wing's airfield on Imbros
24. 2 Wing's airfield on Imbros
25. An unfortunate pilot falls victim to Imbros' crosswinds
26. An Avro 504B sent to No. 3 Wing at Imbros in late August 1915
27. Henri Farman F27, No. 3 Wing, Imbros
28. Maurice Farman No 33
29. A Voisin at rest
30. 3 Squadron aircraft with one of their home-made bombs
31. Samson about to take off with the first 500lb bomb
32. Samson in his Nieuport

In memory of the officers and men of the Royal Naval Air Service, 1911-1918

So much courage, innovation and ability so often forgotten

For my long suffering partner, without whose help this book would never have been written. She put up with being dragged off for days on end to the National Archive and never once complained. She also sub-edited my manuscript.

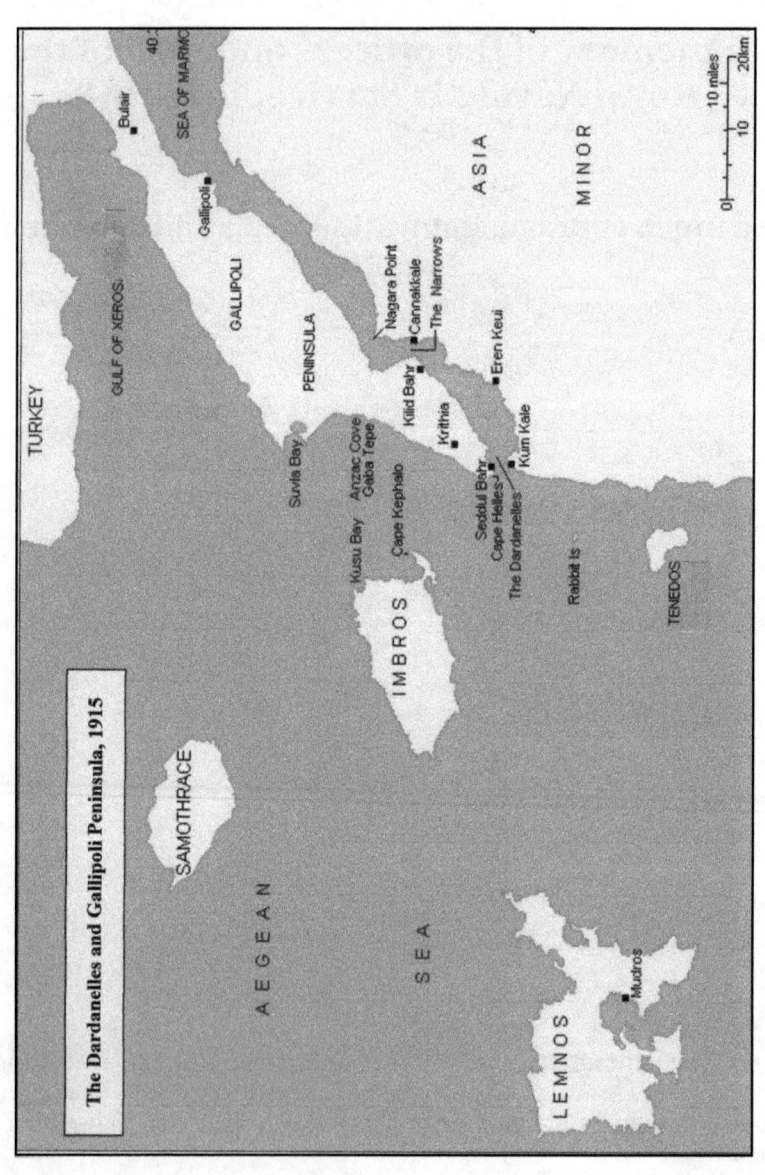

Introduction
The air war in the Dardanelles

The Dardanelles/Gallipoli campaign from February 1915 to January 1916 in the First World War was a single action but in two parts. The Dardanelles was the naval action when the Royal Navy, supported in a small way by the French and also some Russian and Australian ships, tried to force the channel of that name leading from the Mediterranean to Istanbul and the Black Sea and make Turkey surrender. In this they failed. And when the Navy failed to overcome the Ottoman defences, an invasion of the Gallipoli peninsula was launched by the Allies, using British, French and ANZAC (Australian and New Zealand Army Corps) troops to reach the Turkish capital by land. In this action, the Gallipoli campaign, the naval forces played a supporting role.

The Dardanelles operation was strongly supported by Winston Churchill, then First Lord of the Admiralty, and Lord Kitchener, Secretary of State for War. They felt that if the campaign was successful and Turkey was knocked out of the war, then the whole enemy alliance of Germany, Austria-Hungary and Turkey might well come tumbling down like a house of cards. The naval bombardment began on 19th February 1915 but was halted by bad weather and did not resume until 25th February. Demolition parties of Royal Marines landed almost unopposed and knocked out some Turkish guns, but bad weather again intervened and called a halt to the operation. The bombardment did not recommence until 18th March. The attempt to force the straits by naval action alone used mostly obsolete warships and those too old for Fleet action. However, after three battleships had been sunk and three others damaged, the Navy abandoned its attack, concluding that the fleet could not succeed without the help of the Army. Landings began on the Gallipoli Peninsula in two places on 25th April, at Cape Helles (29th British Infantry Division and the Royal Naval Division) and at ANZAC beaches. A French brigade landed at Kum Kale on the Anatolian coast opposite, but was later withdrawn. By September it was clear that without further large reinforcements, there was no hope of decisive results. Lieutenant General Sir Charles Monro took over command in October and recommended the withdrawal of all the military forces and abandonment of the campaign. His advice was acted on.

The Royal Naval Air Service (RNAS) supported both the land and sea operations with daily reconnaissance, bombing, photographic and spotting flights for the naval bombardment. It put quite a strain on their resources. However, if ever a man was suited to undertake such a task and lead a squadron to do the same, it was Commander Charles R Samson. As commander of a RNAS unit in France and Belgium, he had not only utilised the small number of aircraft at his disposal to their utmost but had also had major input into developing the armoured car, self-propelled gun and armoured personnel carrier and introducing them to British military life. A charismatic leader, bent on taking the war to the enemy with whatever he could lay his hands on, he inspired his men to follow his lead. Unfortunately, the resources they obtained were sometimes appropriated from other units – hence their nickname of 'The Motor Bandits'.

With very little notice and no reason given, Samson received orders on 25th February 1915, that his squadron was being relieved at Dunkirk and brought back to Britain. No 3 Squadron was devastated, officers and men alike. At that time, it was the most experienced and most decorated British unit in France and Belgium, both in the air and on the ground, with more combat experience than any other British aviation unit on the Western Front at the time. It had a maximum strength of some 500 men, a mix of RNAS and Royal Marines, and had, incidentally, developed an excellent way of spotting for the big guns of the Dover Patrol off the Belgian coast. While the Belgians and French would miss this unit, the Germans would be delighted they were gone but still would not remove the bounty they had put on their heads. However, the Royal Navy desperately needed Samson and his squadron in the Dardanelles to support the naval action. It was being replaced in Dunkirk by No 1 Squadron RNAS, half-trained and with very little combat experience, commanded by Wing Commander Arthur Longmore.

Samson tried to phone Commodore Murray Sueter, the head of the RNAS, to find out what was happening and why, but all he got was the run-around and told not to worry. For the next few days the men packed up the camp, settled bills and said some very sad farewells. The rumours were rife: they were going back to carry out coastal patrols or - the worst thing possible - becoming a training squadron. Samson did learn from Murray Sueter that they would not be in England long before they were to go to foreign parts but for now he and his squadron were to report to Dover. He was ordered to return to England with all serviceable aircraft and transport but to leave behind all his armoured vehicles and guns. Some of the officers and men were hoping for a spot of leave as they had been on active service for around six months without a break. A number of them were over-tired and run-down and a chance to see their families would be really good.

The Dardanelles/Gallipoli air operation was, of course, far larger than Samson and his men could carry out on their own so other brand-new units of the Royal Navy and the RNAS were brought in to help. The first to arrive was HMS 'Ark Royal', the first designed and built aircraft carrier in the Royal Navy. It carried seaplanes, underpowered machines that very often could not carry out the duties assigned to them, which led to the Navy feeling they had been let down by the RNAS. The answer was to send for Samson and his men - urgently. No 3 Squadron moved to the island of

Tenedos and began operating eighteen aircraft in support of the Gallipoli Campaign. In the first weeks of the campaign they took over 700 photographs of the peninsula using a hand-held camera and conducted other ground support tasks, including spotting for naval gunfire, reporting the movements of Turkish troops and, of course, dropping over 100 bombs. On 21st June 1915, the squadron was renamed No 3 Wing RNAS and a little later was moved to Imbros. Its epic achievements continued: on 19th November, during a raid against a railway junction near the Maritsa River in Bulgaria, Squadron Commander Richard Bell Davies won the Victoria Cross for landing and rescuing a pilot who had been shot down in the face of intense enemy fire.

The next new RNAS unit to arrive in the Dardanelles was HMS 'Manica', a kite balloon ship. This overcame the problem that there was no room to raise a spotting balloon on land by putting it on a ship, and proved to be a great success. It was followed by two more kite balloon ships. But first the Navy had to overcome the problem that the sausage-shaped kite balloon was not known in Britain and no one had seen one, except for the personnel of 3 Squadron. In Britain at this time the only observation balloons were small spherical ones used by the Royal Engineers in the Boer War which started in 1899. The Balloon Section went on active service for the first time and its operational successes led to the demand for greatly increased production by the Balloon Factory. Along with the pressures of operating under war conditions and the need for new equipment, the Factory developed two new classes of balloon. These were still in service with the British Army at the start of the First World War but very susceptible to rain and wind. They also had no control in the air and were a failure in France in 1914. Samson had seen a Belgian kite balloon that could operate in all weathers and demonstrated it to an RNAS balloon section that had come over to Dunkirk. The design was taken back to Britain and copied. 'Manica' was so very successful at directing fall of shot for the battleships that the Navy sent three kite balloons to the Dardanelles in all. They flew 120 missions, just 5% of the total flown by the RNAS, but each a mission that would last for some 8-10 hours. As soon as the Turks saw a kite balloon rise up out of its ship, their artillery would go silent and be pulled back into cover. Two Sea Scout airships, another brand new weapon system for hunting submarines that was developed in action, were also sent out and proved a great success. Yet again the RNAS were leading the way.

A greatly improved aircraft carrier called the 'Ben-my-Chree', with far better aircraft and greater speed, came out to the Dardanelles in June to support the Gallipoli Campaign. This was typical of the RNAS. They did not sit around waiting for a scientist or an engineer to develop a new weapon or way of delivering it like all the other services involved on the British side during the Great War - they went out and did it themselves, then showed others how to do it. One of her aircraft made the first ship-launched aerial torpedo attack on a ship in August 1915. After Gallipoli was evacuated at the end of the year, 'Ben-my-Chree' became flagship of the East Indies and Egypt Seaplane Squadron that operated in the Eastern Mediterranean.

The number of innovations in aviation that the RNAS were responsible for in the early days of the First World War was incredible. Nothing seemed to faze the best of its officers and men: they were given an order and found a way to carry it out. In the case of No 3 Squadron, they very quickly discovered that the small 20lb Cooper bomb was too small to do any real damage and swiftly moved up to the 100lb, until then mostly carried by RNAS seaplanes. Samson even managed to stagger into the air with a 500lb bomb, built by him and his squadron, and drop it on the enemy. Once in the Dardanelles, they also mounted machine guns on a number of their aircraft to convert them into fighters to attack the German Taube bombers and later to try to engage the Fokker Eindecker monoplane. Samson and his men still had a price on their heads but this time they would only fight in the air. The days of charging around the countryside in their armoured cars shooting up Germans had long gone but developing new weapons and ways of fighting was still very much in the forefront of the RNAS.

The main task of the RNAS at Gallipoli was that of intelligence gathering, either by a pilot and observer making out a report or by handing over a film for developing. They would carry out daily photographic reconnaissance missions and, in the first few weeks of landing on Tenedos, had taken some 700 photographs, which they tried to pass on to the Army. Here, success depended on the officer in command. One man in particular, Major-General Aylmer Hunter-Weston, commander of the 29th Division, felt aerial photography was a waste of time and would not even look at the photographs of the Turkish positions taken by the RNAS he and his officers were shown, considering them forgeries. The division landed at five beaches around Cape Helles at the tip of the peninsula. Three of the landings faced little or no opposition but were not exploited. The two main landings, at V and W Beaches on either side of the Cape, met with fierce Turkish resistance and the landing battalions were decimated. If ever there was a case of lions led by donkeys, this was it. Hunter-Weston was described by his superior Sir Douglas Haig as a "rank amateur", and earned the reputation "as one of the most brutal and incompetent commanders of the First World War". But more about him later.

To be fair, the initial disbelief is understandable as a lot of the senior officers had never seen anything like these pictures but Samson took a number up for their first-ever flight in an aeroplane to convince them that they were real and genuinely of the Turkish positions. The most open-minded took to the new technology with gusto and incorporated it in their plans. It was prejudiced dinosaurs like Hunter-Weston who refused to understand - and condemned their troops to needless massacres. The RNAS really came into its own when they delivered reports and pictures of the massing of the Turkish 5th Army in front of the ANZAC lines. They gave these men the warning and support they required not just to stop, but to help destroy the Turkish attack, which would not be repeated until January 1916 when the Turks attacked - and discovered the empty ANZAC trenches.

The role of the Royal Navy at Gallipoli was to support the landings, using naval guns instead of field artillery, of which there was a severe shortage in 1915. However, with a few spectacular exceptions, the performance of naval guns on land targets was very poor, particularly against infantry in entrenched positions and artillery dug in or placed in the old forts. The ships' guns lacked elevation so fired on a flat trajectory which, coupled with the inherently unstable gun platform, resulted in poor accuracy. However, the guns did prove effective against exposed lines of troops. On 27th April, during the first Turkish counter-attack at Anzac, the Turkish 57th Regiment attacked down the seaward slope of Battleship Hill within view of 'Queen Elizabeth' which fired a salvo of six fifteen-in (380mm) shells, halting the attack completely. On 28th April, near the old Y Beach landing, 'Queen Elizabeth' sighted a party of about one hundred Turks. One fifteen-in (380mm) shrapnel shell containing twenty-four thousand steel pellets was fired at short range and killed the entire party. For the rest of the campaign, the Turks were very wary of moving within view of battleships. All the Allied forces suffered from chronic shortages of artillery shells. The battleships had very few high explosive shells so used solid shot, which was designed to attack other battleships and not stone or dirt forts. The Army guns were limited to two rounds per day and, like the Navy, were very short of high explosive shells. They attempted to cut wire with shrapnel shells, which proved to be a great failure.

The RNAS experience in the Dardanelles/Gallipoli campaign can be characterised by experimentation and an attitude of make do and mend. The home-made 500lb bomb and incendiary devices, and parachute mines to destroy the Nagara anti-submarine net. The development of the 'Ark Royal' and 'Manica' while carrying out their duties and under fire. These ships would lead to the fleet carrier of World War Two; the RNAS were on the leading edge of developing modern weapon systems and technologies.

But at the centre of the story are No 3 Squadron RNAS, Samson's squadron, the original 'Motor Bandits' but now without their armoured cars. By November 1915, 3 Squadron had been in action constantly for sixteen months, again far longer than any other British unit at this stage in the war. They had not been rotated or rested. They were shot, dog-tired and in some cases their nerve was gone. Yet day after day they went up. Not surprisingly, some did not make it back and accidents were happening that should not have done. But the Navy needed Samson and 3 Squadron and could not afford to let them go home.

Chapter one
The move to Tenedos, February-March 1915

At 2355hrs on 1st February 1915, HMS 'Ark Royal'[1] slipped her moorings at Sheerness and headed out to sea and to war. She was the first ship in history designed and built as a seaplane carrier. Purchased by the Royal Navy in 1914 shortly after her keel had been laid and while the ship was only in frames, this allowed her design to be modified almost totally to accommodate aircraft and set her at the cutting edge of technology. Sadly the new design did not go as far as the engine, which was still the original one: 'Ark Royal' was so slow she was unable to keep up with the Home Fleet. The other big problem was that her aircraft could not take off in the North Sea as it was too rough.

All of which helps to explain why 'Ark Royal' was being sent out to the Dardanelles. She would carry the first seaplane unit of the Royal Naval Air Service (RNAS) to war in the Eastern Mediterranean and sailed under the command of Commander R H Clark-Hall, who was also in command of the pilots and men of the RNAS she carried. The officers were:[2]

Squadron Commander R H Clark-Hall (acting Commander)
Flight Commander H A Williamson
Flight Commander C F Kilner
Flight Lieutenant R H Kershaw
Flight Lieutenant C R Bromet
Flight Lieutenant C Hornby
Flight Lieutenant J W Allsopp
Flight Lieutenant W H S Garnett
Flight Lieutenant N Sholto-Douglas
Flight Lieutenant R Whitehead
Flight Sub-Lieutenant E H Dunning
Warrant Officer W H Ellison

The ship and her crew would develop a very close working arrangement with Commander Samson and 3 Squadron.

As the 'Ark Royal' moved into the Channel a storm blew up and a lot of the men became seasick. The ship was hit by a second storm as she passed through the Bay of Biscay and now most of the crew were laid low. It must have been a relief to enter the Mediterranean and at 2310hrs on 12th February 1915, the 'Ark Royal' tied up to a buoy in Bighi Bay, Malta. Here they carried out a lot of training in the art of handling aircraft off the deck and into the water, very necessary in view of the lack of experience of pilots

---

[1] The National Archives (TNA): AIR 1/479/15/312/239
[2] TNA: AIR 1/681/21/13/2209

and crew. Clark-Hall had been Squadron Commander for Aircraft Armament on HMS 'Hermes', the Navy's first attempt at a seaplane carrier in 1913, but this was his first sole command. Captain Cecil F Kilner, Royal Marines Light Infantry (RMLI), the Flight Commander, was a veteran of the Cuxhaven Raid but six of 'Ark Royal's' officers had only taken their pilot's licence since the outbreak of war, four of them only since 24th October 1914. It was unlikely that any of these had had much practice, if any, with a seaplane.

On 13th February at 1650hrs Captain Kilner took off in No 136, a Shorts' seaplane, and returned some 35 minutes later at 1725hrs. At this point, the training seemed to be going well but on the morning of the 14th it all started to go wrong. At 0700hrs the crew hoisted seaplanes No 136 and Wight No 172 onto the flying deck, followed at 0830hrs by Sopwith seaplane No 808. At 0845hrs, No 808, with pilot Lieutenant Garnett in charge, was placed in the water. He started to taxi the aircraft out when he lost control and the aircraft capsized. An hour later the crew of the 'Ark Royal' managed to salvage the aircraft and hoist it on board. This was vital as aero engines were like hen's teeth and far too valuable to be allowed to go to waste. The seaplane was placed in the turning room just under the bridge, where it was allowed to drip dry. This was an area for pre-flighting the aircraft and where engine testing and other live testing of the engine could be carried out.

There was no time for any more practice just now. At 1715hrs the 'Ark Royal' slipped her moorings and headed out into the Mediterranean on route for Tenedos, a small island off the Turkish mainland, which was reached at 0810hrs on Wednesday 17th February 1915. 'Ark Royal' dropped anchor and in the afternoon, three seaplanes were placed in the water and pilots Bromet, Kershaw, Kilner and Whitehead all carried out half-hour test flights with no problems. They then carried out a reconnaissance of the forts guarding the entrance to the Dardanelles, their first operational sortie. At 0710hrs on the 19th Kilner left the ship in seaplane No 136 and carried out a reconnaissance from Bashiki Bay to Gapa Tepe, returning to the ship at 0910hrs with copious notes of what he had seen. At 0920hrs a seaplane was sent to help HMS 'Cornwallis' with her fall of shot, but it arrived after the 'Cornwallis' had finished firing. Using a searchlight, the aircraft was told to inspect the damage at Forts 3, 4 and 6. It returned to the 'Ark Royal' and reported all guns intact and no damage to any of the targets. The pilot had not wished to tell the 'Cornwallis' that it had missed all its targets, which did not go down at all well with its captain. He needed to know what had happened and to be told promptly. In the afternoon two aircraft were sent out to spot for HMS 'Inflexible' but both aircraft suffered radio failure and had to return to the ship. Due to bad weather there was no more flying until late on the 25th when seaplane No 173 was placed in the water and Whitehead attempted to take off at 1800hrs, returning to the ship at 1915hrs having failed to do so.[3]

On Friday 26th February the 'Ark Royal' moved from Tenedos to Rabbit Island to shorten the flying time to the entrance to the Dardanelles. At 0740hrs Lieutenant Douglas took off in Short seaplane No 922. He reported there were no Turkish troops in the Yeni Kioi area, but a number of new guns had been moved into the area and that Fort 6 now contained seven guns. Also that there was a lot of enemy merchant shipping movements above the Narrows. Four further flights were tried that day but all four failed for various reasons: petrol tank bursting, low pressure in the fuel system, sea state did not allow take-off and could not gain enough height. The weather now closed in and the sea was too rough for take-offs.

On Monday 1st March Lieutenant Bromet and Flight Commander Williamson took off at 1504hrs and carried out a widespread reconnaissance. They spotted extensive trench systems and gun pits between Forts 6 and 8, but no guns in position, then a large artillery park and, as they flew across the Narrows, a row of seventeen mines. They returned to the ship at 1612hrs. At 1710hrs Douglas left the ship in No 922 but one of his floats was torn off while he was trying to take off. He was towed back to the ship and the seaplane was salvaged. Garrett tried to leave the ship in No 808 but failed to take-off and returned to the ship with an overheated engine.

All in all, it was not a terribly auspicious start for the unit. The 'Ark Royal' had been on station for two weeks but had only managed to get aircraft up on four of those days. It was a brand new, top-secret fighting machine which lacked experience in all departments. The RNAS crew of the 'Ark Royal' were still very new and inexperienced and were having to learn on the job, not good for the reliability of the machines. The pilots were also very new at flying from open choppy water - it was definitely not the same as being able to fly a landplane - and were still learning how to use the waves to help them take off and get into the air. They needed time to learn and to get things right so that they would be better able to help the Fleet, but the Fleet was on active service and could not give the ship and its crew the time it needed. Which was why Samson and 3 Squadron were ordered to the Dardanelles. No 3 Squadron RNAS, under the command of Commander Charles R Samson, had been in action since the start of the war. They arrived in France on 27th August 1914 and immediately set about finding ways to attack the Germans. Samson and his men very quickly took up the idea of the Belgian armoured car and developed their own version, built by the Forges et Chantiers de France shipyard in Dunkirk. When the

---

[3] TNA: ADM 116/1352

officers and men were not flying they were out attacking the enemy in the armoured cars and the squadron very quickly made a name for itself at Douai and Antwerp. They soon became a real problem for the Germans, who had no option but to put a price on their heads. On the Allied side of the lines they were called the 'Motor Bandits' or, if you had just lost your truck, they were the 'Motor Bastards'. They very quickly became the most decorated and experienced British air unit and armoured car unit, so it came as a great shock to all concerned that the Motor Bandits were ordered home.

The Admiralty had ordered Samson and his men back to England with immediate effect and no reason given. There were a number of very worried men: maybe they had borrowed one lorry too many. They would find out soon enough. February 27th was a day of farewells and a very sad day for Samson and his officers and men and those forces and local people who relied on them. They had made a lot of good friends in the Dunkirk area but a spot of leave would be really nice. The thought of leaving the cold, damp, and very makeshift billets behind was not very upsetting but the thought that they would not attack the German again was very sad. None of them wanted to end up as instructors or teachers at a training station which was what they all thought would happen. There was still a lot of fighting to do and they wanted to be in it until the end. Samson went off to General Bidon's HQ[4] and said his farewells to the general and his staff. After that he went to have a last lunch with the Commandant of the French squadron that shared the airfield with them - and what a lunch it was! That evening all the pilots met up and in the general euphoria a sweep was organised amongst them for the first one back to Dover. Flight Lieutenant Reggie Marix joined the sweep even though at the time he did not have an aircraft but he was off to Paris to pick up a brand new 200hp Breguet and he would join the race from there, with a suitable handicap.

The fog was far too thick to fly in on Sunday 28th February. It was as if France did not want to let the Motor Bandits go but intended to keep them there to help fight the German and chase him from her lands. Samson and his pilots decided one last lunch was required and retired to Café des Arcades in Dunkirk. After lunch the fog was still there and just as bad, but somehow Samson felt that it had cleared a little. This might have been down to the wine with lunch but a number of the pilots took off. Samson had been told that Marix had left Paris several hours ago and he knew that a bit of fog would not stop Marix. He wanted to win the sweep himself and was soon in the cockpit of his old faithful BE2, No 50, taking off and heading for Dover. Samson could not see the hand in front of his face after a few minutes but he pressed on. A little while later he realised he had been a first class fool as the weather failed to clear but he still pressed on flying

---

[4] French Commandant of Dunkirk

blind. Suddenly the fog thinned and out he popped a mile from Dover with the castle right in front of him. What a relief! He was very pleased with himself that his dead-reckoning navigation skills were still good.

He flew past the castle to the airfield on the heights next to it where he found Derroussors, Lord Edward Grosvenor's old mechanic, waiting for the squadron to land, and in particular No 1241, as he was the mechanic for that aircraft and had kept its engine running without a miss. On good nights he could be found sleeping under the aircraft and when it was up, he could be seen looking out for its return on the airfield. He asked Samson where his aircraft was and Samson could not resist pulling his leg, saying it was broken in Calais. Derroussors rushed off to a shed, came back with a tool box the size of a steamer trunk and loaded it into No 50. Samson asked him what he was doing and Derroussors demanded that he fly him to Calais so he could fix his aeroplane. Samson then explained it was only fog-bound and would be over soon. The most of the squadron turned up later that afternoon, the last one landing the next morning. The men came over with the transport, their tools and a few other bits they felt were needed.

They were all billeted in Dover, with the officers staying at the very splendid Burlington Hotel, which looked very like Osborne House on the Isle of Wight. There was no barrack space at the airfield for the men so they were placed in boarding houses in the town. The landladies were a bit taken aback when this group of men arrived in very dirty boiler suits and odd bits of uniform but they were all quickly settled in. That evening Lieutenant C Collet was hard at work carrying out the First Lieutenant's duties when the door opened and in walked Lieutenant R Bell Davies. Collet was surprised to see him but when Bell Davies said he was reporting for duty, he handed over all the duties of First Lieutenant to him with immediate effect as he hated the job, but Bell Davies enjoyed the work and soon got stuck in.

Samson received orders to report to the Admiralty on Monday to collect his new orders and left early on 1st March, driving up to London in his Rolls-Royce saloon car, which his men had cleaned and polished. On arriving in London he duly reported in to the Admiralty and, having got his new orders, leapt back into his car and now raced back to Dover, breaking a number of speeding laws on the way. On the Dover Road somewhere in Kent, Samson was pulled over for speeding by a local policeman and as he did not have his driver's licence with him, he was charged by the constable with both speeding and that offence too. He had tried to explain that he was carrying urgent orders from the Admiralty and had to get back to his squadron but the constable would have none of it. The man in front of him was very dishevelled and unkempt and did not look like a real naval officer on urgent official business. Samson however did not treat the incident very seriously and went on his merry way. A few months later, a large document for his attention arrived on Tenedos. It claimed that as he could not be traced the case was dropped but the chief constable of Kent had also written on it 'that Commander Samson would not be proceeded against, as he evidently had been in a great hurry.'

Once back in Dover, Samson ordered all his men to a meeting just after lunch and he stepped forward and with a great big grin on his face said one word:

'DARDANELLES'

A lot of the men were surprised and very confused as they had no idea where the Dardanelles was or who they were going to fight. This was probably the case with the majority of British and Dominion forces sent there!

All leave was cancelled as of that instant as they were required in the Dardanelles as quickly as possible. The first thing Bell Davies had to do was sort the men out. The Central Air Office, Sheerness Sub-Depot, was supposed to look after the squadron for all supplies, food, stores and pay and allowances. They were also supposed to fit the men out with new uniforms, overalls and working clothes, but they were not expecting the squadron. They could not help them out and very quickly the system broke down and the squadron was left to its own resources. The officers were in the Burlington Hotel and could charge things to the squadron bill but as the men were in local lodging houses in Dover, the landladies were not surprisingly a little concerned about their prospects of being paid by these penniless men dressed in rags. The officers pooled their money and gave what they could to the landladies.

The following day Bell Davies talked to the pay department at Sheerness and then sent two armed officers to collect what money he could get to pay the men. A second group of men was sent up to Sheerness to raid the stores for what bits of uniform they could find and a selection of overalls and other work clothing. Another party was sent to Chatham to see what could be acquired in the way of stores and clothing. All the parties returned in the early evening clutching their ill-gotten gains. The Motor Bandits had struck yet again! There was not enough money to pay the men and officers all their pay to date and allowances, so Bell Davies shared out what they could. A representative from Harrods had been hanging about the hotel all day and, overhearing Bell Davies and some others discussing the uniform problem, he stepped forward and said he could supply the whole squadron with ready-made suits. Bell Davies dismissed him, not believing it was possible in the few days left, but in the end he did supply suits for the whole squadron. What clothing was available was given to the advance party and what working gear they had found was again shared out until more could be acquired at a later date.

Samson decided that the advance party would be made up with himself in command, five officers (Collet, Lieutenant E Osmond, Marix, Flight Lieutenant G L Thomson and his brother Lieutenant Bill Samson), and 30 men. Their transport would consist of 12 motor lorries, two light tenders and two touring cars. He also decided that they would take two BE2 aeroplanes so that on arrival he would certainly have at least one aeroplane that they could put together and fly[5]. They would also carry a selection of bombs of varying size and weight, enough fuel and oil for several days of continuous flying and a selection of general spares. The Navy had also placed an order with the French firm of Henry & Maurice Farman at Boulogne-Billancourt for ten replacement aircraft for 3 Squadron. Samson felt the Shorthorn by Maurice Farman was the best bomber and reconnaissance aircraft then available.

On 1st March 1915 the Royal Navy placed an urgent order with Sopwith for three 100hp Schneider single-seater floatplanes, which had to be ready and shipped to Devonport and loaded on to the SS 'Moorgate' by 16th March. The first aircraft, No 1437, was finished and ready to be packed and sent down to Devonport on 7th March, while the rest of the packing was finished by the 11th.

The next few days were very hectic for the men of 3 Squadron as the advance party was made ready to depart. No 50 was taken apart, given a good service and over-hauled and then packed up and placed on the back of one of the trucks, all under the close supervision of Warrant Officer J J Brownridge. All the spares, fuel and bombs, personal equipment and some tinned rations was placed on or in the other vehicles. There was no room at Dover harbour for Samson, his men and the vehicles, so they were ordered to embark at Folkestone.

Bell Davies meanwhile had had a good look at the logistical problems of getting the rest of the squadron and 'Nigger', Samson's captured German horse, down to Devonport Docks in Plymouth. He thought at first of putting the men and stores on the train, driving the vehicles down and flying the aircraft down to Plymouth, but there was no place to land close to the docks. Now he had a complete rethink about the problem and in the end decided it was best if they all went on the same train - vehicles, aircraft, men and Nigger. So he took his problem and went to see the station master at Dover station, who turned out to be very helpful.

Back in the Dardanelles, Thursday 4th March was a very good and busy day for the 'Ark Royal'. Flying started at 0800hrs with Douglas in No 922 taking off first; he was spotting for the 'Inflexible' and the 'Irresistible' with all signals being relayed by HMS 'Usk'. The next machine up was No 808

---

[5] TNA: AIR 1/361/15/228/50

with Garnett at the controls and also tasked with the same job. For two hours they both directed the fall of shot from these two ships, Garnett returning to the 'Ark Royal' at 1105hrs. Flying started in the afternoon at 1227hrs when Douglas took off again in No 922, being relieved by Garnett in No 808. As the ships did not require Bromet who was flying No 172, he went off on a reconnaissance flight over Yeni Shehr. He came under intense small arms fire and started to take damage so turned away and headed back to the 'Ark Royal'. He landed at 1610hrs and immediately started to sink as his floats were full of bullet holes and he had also sustained damage to the leading edge, elevator and his rudder. The upper control section broke away as the aircraft was being hoisted on to the ship because of the large amount of water in the floats.[6]

Once again 'Ark Royal's luck did not hold: Friday 5th March was a very bad day for the ship and its crew. At 1000hrs she slipped her moorings and joined the 'Queen Elizabeth' at Gaba Tepe. At 1114hrs Garnett and Williamson taxied out in No 808 and took off, climbing to a height of 3,000ft and heading off in the direction of the Dardanelles. Three miles from the ship the aircraft went into a spin and looked to be out of control. HMS 'Usk' spotted the crash site and went to rescue the crew. The aircraft was a wreck but they did manage to salvage the engine. Garnett, the pilot, was only slightly hurt but the observer, Williamson, was very seriously injured. Spinning was a big problem for all aviators at this date and proper instruction on what to do to get out of one would not come for another year. At 1214hrs Douglas left the ship flying No 922, unexpectedly returning at 1310 and making a poor landing. He had been wounded by ground fire. Kershaw took over No 922 once it was refuelled and carried out the reconnaissance mission, returning to the ship two hours later.

6th March was not a good day either. At 1305hrs Kilner left the ship in No 136 and returned 23 minutes later with engine failure. At 1340hrs Kershaw left the ship in No 922 and returned 42 minutes later with engine failure. Now Bromet left the ship in No 807 and also returned with engine failure. Even given the unreliability of them at this time, it was not a good day for aero-engines. Two days later Bromet left the ship in No 172 but suffered engine failure. At 1235hrs Whitehead and Lieutenant Lawrence H Strain left the ship in No 173 and carried out a reconnaissance over Chanak, but due to low cloud could not spot for the Fleet. On 10th March two seaplanes, Nos 172 and 136, failed to fly due to engine failure. Kershaw did manage to take off in No 922 and carried out a reconnaissance from Kavak River and up to the Bulair lines.

It is clear that the 'Ark Royal' was failing to get seaplanes in the air a lot of the time. This could be due to poor weather and/or the sea state preventing

---

[6] TNA: ADM 116/1352

the seaplanes from taking off. There were also plenty of technical problems, especially with the engines, which meant the aircraft could not fly or returned early from missions. Another very serious problem for the Navy was the lack of detail in the reconnaissance reports because of the inexperience of the observers and pilots. We must remember that the 'Ark Royal' was brand-new and had only been with the Fleet a few months and this goes for the crew as well. From Commander Clark-Hall at the top to the lowest fitter and rigger, they were all very inexperienced and lacked combat experience and sea time.[7] The 'Ark Royal' and its crew were still very new at their work and required instruction from experienced observers and pilots and ground crew.

By the end of March the 'Ark Royal' had been on station for 44 days and had been able to put aircraft in the air on only twenty of those days for a total of 60 flying hours. The fleet had expected seaplanes in the air every day and for at least eight hours per day, carrying out spotting and reconnaissance missions. The information brought back was then placed on a rough hand-drawn map and passed on up to the fleet. These maps were about as much good as a chocolate tea pot. Either Clark-Hall had forgotten how to put the information onto Admiralty Charts or just did not know. In contrast Samson and 3 Squadron would put their information directly onto Admiralty charts supported by photographs and then pass copies to both Naval and Army HQs. They had built a very good reputation with the Home Fleet, and in particular the Dover Patrol, for good co-operation on spotting for the ships' guns and on producing intelligence reports and maps. The Admiralty supposed and indeed took it for granted that all RNAS units must be trained to the same standard as No 3 Squadron, but Clark-Hall and the crew of the 'Ark Royal' were sadly below that.

Back in England meanwhile, by 10th March the advance party of 3 Squadron was ready to leave Dover early the next morning and the other aircraft were broken down into small loads to fit onto a train, all except for the Breguet pusher biplane. Bell Davies and several other officers felt this was 'a huge and horrible affair constructed of steel'[8]. The only pilots able to fly this monster were Marix and Samson but neither with great success due to the poor engine. Loading of the advance party started at first light on 11th March. Collet took the two heavy trucks down to the docks first, with Samson and the others following on after breakfast. The harbour was equipped with two 5-ton cranes which in peacetime were used to load cars onto the cross-channel steamers but Collet very quickly discovered that these could not lift the fully-laden trucks onto the ship. They were far too heavy. This was a major problem but he set about having the fully-packed

---

[7] TNA: ADM 116/1352
[8] Richard Bell Davies, *'Sailor in the Air'*, London 1967, page 117

bodies removed from the chassis and their loads spread amongst the other lorries. This was a simple operation but he was worried about fitting the bodies back onto the chassis once unloaded in Boulogne.

Samson and his party were first to be unloaded when they came alongside in Boulogne but Collet's fears were justified for it was not an easy task to bolt the bodies back onto the truck chassis. Samson took the cars, seven men and the tenders and pushed on to Paris as he wanted to call in at the Farman works in Boulogne-sur-Seine and see if his order had been finished. The liaison officer at the factory, Lieutenant Thurstan, confirmed the order was finished and had been despatched to Marseilles several days before. Samson and his officers were put up at the Ritz, while the men went to a much cheaper hotel.

Samson had left Collet and Osmond with twenty men to put the trucks back together. All attempts failed and they ended up having to unload each truck body, bolt it the chassis and then reload the vehicles. Sixteen hours later the convoy turned up at the Ritz just as Samson and the others were finishing breakfast. Samson asked for the bill which he was only too happy to pay but the Ritz management would not hear of it. Impossible! Unthinkable! Not the Hero of Douai and his party, they were heroes of France! Samson met Collet and Osmond in reception, the latter looking much the worse for wear, and the men were just too tired to go on. Samson replaced Osmond on the trucks with Lieutenant Butler and then turned to the main body of men and told them they had half an hour to see Paris after having first had breakfast at the Ritz. Their ship, the SS 'Abda', would be sailing on 17th March at noon so they had just four days to get from Paris to Marseilles. Samson decided that he, with the two cars and one tender, would push on to Marseilles, with the trucks following on making best speed. It was going to take the trucks some 30 hours with a very strong tail wind pushing them along on the road and as long as nothing went wrong, but Samson had great faith in his Eastchurch men, they would make it. Their route to Marseilles was going to be Bourges, overnight stop, on to Clermont-Ferrand, Avignon and finally to Marseilles. The trucks would stop if and when they could and they were also to look out for anything that could be of use in the Dardanelles. True Motor Bandit standing orders!

Back in England, Bell Davies was still having a large number of problems getting money, clothing and stores for his men. This included their rum and tobacco ration. They had stripped the Breguet down as far as possible but due to its steel frame, which meant it had to remain on its undercarriage, it was still a big lump. It was going to be towed from the airfield to the station. There were several low bridges *en route* that it would not fit under so a new route to the station had to be found. Bell Davies took the measurement of the Breguet to the station master at Dover station and found that when placed on a standard flat car it was too tall to pass through the large number of tunnels between Dover and Devonport docks.

However, the station master knew that the Midland Railway possessed some low-bogey trucks and arranged for one to be brought to Dover. A cross-country route from the airfield past the castle was found but it was a muddy track and the vehicles on the airfield could not tow the Breguet along it. No problem was insoluble for a Motor Bandit. A traction engine passing the airfield was stopped by Bell Davies and hired for a day to tow the Breguet to the station - and an impressive sight it made on the streets of Dover.[9] The last problem for now was the horse 'Nigger', which had been captured from an Uhlan detachment in Belgium. Samson was insistent that the horse came out to the Dardanelles. Now the Dover station master found a horsebox wagon to transport the horse and a handler. One of the young drivers had become very fond of the horse and had been made 'Yeoman of the Horse'. He would travel with his precious charge.

15th March was a very busy day for the Motor Bandits. At the airfield in Dover everything was taken down towards the station and made ready to load on the special train at first light. All the men of 3 Squadron mustered at the station, where they were issued with haversack rations and boarded the train. Next stop Devonport harbour, Plymouth! Sopwith had just finished (and only just in time) a third 100hp Sopwith "Schneider" single-seat floatplane, No 1438, and crated it together with a set of major spares and No 1437. They were sent to Devonport to sail to Dardanelles on the SS 'Moorgate' which would sail on 19th March. Sopwith 80hp Tabloid "SS3" single-seat landplanes Nos 1203 and 1204 plus Nos 964 and 965[10] would also be sailing with them. This shipment had to come down by a special train as a normal goods train would have taken a week to get to the dockyard. It did not arrive in Devonport until late on the 17th but was still all loaded on the ship that day.

At Plymouth the men were placed in the naval barracks while the officers went to the Royal Hotel. All the stores and equipment were unloaded from the train and made ready to load onto the SS 'Moorgate'. The Breguet yet again caused problems: the special low wagon was too long to fit on the dockyard railway so the aircraft had to be unloaded outside the dockyard and pushed, with great care, up to the ship. The men and Nigger were to travel on the SS 'Inkosi', which had been converted into a troopship to take them to the Dardanelles. A horse box was borrowed from the local barracks and it was swung onto the 'Inkosi' with Nigger inside.

3 Squadron were joined on the ship by a detachment of the Royal Naval Air Service Armoured Car section under the command of Lieutenant Commander Josiah Wedgwood, who had not distinguished himself when leading a section of armoured cars in Belgium. Bell Davies, as senior

---

[9] Richard Bell Davies, op. cit., page 118
[10] TNA: AIR 1/361/15/228/50

military officer on the ship, was Officer Commanding Troops but as Wedgwood was older then himself, he felt uncomfortable about this as he did not want to hurt the man's feelings. Fortunately Wedgwood was fine about the situation and was even very helpful during the voyage. The SS 'Inkosi' slipped her mooring just before midnight on the 17th and headed out into the Channel. The men quickly stowed their gear and came on deck to watch as England and the Eddystone light grew smaller in the moonlight. The SS 'Moorgate' left Devonport late on 19th March.

The first part of the voyage was fine until the evening the ship entered the Bay of Biscay when the weather changed and the sea became rough. The men were housed in the hold of the ship, which had been converted to living areas where they could sling their hammocks. Very few of the men had ever been to sea so there was a steady flow of men to the latrines and up onto the main deck. There was a lot of cursing and swearing as the ship lurched about and the men lost their footing or missed the ladder as the ship rolled. Mechanic Arthur Beeton, who had worked on small boats on the Hamble River, faired a lot better than most. He laid in his hammock and was woken by its increased movement as it swung from side to side. In the morning he and a few other stalwarts headed for the galley and were met with the smell of bacon. Sadly having eaten the greasy fry-up, Beeton had no option but to run for the heads (latrine). For the next three days the men of the RNAS on the ship were very ill; many of them just wanted to die.[11]

Nigger collapsed in his box with a case of colic. Colic is used to describe a symptom of abdominal (belly) pain, which in horses is usually caused by problems in the gastrointestinal tract. It is one of the most common causes of death in horses. Fortunately there was a CPO with the armoured car section who was a Master of the Hunt and who knew a lot about horses. Under his direction, they gathered together bits of rope and a hammock, which was passed under Nigger and kept him off his feet. Slowly the horse got better and came to enjoy being in his hammock.

SS 'Inkosi' passed Gibraltar and Tangiers and the sea state greatly improved. The men recovered from their seasickness so Wedgwood started to drill his men with their Vickers guns. The ship called into Malta and all the men were given a few hours shore leave. For the armoured car crews, this was their first time in a foreign country and a lot of them went off to find a good meal. But Malta like many other countries was suffering from rationing and the only thing they could find was pigeon. They all got back on the ship, which left port that night and headed towards the Dardanelles. Beeton and several men were sick having eaten the pigeon dinners.[12]

---

[11] Leading Mechanic Arthur George Beeton, IWM Sound Archive, catalogue number 8323
[12] ibidem

The 'Ark Royal' meanwhile had acquired several mines, painted them up like the Turkish mines and then placed then around the ship. Her seaplanes flew over them to see if they could spot them. Not a bad idea except that the sea bed off Tenedos is sandy and the mines showed up at the 18ft mark[13]. However, the Dardanelles is a very different proposition. It is a dark and murky sea lane with no visibility below 10ft so it is very doubtful that the pilots and observers could see the mines in the Dardanelles or in Erin Keui Bay. Therefore reporting no mines in the Erin Keui Bay area on 17th March was so very wrong and cost three battleships.

Samson and his party had a good run from Paris to Marseilles and would stop every so often to await the trucks, which were rather slow but making steady progress. They spent the night in Bourges and picked up a few extra bits and pieces to make life a little more comfortable. His advance party reached Marseilles on the evening of the 15th and went to the Hôtel du Louvre et de la Paix. The cars and tender were taken to the docks and parked up near the ship. In the early hours of the 16th, the main convoy of twelve trucks and a tender arrived and went straight to the docks and found the ship. The SS 'Abda' had been chartered because of its speed of 20 knots as the Admiralty put it 'No matter what the price': she was required to move Samson and his men and move them fast. Samson arrived the next morning at 0600hrs just as the last of the trucks and cars was being loaded into the hold. He and his party plus the French aircraft direct from the Farman factory were all put aboard this small luxury passenger ship. The aircraft were stowed in some ten very large packing cases on deck so Samson could not inspect them before they sailed.

The SS 'Abda' was a very comfortable steamship and Samson and his party had a very restful seven days sailing through the Mediterranean to Imbros, a small island in the north Aegean Sea some twenty miles from the Dardanelles. On 23rd March, as 'Abda' approached the anchored fleet off Imbros, it was intercepted by a picket ship and given directions to the flag ship and told where to anchor. Samson went to report to Rear-Admiral Rosslyn Wemyss, on HMS 'Euryalus', a Cressey-class armoured cruiser. The admiral, however, was ashore at Moudros, not on his ship. During the Dardanelles Campaign, the town of Moudros and its harbour were used as an Allied base, under the command of Admiral Wemyss. The British Empire troops and many others used the spelling 'Mudros'. Samson reported to the Admiral and was greeted with a very miserable and downbeat command centre. On 18th March the fleet had lost HMS 'Irresistible' and HMS 'Ocean', the French battleship 'Bouvet' was sunk and two more vessels badly damaged. He returned to the 'Abda' with no instructions so when HMS 'Queen Elizabeth' steamed into the harbour with Vice-Admiral Sir John de Robeck on board, Samson went across and

---

[13] TNA: AIR 1/681/21/13/2209

reported to him. Admiral de Robeck, commander of the Eastern Mediterranean Squadron, the Royal Navy's force at the Dardanelles, was delighted to see Samson and his 3 Squadron. The seaplanes from HMS 'Ark Royal' had proved to be useless and quite unsuitable for the job in hand. At long last he would have land planes that could fully support his fleet, for eight hours a day every day. Samson had a long consultation with the Admiral and his Chief-of-Staff, Roger Keyes.

They told Samson that his base of operations was going to be the island of Tenedos. This was 30 miles south of Imbros and just 11 miles across open water from Gallipoli. Admiral de Robeck had given the task of building an airfield to the captain of the 'Ark Royal', Commander Clark-Hall, who knew Samson well from the old Eastchurch days. The best piece of land for an airfield was being used as a vineyard. Clark-Hall managed to get the farmer to agree to the vines being dug up and the field, which was flat and 'L' shaped, turned into an airfield 600 yards long and 300 yards wide, thanks to a band of over 200 Greek labourers and some of his crew. This was situated on the north coast at the western end of the island, some three and a half miles from the town of Tenedos and half a mile from the landing beach. At the seaward northern end was a patch of scrub then some cliffs with the sea also at the southern end. The site for the tented area to one side of the main runway was 200 yards by 150 yards. All the vines had to go but compensation was given to the land owner: six months' rent up front, £1,010 pounds for the loss of his crop[14] and the field rented for a whole year. He was, not surprisingly, very pleased with life. Clark-Hall managed to add to his workforce some 60 local men and 10 very local donkeys. The whole work party also managed to carve out a rough track from the beach up to the airfield. Samson promised the Admiral that once he had unloaded the aeroplanes, his men would have an aeroplane in the air within 12 hours. He was ordered to return to his ship and make for Tenedos and to start his unloading in the morning with the help of the crews from HMS 'Vengeance' and 'Ark Royal'.

The Admiral was shocked that none of the aircraft carried radio and promised to have some sets sent out from Britain and fitted to them. They were essential for reporting back while spotting for the warships' fall of shot. The main task for Samson and his men was finding the Turkish guns emplaced in the forts or dug in infield positions, and then spotting for the naval gun fire until they hit these targets. The problem the Navy faced was that a number of the batteries were placed in valleys or in gullies that could not be seen by the battleships.

To give some idea of the task that faced the Navy, the Turkish Çanakkale Fortified Zone was responsible for the defence of the Dardanelles. It was a

---

[14] TNA: AIR 1/361/15/228/50

corps-sized unit, commanded by Brigadier General Cevat Paşa, and composed of two infantry divisions, the 9th commanded by Colonel Halil Sami Bey and the 11th commanded by Colonel Refet Bey, as well as coastal and mobile artillery and other supporting units. The fortifications of the Dardanelles consisted of the outer, intermediate and inner defences, a number of forts, fixed gun batteries and mobile batteries, some with very elderly guns. The outer defences were the two historic forts at the entrance of the Straits: Kumkale and Seddülbahir. These were equipped with thirteen heavy and seven medium guns, which were obsolete. The intermediate defences were protecting the interior minefields and they were equipped with medium guns. The inner defences were the most powerful ones, but their guns were also antiquated and ammunition was scarce. The forts protecting the shores of the Dardanelles were reinforced with guns from old dismantled warships. There were 230 artillery guns of different sizes (howitzers, mortars, etc), but most of them were around 25-30 years old and only 82 pieces were good enough to match the artillery of the Allied fleet. Guns brought from the nearby defensive lines close to Istanbul and the depots of the Ministry of War were in use as well. The German General Staff had dispatched Vice-Admiral Ernst Adolf Julius Guido von Usedom, who was an expert in coastal defences, to assist in this. He was accompanied by 500 German artillery specialists.

Although the Fleet hit the forts many times, or so they thought, large amounts of dust and smoke were thrown up covering the target, which was invisible from the ships anyway. The bottom line was that at the end of the day, the forts were still firing. As the ships retreated, the lesson learned was that it was exceedingly difficult for them to destroy the Turkish guns; a direct hit was required for this. As most of the battleships could not elevate their guns high enough, they could not drop rounds into the forts. The seaplanes from the 'Ark Royal' had tried to provide a spotting service but they were too slow and flew too low and got shot up. Another problem the Navy had discovered was that their maps were not accurate and a very important job for Samson and his pilots was to carry out detailed reconnaissance of the Gallipoli peninsula.

The Royal Navy and the French took on board the ineffectiveness of the seaplane carrier 'Ark Royal' and sent two squadrons of land-based aeroplanes to provide air support. As Samson had driven down through France to Marseilles, the French had been forming MF 98 Squadron T (Tenedos) in the Lyons region to give an air component to the French land and naval forces that were attempting to force the Dardanelles. The squadron was under the command of Captaine Antoine Césari, a veteran of the Battle of the Marne. They moved down to Marseilles on 24th March with their aircraft, all their camping equipment and a number of workhorses, and sailed on 28th March on the ship 'Ganga', steaming in the direction of Tenedos. But Tenedos was not ready and they were diverted to Alexandria in Egypt where they docked on 4th April.

At first light on 24th March Samson and his squadron were on the south side of Tenedos and at 0600hrs joined HMS 'Vengeance' on the north side of the island. At 0700 hrs the men from 'Vengeance' and 3 Squadron started to unload the 'Abda'[15]. They managed to get two large Hervieu-type hangars ashore, some food and other stores, but the weather closed in and all work had to stop. The working party from 'Vengeance' returned to their ship to hot food and a comfortable hammock at 1600hrs but Samson decided that he and his men would stay on the island. They would put up the two hangars, which were basically very large tents, and then sleep in them. The men struggled for hours in the teeth of the gale and, with a lot of shouting and swearing, the hangers were erected. Samson and his men bedded down in them. They had a very miserable night; they could not light a fire as they had no firewood and everyone was cold and wet and hungry. While it was true that they had become a little soft since leaving France, the Navy were not good at looking after a shore party and there was no way to get hot food and other rations to the men on the island. A shore party was supposed to return to its ship at night but Samson's squadron did not have a Royal Navy ship to return to. The gale increased on the 25th and into 26th March so no work was done. Rear-Admiral Thorsby landed on the 25th and had a long discussion on how they were going to get the very large and very heavy Farman packing cases off the 'Abda'.

On Friday 26th March at 0645hrs, the 'Ark Royal', 'Vengeance' and the 'Abda' weighed anchor and sailed round to the north side of Tenedos, as the worst of the storm had passed. At 0900hrs the 'Abda' came alongside the 'Ark Royal' and the large Farman packing cases were lifted onto the deck of the 'Ark Royal' using the large derrick on the seaplane carrier. The crew of the 'Vengeance' landed at 0930hrs. They had made a couple of rafts using motorboats and a ship's boat: a wooden platform was placed over and between the two vessels and lashed into place. The platform was large enough to take the Farman crates with no problem. Samson's fully-loaded vehicles were also placed on the rafts and brought ashore. No 50 had been unloaded from the truck and was run ashore on its own wheels. Once the crates and vehicles got to the beach, the working party of 100 men from the 'Vengeance' took over and manhandled the crates up the slope to the airfield. As soon as No 50 arrived at the airfield, six of Samson's men started putting the wings back on and getting her ready to fly. That evening No 50 made the first take-off from Tenedos and flew around the island.

'Ark Royal' was continuing to have her usual problems. At 1345hrs Bromet took off in seaplane No 172 but half an hour later returned with engine failure. At 1450hrs Douglas took off in seaplane No 922 and also returned in half an hour with engine failure. Bromet then took off at 1547hrs in 172 again and headed to the Gallipoli peninsula to carry out a reconnaissance

---

[15] www.naval-history.net: Log book home page, HMS 'Vengeance', page 41

mission over Chanak, returning to the ship at 1730hrs having his persistence rewarded by completing a good mission. Whitehead left the ship in seaplane No 173 but returned 40 minutes later with engine failure. No 173, a Wight pusher seaplane, was so unreliable that it was taken apart for spare parts on 27th March 1915[16].

On the 27th 'Vengeance' landed her 100-strong working party again at 0730hrs and they started to knock the airfield into shape and finished the unloading of the supplies from the 'Abda'. At 0930hrs the captain of 'Vengeance' decided that the airfield would provide a good training ground for the Field Gun Team so the team, limber and one 12lb gun was landed on Tenedos. They all returned to the ship for their lunch and at 1300hrs continued to land stores for 3 Squadron. The men were formed into a long line and passed the 2-gallon petrol tins from man to man, followed by the small supply of bombs that Samson had brought for No 50, but as the 'Ark Royal' had sailed with no bombs Samson gave Clark-Hall half his and a few spare bomb racks.

It took two full days to unload all of 3 Squadron's equipment and get it up to the airfield. The most exciting moment came when it was time to off-load Nigger. He was hoisted over the side and lowered into the water behind a ship's cutter, then he was got on shore with a combination of men pulling and him swimming. As soon as his legs were on firm ground, Nigger was off like a racehorse in the Grand National with his 'Yeoman', Able Seaman Elsden, hanging on to the tow rope for all he was worth. They were off - Nigger in full flight and poor Elsden being pulled along behind. Through the soft sand they went and up the road towards the airfield, Nigger dragging his hapless yeoman through some thorn bushes as he careered onwards, but it was during this headlong charge that Elsden spotted a tree stump. As they passed, he managed to get a few turns of the rope onto the stump which brought Nigger to a sudden halt,[17] much to his relief!

By nightfall on 27th March Samson had his BE2 No 50, two Maurice Farman Shorthorn 100hp aircraft and eight Henri Farman 80hp Gnome engines unloaded. He was very disappointed to see these 80hp aircraft as he felt these were purely fit for peacetime flying or as trainers. With a top speed of only 60mph they were far too slow and could not carry an observer over enemy-held territory.

Tenedos is only about 22 miles square, with a population of about 600 and a garrison of 40 or 50 men in 1915. The airfield was some three and half miles from the village of Tenedos with only a dirt track linking the airfield

---

[16] www.naval-history.net: Log book home page, HMS 'Ark Royal', page 15
[17] Richard Bell Davies, op. cit., page 119

and the town. The military and civil governors and all the high society of the place were seated in and around the little smoky cafe near the sea when a breathless boy announced that the "Ingleezi" were landing. On hearing this the Mayor charged the head of police to go and investigate what was going on and find out if it was an invasion by the English. The story is now taken up in and Australian newspaper:

'Detaching a red pepper from one of the bunches which have always hung around the eaves of the cafe, and lighting his cigarette, the policeman gloomily started off for an hour's walk, which brought him in sight of a hundred or so soldiers busy working setting up tents and sheds for aeroplanes. Such audacious contempt of the authority of Tenedos outraged the feelings of the gendarme, and he was advancing with the idea of entering a protest, when he was pulled up by a sentry, who asked him what he wanted. Very politely the Greek stated his rank, title and mission, but the only reply he received is given as: "Look here, friend, it's no business of yours what we are doing." So he had nothing but to retrace his steps to where the governors were awaiting him, taking counsel as to the best course to adopt. They were still engaged in this knotty discussion when a messenger came to say that a British officer was waiting to see them at the Citadel. The civil governor begged his colleague to delay until he had time to put on a collar, and the pair arrived before the Citadel just as a company of British marines were marching through the gates, saluted in dismay by the Greek sentries. It was what the French would call an epic scene, and though intensely comic to some of the onlookers, must have been a sore trial to the two deposed officials, who were bidden to follow the soldiers.

Inside the Citadel they found a lieutenant-colonel most polite, but no waster of words. Without any further preface he simply told them that troops were going to be landed, and the Citadel must be immediately cleaned in readiness. "'Now take me to the post office," was his next request, and there the post master humbly rose and begged the colonel to take his solitary arm chair. Seating himself, the officer remarked, "I shall come here twice a day to censor the letters and the telegrams. From now you are forbidden to dispatch anything without my permission." That was all, and without waiting for an answer the colonel mounted his horse and rode away. The governors decided it was best to yield to the strangers who had invaded their island territory, and an army of several hundred of the inhabitants were soon at work, sweeping away the heaps of century-old dust and filth accumulated in their Venetian Citadel, the pride of their hearts. The British colonel had in sooth accomplished a miracle.'[18]

The colonel was, in fact, Commander Samson on Nigger. As Admiral de Robeck was due to visit the next day he wanted the fort and the town

---

[18] The Colac Herald (Victoria : 1875 - 1918)

cleaned up, as it was a festering midden that time had passed by. Samson knew he could not stop his men coming down to the village and the tavern but he was going to make sure it was a fit place for both them and the Royal Marine garrison. The Tenedos Post and Telegraph Office was in fact a cable station for the Eastern Telegraph Company and linked Constantinople to Alexandria in Egypt. This cable had been cut at the entrance to the Dardanelles on the start of hostilities.

On hearing of the invasion of Tenedos and some other Aegean Islands by the British, the Germans set about putting out propaganda against the British:

'THE OCCUPATION OF TENEDOS.
Most laborious efforts are still being made to frighten the Greeks about the occupation of certain islands in the Aegean for the purposes of the operations against the Dardanelles. Having already declared that the British are sure to annex Lemnos, the "Cologne Gazette" now says that the same fate has befallen Tenedos. It publishes descriptions in a French newspaper of the arrival of the British in the island, the closing of the telegraph office, and the establishment of a censorship, and says; "Where are the neutrals with their protests against this violation and with their cries of horror? They are all of them dumb. Perhaps they think that is but a trifling offence and painless for those concerned in comparison with Belgium. We will wait and see. Who is simple enough to believe that, when Russia is master of Constantinople and the Dardanelles, England, though she may a hundred times have guaranteed their freedom on paper, will ever again leave Lemnos and Tenedos?" '[19]

Come Sunday 28th March, 'Ark Royal' was still having problems with its aircraft. Two failed to take off for a spotting mission for HMS 'Majestic' while a third managed to take off but suffered radio failure so could not do the spotting. At 0930hrs an aircraft was seen approaching the 'Ark Royal' at 6,000ft and once its large black crosses were spotted, the ship fell in at action stations. It was a German Taube monoplane flown by Lieutenant Erich Serno of the 1st Aircraft Company. Two bombs were dropped: one fell 100yards in front of the ship, the other fell just 10ft from the port side opposite the main aircraft hold. One aircraft was damaged.

By late afternoon Samson and his men had managed to put together four aircraft including Samson's BE No 50, the two large Farmans and one small 80hp Farman. Samson flew one of the Farman's around the island and then landed, handing it over to Marix to take for a good shake-down flight. At 1830hrs on 28th March Samson took off from Tenedos in No 50 and headed for Gallipoli. Cruising over the entrance to the Dardanelles he could see a British destroyer patrolling but he was not worried as it was a

---

[19] 'West Coast Times', Australia, 11 June 1915, page 2

Royal Navy ship - until the ship opened fire. Samson turned and headed back to Tenedos but so did the destroyer. They closed in on the 'Ark Royal' which signalled the destroyer, HMS 'Usk', that the aircraft was a friend. 'Usk' replied 'Think I knocked a tail feather out of him', but there was no damage to Samson's aircraft. The 'Usk' had been working closely with the seaplanes of the 'Ark Royal' and knew them well and their Union flag markings. The only land planes in the area until now were the German Taubes like the one that had attacked the 'Ark Royal' and Samson's aircraft did not carry the Union flag but the new national roundel marking.

Meanwhile, the rest of Samson's squadron was on its way to join him on the SS 'Inkosi'. As the ship left Malta behind and headed towards Tenedos and the Dardanelles it was decided to hold a cricket match between the RNAS Armoured Car Section and 3 Squadron RNAS personnel. I will let Lieutenant Bertie Isaac, the Intelligence Officer for 3 Squadron, continue the story:

'We played cricket on deck and it was a great match, 1 round per side and both sides very confident. The Air Service against the Armoured Car squadron. They were in first and made a respectable 112 runs and we considered ourselves beaten as our wickets fell for just 18 runs; I went in and made 95 runs not out! There was great rejoicing. Everyone standing drinks for one all over the ship. I must have remembered some of my cricketing days at Wellington.'

Meanwhile Clark-Hall was desperate for his new aircraft and spares that were coming out from England in the same ships as 3 Squadron and due in the Tenedos anchorage in the next few days. On Monday 29th March the Royal Marines garrison that had occupied the fort on Tenedos was changed and now was made up from the detachment on the 'Ark Royal' commanded by Captain Panton, who would remain in command for the next year. His duties would include looking after the post office and the telegraph and censoring all the island's mail. Now that Samson was on Tenedos, things were going to change both on the island and on the 'Ark Royal'. Samson's men were now flying five missions a day, each one lasting over two hours and each time an aircraft went up, it took a bomb with it. However, until the 'Inkosi' and 'Moorgate' arrived he was going to be short of bombs. By the end of the month he and five of his pilots had gained a lot of experience on taking off and landing on their new airstrip.

On the 'Ark Royal' things had gone from bad to worse. The next time the 'Ark Royal' would be able to get any aircraft in the air would be Sunday 4th April. Short No 136 was grounded until a new engine came out, Sopwith No 808 had been destroyed, Sopwith No 807 had been damaged and was awaiting spares, Wight No 173 consistently failed to develop full power. Wight No 172 and Sopwith No 922 had performed the bulk of the flying, such as it was. They had set out on 75 missions and only managed 25, but only three of these were spotting missions for the Fleet. On the whole the seaplanes failed to meet the main requirement for the Fleet, which was accurate spotting. This also explains the failure of HMS 'Queen Elizabeth's indirect bombardment across the peninsula. The reconnaissances served to confirm information already in the possession of the fleet and were useful in confirming the small amount of damage done and the absence of torpedo tubes but the reports about the position of gun batteries were backed up by badly-drawn sketches of the emplacements, not to scale and not accurate enough to be placed on a map. These reports were insufficient to enable the guns to be destroyed even when the position was accessible to ship's fire power.

The major problem facing Clark-Hall and Kilner was that the inexperience of their pilots meant they were failing to get their aircraft off the sea and so could not support the Fleet. Rather than facing up to the fact and trying to rectify it by some belated training, multiple excuses were offered: poor and underpowered engines, the W/T system (radio) kept on breaking down, too much smoke and dust for the observer to see the target after the first salvo. Last of all it was the wrong type of sea:

The short choppy sea which was prevalent in these waters during the strong winds of winter, made it exceedingly difficult for either the Sopwith Seaplanes or the Wights to get off the water.[20]

On 11th April Clark-Hall carried out and then wrote a full report on the state of his aircraft to demonstrate how they were responsible for his failure:

'The original six machines with which the ship left England

No. 136 200C-U Short – In good order. Has now had new planes fitted. The most valuable and the only rough weather machine in the ship. Has suffered considerably from engine trouble, and on stripping down a fractured ball race and other damaged parts were found. No spare one on board. Cabled for, but not yet arrived. These parts have now been removed from No. 173.

No. 172 200C-U Wight – Has done very good work, but will not get off anything except very slight sea. Still in very good condition.

No. 173 200C-U Wight – This machine has never given good results. It has now been disassembled and No, 176 will take its place. The necessary parts have been removed from the engine to complete the repair of 136 and 172. It is not possible to stow more than two Wights in the hold with other machines on account of their great breadth.

---

[20] TNA: AIR 1/681/21/13/2209

No. 807 100 Mono Gnome Sopwith – Owing to insufficient surface this machine has never been able to climb and has given poor results. It is now used as a single seater, and as such is capable of some further service.

No. 808 100 Mono Gnome Sopwith – completely wrecked on the 5th March 1915

No. 922 100 Mono Gnome Sopwith – Has done very good service and is still in good flying order. All these three Sopwith machines are dependent on a calm sea to enable them to get off.'[21]

The Fleet may have felt badly let down by the 'Ark Royal' and the RNAS up until now and believe that air support in the Dardanelles had failed. However, Samson and his Squadron had arrived and a sea-change, so to speak, was on its way.

---

[21] TNA: ADM 116/1352

Chapter two
Tenedos, April 1915

With the arrival of Samson and 3 Squadron's advance party, Commander Clark-Hall and Captain Kilner of the 'Ark Royal' realised that their commands might be under threat as so far their seaplanes had let the fleet down and had not fulfilled their mission. However they might have felt about him under the circumstances, Samson's attitude to them was one of friendly co-operation. One of the first things he did was to share his meagre supply of bombs with them so that they could start to take the attack to the Turks.

At lunchtime on 1st April, the SS 'Inkosi' steamed into Mudros with her precious cargo of the rest of 3 Squadron and some very important spares. At long last they had arrived! From the ship they could see the Army setting up its camps and drilling with horses and guns. The ship moved on slowly, passing close to HMS 'Inflexible', who had a bad list on her; they could see where she had been hit several times. As the 'Inkosi' passed, they could see the bodies of the dead being taken out and placed into a launch for burial ashore on Mudros. A grim arrival for the newcomers! The ship was given permission to pass and move on to its anchorage at Tenedos.

As they approached the island, a Maurice Farman flew over followed by Commander Samson in his BE No 50 and finally a Henri Farman. A great cheer went up from the men of 3 Squadron on the 'Inkosi'. Their fearless leader had made it and was in the air! Just what they needed to see after the 'Inflexible's losses! Samson passed over the ship and headed out over the sea to the Dardanelles where he flew over a Turkish fort and seeing the gun crews running to their guns, dropped his three bombs. They did little damage but he had let the Turks know 3 Squadron were in town. All that was needed now was the SS 'Moorgate' to arrive with the rest of the aircraft spares and other supplies both for 3 Squadron and the 'Ark Royal'.

The personnel of 3 Squadron at this point in time was as follows:

Wing Commander C R Samson
Squadron Commander R Bell Davies
Flight Commander E Osmond
Flight Commander R L Marix
Flight Commander C H Collet
Flight Lieutenant E H Newton-Clare
Flight Lieutenant R E C Peirse
Flight Lieutenant W H Wilson
Flight Lieutenant C H Butler
Flight Lieutenant G L Thomson
Flight Sub-Lieutenant W S Newton-Clare

Lieutenant W L Samson
Lieutenant F R Samson
Lieutenant C R Aspinall
Lieutenant B Isaac
Sub-Lieutenant W E Whittaker
Warrant Officer J J Brownridge
Two doctors and 110 ratings.

The remainder of 3 Squadron started to move ashore on 2nd April, bringing with them a load of camping supplies, six more Hervieu canvas hangars and other necessities urgently required to set up an effective airfield. As befitted the Motor Bandits, this included a number of motorised units: one mobile workshop lorry, one searchlight lorry, one W/T (radio) station and a mobile acetylene-welding plant, both mounted on lorries. The men were delighted to be back on dry land and reunited with the rest of the squadron. They soon set to building workshops and had all the aircraft unpacked and started fitting the wings and engines.

Sunday 4th April was Easter Sunday but today in the Dardanelles it was no Bank Holiday. At long last the pilots of the 'Ark Royal' were taking the fight to the enemy. As Samson flew around the area the difference between Europe and Gallipoli was very clear. The North Sea had been grey and very cold while the farm land around Dunkirk was green, flat and lush. The waters of the Aegean were blue, warm and very welcoming after several hours flying and the island of Tenedos was dry and very dusty and mostly turned over to cultivating vines, peppers and olives. The western side of the island was made up of very high cliffs which as you move to the east fall away to sea level by the time you reach the town of Tenedos. The airfield was linked to the town by a very rough cart track, which was only just passable for a wheeled vehicle. There was very little fresh water on the island so this was rationed and the men were excused shaving unless it rained. At the end of the working day, all the officers and men were encouraged to go for a swim as this helped keep them clean and they could wash their clothes in the sea, but salt was left on the material and this could act as an irritant. Whenever the 'Ark Royal' anchored off the airfield, bathing parties would go out to the ship as she had a large bathing room.

On 4th April Admiral Sir John de Robeck sent a report in to the Admiralty praising the work of Samson and his 3 Squadron. He had unloaded 18 aeroplanes and got five of them ready for operations within two days of landing, plus his men had got the two French seaplanes they had found abandoned on the beach working again. They then took the floats off them and put each one on a fixed wheeled undercarriage. He also gained a French pilot who had remained with the machines and did not want to lose his aeroplane. Not one to let the grass grow under his feet, Samson had already put in an order for four new 100 HP Maurice Farman engines and aeroplanes.[22]

The isthmus of Gallipoli is a lot like Tenedos in that it is very dry and dusty. It is 52 miles long and has a maximum width near its centre of 12 miles. The neck of the isthmus near Bulair is only 3½ miles wide and from ANZAC Cove across the width is only some six miles. All the beaches are narrow and back onto steep sandy soil cliffs that rise up for several hundred feet directly from the beaches. Once at the top, the land becomes one continuous ridge system that runs north and south making defence very easy and attack very costly. From the top of the isthmus to Suvla Bay on the Bay of Xeros' side it is a constant chain of hills that precludes any landings apart from a few gullies. The hills surrounding Suvla Bay rise to a height of 670ft. A large feature in the area is a salt lake that is wet in winter and dry in summer and can be driven over as a thick crust is formed. The hills and mountains are covered in a coarse scrub and olive trees. As you come down from Krithia there are a number of spurs that lead towards Cape Helles. The ravines between the spurs are full of dense gorse. The land behind Krithia runs gently down to the coast on the Dardanelles side of the isthmus allowing the positioning of many forts and other defences and several towns. There is also a shortage of water on the isthmus as the very few rivers or streams mostly dry up in the summer. Water was only available from wells, which would make life very difficult for both sides.

There were no paved roads on the isthmus, only glorified cart tracks that in heavy rain would be washed out and turned into a muddy quagmire. Chanak was both a very important trade centre and the headquarters of the general officer commanding the Turkish defence force. The town is situated at sea level at the Narrows and on both sides of the Dardanelles. There were a large number of short jetties and good facilities for landing troops and supplies, including a pier at the north end of the bay that would allow a tug or lighter to come alongside. Next to this was an arsenal from which ammunition and supplies were issued to the forts. Krithia is a small village about four miles from Cape Helles and had a population of some 450 families before the fighting started.

The Straits were closed by a series of ten lines of mines making up a minefield five miles long, laid across the Straits near the Narrows and containing a total of 344 mines. Most of these were contact mines: they had to be struck by a ship to detonate. There was a supply of 30 mines that could drift down the Narrows on the current if required.[23] The Turks brought up 12 field gun batteries that were dug in to cover the minefield

---

[22] TNA: AIR 1/361/15/228/50
[23] TNA: AIR 1/681/21/13/2209

and could not be spotted by ships until they were level with them but could be spotted from the air. Thirty-two 15cm howitzers were also brought up and dug in, one-third on the European side and two-thirds on the Asian side. The Royal Navy were not bothered by these guns as they felt they did not have the penetrating power to pierce the deck of a battleship or damage the superstructure. More of a concern were the twelve searchlights emplaced to cover most of the Straits which would play a big part in the defence of the minefield. The Navy tried to carry out several sweep operations during the night and the lights made these impossible to carry out and also very costly.

From 19th March to 24th April there was only nine days of bad weather which made flying impossible for 3 Squadron, and a few other days when it was impossible for the seaplanes to even try to fly, but 3 Squadron in this period carried out numerous missions:

42 reconnaissance or bombing flights by aeroplanes during which 65 bombs were dropped.

12 reconnaissance flights by seaplanes during which 15 bombs were dropped.

15 spotting flights by aeroplanes

10 spotting flights by seaplanes

18 photographic flights by aeroplane

10 evening aircraft patrols by aeroplanes

One thing Samson picked up on very quickly was that his map from the Admiralty and what he was looking at on the ground from his aeroplane were two very different things.[24] He decided that one of his first tasks was to improve the charts and maps so that the Army, Navy and RNAS were all working from the same type of map with the same information on it, with the enemy positions clearly marked and with valleys and ravines all in the right place, as at times there had been some confusion between the spotter aircraft and the fleet over the position of a battery. Samson was a strong believer in the new science of aerial photography: one aeroplane with a camera could bring back a vast amount of information with far greater accuracy than any hand-drawn map. It was such a new science that most of the senior military officers he dealt with in Gallipoli did not believe what they were seeing. Flight Lieutenant C H Butler and Flight Lieutenant G Thomson were the squadron experts on aerial photography and had brought a small camera with them with which they took some 700 pictures. This small hand-held device was used until they were given a proper aerial camera by the French squadron L'escadrille MF 98 T, who came to share Tenedos airfield.

---

[24] TNA: AIR 1/681/21/13/2209

Life on the island of Tenedos was not idyllic. The heat and dust made life very laborious but worst of all were the flies. Arthur Beeton and some of his mates had a cure for them:

'We found the flies in these bell top tents went up into the top of the tent, in the peak every night. So we found the fire extinguisher – which every tent had – a couple of squirts and they all died and we got rid of them. When the extinguisher ran out we took it to the Store Keeper [Warrant Officer J J Brownridge], he was one of them old naval types, 'there has been no fire you're not having any', so we filled it with petrol, we found it just as good. We squirted it in the tops again and the flies all died. Until a plane caught fire just outside and all the officers that ran to it collared the first fire extinguisher they could get. They squirted petrol, and the petrol caught alight and came back to their hands you see. Oh there was a row about that.'[25]

Another problem that affected a number of the men and all the pilots and observers was the glare from the sun. The clear air was great for taking photographs, but the constant glare of the sea and the large clear areas of sandy soil caused severe eye strain, especially for the aircrew when carrying out reconnaissance flights.

Samson encouraged closer liaison with the fleet, especially for the pilots and observers. A signal was made to the airfield each evening before the next day's spotting flight, giving the hour of day the shoot would take place and its location, and the name of the ship involved. On occasions the gunnery officer and captain of the vessel would land and discuss the next day's target and what they hoped to achieve. All this helped create a closer working relationship between the observer in the aircraft and the gunnery officer. The system for spotting was as follows. Once over the target the aircraft would fly a figure 8 and radio the ship that they were ready. The ship would fire one round and the observer would correct. The message would first state the distance the shot was over or short of the target, then it would state if it had pitched left or right of the target. For example, if the shot was long by 200 yards and to the left by 50 yards, the message would read: S 200, L 50. The ship would signal the aircraft by searchlight confirming the new direction and asking permission to open fire and the aircraft would then order the ship to fire. Samson felt there was too many messages; a lot were cut out and searchlight signalling was stopped.

At first the observer in the aircraft used to spot rather than the pilots, as this gave them both training and experience, but a number of Samson's pilots did not require an observer as they had learnt their lessons on spotting with the Dover Patrol off Belgium. While aircraft spotting was going on, the Fleet had to maintain radio silence, which they were not

---

[25] Arthur Beeton, IWM Sound Archive, catalogue number 8323

always very good at, as if other ships were transmitting they could block the aircraft's signals. In the first few days of spotting, the signalling was slow and not very accurate so Samson opened a signal school for the observers and pilots who were having problems, using two of his men who were experienced signallers. If they were not up flying then they were at school learning Morse. This dramatically improved the speed and quality of the signalling, to the extent that HMS 'Prince George' wrote in a report on 9th April 1915:

'An aeroplane spotted for us and gave us a fine object lesson in what can be done in this respect. It was about 6,000ft above the battery flying in a figure of eight, but at the distance looked as if it was stationary over the target. It sent the results of each shot by W/T immediately it fell, and the rapidity with which it spotted and transmitted was quite a revelation to most of us.'

On 4th April the 'Ark Royal' managed to get several seaplanes in the air. The first was Douglas in No 922 who took off at 0612hrs and headed to Smyrna harbour, followed at 0657hrs by Bromet in No 172, heading to the same destination. Bromet returned at 0820hrs and reported that he had attacked three torpedo boat dropping one bomb on each but all three missed. At 0855hrs HMS 'Usk' was spotted approaching the 'Ark Royal' with Douglas and No 922 in tow: he had suffered an engine failure. At 1230hrs a second strike against Smyrna harbour was launched. First up was Douglas in a repaired No 922 followed by Bromet in No 172. The repair did not hold: at 1240hrs Douglas returned his engine having failed again. Bromet checked on the results of HMS 'London' and HMS 'Prince of Wales' shooting that morning on the way to and from the harbour. Both had done considerable damage to the batteries at Morto Bay, and some ten new batteries were spotted and marked up as close as possible on a map.

April 9th was a very busy day as the 'Moorgate' arrived along with HMS 'Manica' (of which more later). Lieutenant Isaac came ashore from the 'Moorgate' at Tenedos to a scene of complete and utter chaos. He walked up the temporary road from the beach to the airfield at the top, stopped and looked around. An aeroplane came down the runway and took off in the direction of the warships that were firing. Isaac could not see what they were firing at but he could see the flash of the guns followed by the sound of the shells heading towards their target. There were two large working parties hauling the crated aeroplanes from the beach up the slope to the airfield. Once there, the working party was directed where to drag the crates to and the men of 3 Squadron descended on them. Samson, Collet and Peirse were up over Gallipoli. Collet was carrying out a spotting sortie, while Samson and Peirse were carrying out a bombing raid and reconnaissance of Turkish positions. Isaac was given a tent-mate and between the two of them they put up yet another bell tent to join the many around the little stone-built house that was used by the officers. The next day Isaac was given a position in the intelligence tent to which every pilot and observer reported on landing and the information they brought back was written down or put onto charts. Isaac's first task was to join up several sets of maps of the Gallipoli peninsula as at the end of each day a new map or a tracing would be sent to Admiral de Robeck and General Sir Ian Standish Hamilton, the commander of the Mediterranean Expeditionary Force. The last bits of equipment were very quickly unloaded from the 'Moorgate' and these included a very large marquee that the squadron had acquired in some mysterious way and was going to use as the mess tent.

Eight of the aeroplanes that had come directly from France had been loaded on the 'Abda' directly and could not be inspected by Samson at the time. On unloading at Tenedos they were discovered to be the wrong type of aeroplane for the job in hand. They were 80hp Gnome engine Henri Farmans, all right for solo photographic missions but nothing else and they soon started to rot in the heat. Samson got on to the Admiral and convinced him that he urgently needed new replacement aeroplanes. The admiral agreed and ordered replacements for Samson.

Besides spotting for the warships' guns, there was the bread and butter job of the intelligence reconnaissance. For a military commander it is vital to have knowledge of what your enemy is doing on the other side of the hill. The pilots and observers located enemy camps, artillery, and entrenchments and made a note of them, these notes being transferred on to a map by Isaac and any other occupant of the intelligence tent. The amended maps were printed on board the SS 'Arcadian', then supplied as a set of three sheets in 1:40,000 scale, over-printed with a red grid, each square equalling 200 square yards, to make the locating of batteries easier. These daily reports from 3 Squadron very quickly began to have an effect as it became very clear that the Turks were not sitting on their hands. On the contrary, they were building very effective and very strong defences. The SS 'Arcadian' had been taken over by the Admiralty in February 1915 and converted to an armed merchant cruiser. General Hamilton came aboard at Alexandria on 7th April 1915 and used 'Arcadian', together with the battleship HMS 'Queen Elizabeth', as his headquarters ship during opening phase of the Gallipoli Campaign. When he took over, he ordered that the 'Arcadian' should be fitted out with a fully-functioning print room with a lithographic press so that multiple copies of intelligence reports, maps, map overlays and photographs could all be copied and distributed around the command. Once Hamilton's staff had transferred to a shore base at Imbros, 'Arcadian' was employed as a troopship in the Mediterranean.

We now return to HMS 'Manica', the other new arrival on 9th April. On 4th March 1915 Lieutenant General William R Birdwood, GOC ANZAC Corps, wired Lord Kitchener urgently, requesting that a man-lifting kite or a captive balloon be sent to the Dardanelles as soon as possible for spotting naval fire and detecting concealed enemy shore batteries, as the seaplanes from the 'Ark Royal' could not give the air support required. The snag was that no land was available to set up a kite or balloon service area so the only thing left was to put it on a ship.

The Royal Navy did not have any spare ships and set about finding a suitable craft. On 11th March an old tramp called the 'Manica' was found, unloading manure from Australia. The Admiralty requisitioned this 3,500 ton steamer, then lying in Manchester, and, after a hasty conversion in Graysons shipyard at Birkenhead, she was dispatched with No 1 Kite Balloon Section to the Dardanelles. The conversion was made by lifting up the long sloping deck from forecastle to waist height, fixing a dynamo to drive a hydrogen compressor, installing a winch and connecting it to the main engines, building a wireless telegraphy house and quarters for officers and men - generally adapting the fittings and appointments to what they conceived to be the requirements of a kite-balloon ship.

Getting a ship was the easy part. The Royal Navy knew what they were doing and what to look for. The balloon would be a far more difficult affair. The RNAS had a few old spherical balloons left over from the Boer War, two hand-power winches, another powered by a petrol engine and some cable, but these balloons were not stable in the air as had been proved at Dunkirk when spotting for the Dover Patrol. A spherical balloon does not take kindly to captivity; it plunges and turns and twists and longs to break away from its tethers. Even in a light wind it never seemed really happy and in a heavy wind it got beyond a joke. The RNAS men at Dunkirk had seen a Belgian and later a French balloon of a type called a Drachen. It had great handling even in a bit of a wind and could rise higher than any British balloon. As it was a German design appeared impossible to get one until it was discovered that the French had set up a balloon factory making them in Paris. An officer who spoke French was dispatched there with the utmost urgency, returning in a very short time to announce that he had borrowed not only a kite-balloon but also a powered winch and cable.

The next step was to marry the ship up with the balloon but there was no time for training as the ship was required urgently in the Dardanelles. The necessary personnel and stores were collected and on 22nd March she was commissioned as HMS 'Manica', under the command of Flight Commander John D Mackworth, with Engineer Lieutenant Robert A Mackenzie RNR as Chief Engineer Officer, and RNR officers and MMR crew. Not only was no training carried out but not even a trial launch or inflation of the balloon from the ship; this all had to wait until the ship reached the Dardanelles. The big question was, would this new idea work? In an incredibly short space of time they sailed from England. They even took with them a ship's mascot, a cat called 'Mowler'. Mowler could be found asleep on the deck in one of the many coils of rope - not a cat to be disturbed as it had been born without any patience! It would jump ship once in the Dardanelles for a far better berth.

None of the crew had been at sea before and the weather was not good, so the voyage from Britain to Gibraltar was a very trying time. Their first port of call was Gibraltar and as many men as possible were allowed ashore to recuperate from the violent seasickness with which they had been afflicted. The C.O. paid his respects to the Admiral, only to incur great wrath by inadvertently flying the obsolete Blue Ensign. However, the Admiral soon became interested in the unusual project and offered all possible assistance. After calling at Malta to take on coal, the 'Manica' proceeded to Mudros, carrying out trial flights off Cape Matapan on the way.

The first was begun with some apprehension as none of the crew knew what to expect. The flying deck was 90 feet by 30 feet and the balloon was nearly 80 feet long, giving little spare operating room in the blustery air which generally prevailed near the surface. Every available man was turned out, the balloon was inflated and the nose allowed to rise to assume the normal operating angle. The basket was toggled on and Mackworth climbed aboard. The order to cast off was given and the balloon rose quickly into the air. All worked perfectly and two minutes later the full altitude was reached. Mackworth had a perfect view and the forward speed of the ship into the wind made the flight very stable. The recovery was similarly text book. The air scoop caught the breeze and filled the ballonet and the lateral sails flapped as they lost lift when the nose went down. The only difficulty was with the parachute stabilisers. These proved too stable and when the lowest hit the water fully inflated, it remained open and filled with water, operating as an efficient sea anchor. This had the effect of pulling the balloon up short by the tail and standing it on end. Fortunately, the master of the 'Manica' saw exactly what was happening and put the ship full astern. This freed the parachute and the landing crew were able to hold the guy-ropes and control the balloon. The parachute trip wires were revised and retried. Everything worked perfectly and before nightfall all of the necessary trials had been completed.[26]

On 9th April 'Manica' arrived in Mudros Bay off the island of Lemnos. As she entered the anchorage a signal was received requesting her commanding officer to report to the flag ship HMS 'Queen Elizabeth' at once. At the subsequent briefing Admiral de Robeck explained that the Turkish defenders could fire comfortably at the Fleet from the high and broken ground of the peninsula. However, from sea level the Fleet could not spot the concealed batteries. Instruction in naval signals and fire observation was given to the balloon observers and trials with the cruiser

---

[26] TNA: AIR 1/148/15/83/2

HMS 'Bacchante' took place off Lemnos on 15th April. It was found that if the 'Manica' kept close to the battleship on the side opposite the target, signals could be repeated to other ships by semaphore. Mackworth reported that:

'The observation is in many respects not inferior to that obtained from aeroplanes, the communications are incomparably better and more reliable, and the chances of a breakdown very much less.'

The first active flight was on 19th April when under direction from 'Manica', HMS 'Bacchante' shelled a Turkish camp just as dawn was breaking.

Squadron Commander Mackworth remained the only trained observer on the 'Manica' for some months until additional observers had been trained at the RNAS Depot at Roehampton and sent out to join the ship. The ease of telephone communications, coupled with the endurance and stability of the balloon as an observation platform, gave excellent results and in fine weather, near-perfect fire control. This so impressed the Admiralty that approval was given for the conversion and completion of six additional balloon ships.

On 10th April the first of the Army spotters that Samson had requested, Major R E T Hogg and Captain Jenkins, reported in to him. Their journey from ship to shore was quite an experience: the pier they were landed on was made out of barrels and boards, the road from the beach to the airfield was rough and the sides were deep soft sand. They managed to get a lift from some locals who had a hand cart to get their gear up to the airfield. These trained artillery spotters were not too impressed at first with Tenedos!

On 11th April Samson was called into a planning meeting on the 'Arcadian' and was given the invasion date and his instructions for that day and those before. From now until the invasion, Samson and 3 Squadron were to fly daily reconnaissance missions over the landing beaches and Turkish defences, taking photographs. Isaac and Butler soon built up a large photographic map of the region, a copy of which was sent to every Division that was going to land. A number of the Army officers could not believe what they were seeing. It looked like a massacre was on the cards for the troops who were to land on 25th April but this new technology was too good to be true for some. Some Generals like Lieutenant-General Sir Aylmer Gould Hunter-Weston decried the maps as rubbish and make-believe.

From now until 23rd April there was a steady flow of ships from Alexandria bringing over the men who would take part in the attack. On a number of occasions while aeroplanes and seaplanes were up spotting for the fleet their W/T messages were talked over by the fleet as other ships sent messages on the same frequency. This was an impossible situation so the spotting aircraft were now given a designated frequency of their own and only the firing ship could be on this channel. An aircraft was sent up to broadcast using the new channel and all the bombarding ships tuned their W/T to it. Sub-Lieutenant Dunning was given the task. He took off in No 807 at 1615hrs and remained up until 1815hrs, having talked rubbish for over an hour on the Morse key.

The 'Ark Royal' left Mudros on the evening of 11th April and headed out to the Gulf of Xeros accompanied by battleships 'Agamemnon' and 'Lord Nelson' and the destroyer 'Usk' to act as a diversion to try to put the Turkish army off the intended attack zone. 3 Squadron were very busy on the 11th, carrying out ten successful missions. Lieutenant Peirse and his observer, Captain Collet, flew the first reconnaissance mission over Gaba Tepe and spotted the Turks digging a number of new trenches and gun emplacements. Back on Tenedos, they gave their information to Lieutenant Isaac. This was now a well-organised information distribution system. He typed up all reports and sent them off for printing and distribution, updated his maps if necessary with any new information, made a new tracing and sent that off for printing as well.

The weather on the morning of 12th April was not good. It was overcast with light misty rain while later thunderclouds rolled in, so no flying was done in the morning. Everyone made good use of this temporary lull in operations. Lieutenant Isaac spent most of the morning digging a drainage trench around his tent trying to save his intelligence office from the flooding. The men set to turning the aeroplane packing cases into workshops and sleeping quarters as the bell tents were not good in the rain, and life improved! Samson's men were very competent and could turn their hands to most things. For some six months they had kept the squadron flying, rebuilding aircraft at times and overhauling them without the use of a repair depot.

In the afternoon 3 Squadron managed to get two reconnaissance flights away. Samson took a special reconnaissance flight with submarine captain Lieutenant Commander Theodore Brodie, who was going to take his submarine E 15 up the Dardanelles to sink Turkish shipping, so that he could see the obstacles that he would have to pass. He had come over to Tenedos just to have a look at the latest intelligence and any pictures of the Straits but Samson offered to take him up and let him look for himself at what he would be taking on. A thunderstorm was moving in so they could not hang about. They took off in a Henri Farman pusher with a 70hp powered engine, giving a very slow top speed of 59mph. This meant that it could not be used for any other type of mission except reconnaissance, and then out of range of Turkish guns. Brodie sat in the front of the gondola in a wicker chair and had an uninterrupted panoramic view of the Straits. This was the squadron's fiftieth mission since arriving and the flow of intelligence both to the fleet and the army was almost unbelievable - except they could see the results with their own eyes.

Lieutenant Warner set about installing electric light in the camp. It had started to get dark on the evening it was finished when Warner walked over to the switch in the mess tent and, with a great flourish, turned it on. Nothing happened and a great cheer went up. Warner's embarrassment level now went through the roof. He called for Platford who was looking after the generator - and had forgotten to turn it on. Another great cheer went up in the mess when the lights came on!

That evening an order arrived from Hamilton's HQ saying a senior officer required a reconnaissance flight the next day. Late the next morning, 13th April, General Staff Officer Grade 3 (Intelligence) Major Charles Villiers-Stuart stepped ashore on Tenedos for his flight. He reported in to Isaac in the intelligence tent. Flight Lieutenant Collet had been assigned as his pilot, just one of eight flights this day for the Squadron. Collet met the Major and started the pre-flight briefing, which was short and very hair-raising. He explained how biplanes could fall and rise very sharply and that he should not be alarmed if the engine stopped suddenly or if he had to put the aircraft into a dive. The main thing was to just sit back and enjoy the ride. Collet then passed him an empty 2-gallon petrol can and told him to hang on to it as this was his life preserver if they had to land in the water. The Major was now looking very worried but Collet, a Captain in the Royal Marines Artillery and an excellent pilot, had had his fun.

At 1420hrs they took off and entered a slow climb, heading towards Gallipoli. As they approached Gaba Tepe, the major could see that the land changed, becoming very coarse and covered in tight scrub which made it very difficult for men to pass. They spotted several gun positions that had been poorly camouflaged and had not yet been reported. Major Villiers-Stuart also saw the magnitude of the Turkish trench system, how far it spread and the miles of barbed wire that had been put into position. Over an hour had passed as they turned for home with the major excited and exhausted. He could hardly believe what he had seen, and in such detail, but now Major Villiers-Stuart would believe the reconnaissance photographs that were sent over to him each day. This was not going to be the cakewalk of an invasion that had been promised by Lord Kitchener and some of the other generals. They landed at 1540hrs and Villiers-Stuart had never been so pleased to feel a muddy field under his feet! He went down to the intelligence tent and started typing up a report that would change things in the ANZAC HQ. Apprehension now swept through the HQ; it was clear this was not going to be an easy attack.

Having read Major Villiers-Stuart's reports and looked at his maps, General Hamilton felt he had to see for himself the source of all this information. On 15th April he came to Tenedos to have a look at the intelligence first-hand but declined to go up in the air. Lieutenant Isaac laid out before the General all the photographs and maps that he had of the landing beaches. For a man who had never seen anything like this in his lifetime it must have looked like black magic or the devil's work. The General told Samson that he had expected to lose at least 50% of his first wave but with this new information he could save a lot more of his command. Showing this new intelligence pack to some of his other planning officers, the General could see a weakness in the Turkish defences that he wanted to exploit. There was an undefended cliff top above Y Beach which he now wanted to use as it could give the British forces a chance to outflank the main Turkish position, and the plan of attack was changed.

On 14th April 3 Squadron carried out a spotting mission for HMS 'Majestic', four general reconnaissance missions with bombs and two photographic missions. The next day one of Samson's pilots found and sketched the Turkish airfield they had been looking for without success for some time. It was just outside Chanak on the Asian side of the Dardanelles. Samson and his pilots were becoming a major problem for the Turkish Army. They were attacking its tented camps and supply trains on a daily basis, sending donkeys, horses and bullocks off in all directions. These would take days to round up again. Colonel Kannengiesser, a staff officer to General Liman von Sanders, gave orders that all defensive construction works had to be carried out in the hours of darkness. As first light broke all work would stop and the work would be camouflaged. All troop movements would also be carried out under the cover of darkness.

On 16th April the 'Ark Royal' got a seaplane up to spot for the 'Agamemnon'. Lieutenant Whitehead took off at 1645hrs in No 176 and flew off in the direction of Taifur Keui where there was a military installation. After a number of missed shots, 'Agamemnon' at long last landed a shell on target and a large magazine exploded. Meanwhile on Tenedos the enemy was striking back. Out of the morning sky appeared a Taube, an enemy aeroplane, and it dropped two bombs. No damage was done to the aeroplanes or the airfield but Warner had rushed to the 12-pounder anti-aircraft gun (AA) and opened fire with some pretty erratic shooting. Samson and Osmond were up spotting for one of the battleships when the big end went in the engine. Fortunately they had the height and speed to turn for home and the wind was behind them. They glided back, getting lower and lower, and just made it.

The early hours of the 17th saw the men of 3 Squadron swarming around two aircraft getting them ready to fly on their missions. Two 100lb bombs per aeroplane were wheeled out and very carefully lifted up and onto the bomb racks. Peirse and Osmond were in one aeroplane while a second was crewed by Collet and Charles Brodie. The two aeroplanes took off one after the other and headed out towards Gallipoli, their targets being a couple of the forts overlooking the minefield, and the harbour of Maidos. Their task was to create a diversion so that the Turks would be looking up and not down as the E15 tried to run the Narrows. Things had not gone well in E15 and she breached in the channel, then ran aground on a sand bar. The Turkish guns opened fire on the submarine and hit it several times, the first shell passing through the conning tower without exploding but killing Lieutenant Brodie, a second exploding in the engine room. The crew abandoned ship and swam to the nearest shore where they were taken prisoner by the Turks. The 'Ark Royal' returned from the diversion work in the Gulf of Xeros and tied up in Mudros anchorage.

On 18th April the enemy aircraft returned and flew over the airfield on Tenedos at 0730hrs, dropping three bombs. No one was hurt and no damage was done to the general operation of the base. Commander Bell Davies was ready to take off, so he jumped into his aeroplane and gave chase, but the enemy was too high and too far in front so he returned to Tenedos. On Samson's orders he and Collet bombed up and paid a visit to the enemy airfield, where they destroyed an aeroplane in its hanger and damaged other buildings but the thing that really hurt was the destruction of the fuel store. This greatly restricted air operations. The Turkish air force was now effectively grounded and would remain so until after the landings on the isthmus of Gallipoli. In one stroke Samson had gained air superiority over the battlefield. One aeroplane went up on a spotting mission for HMS 'Triumph', but due to a W/T failure no firing was carried out. A detailed reconnaissance was carried out of the beaches from Tekke Burnu and Cape Helles using three aeroplanes. 'Ark Royal' launched one seaplane at 1630hrs, No 176 flown by Lieutenant Whitehead; it returned at 1800hrs having carried out W/T testing.

On 18th April, 'Manica' and the cruiser HMS 'Bacchante' were ordered to leave Mudros at night and creep up to the peninsula just before dawn to engage any suitable targets of opportunity that might be found. What the Turkish reaction would be to the balloon was not known. They were not even aware of the presence of a balloon ship – indeed, they had no reason to know that such a thing existed - and had taken no special precautions. There was no camouflage to try to hide the very smart white tents. The first active flight was on 19th April when under direction from 'Manica', HMS 'Bacchante' shelled a Turkish camp just as dawn was breaking.

Mackworth wrote in his report:

'The enemy were not aware of the presence of the balloon ship, and had taken no special precautions against being overlooked. The consequence was that when Manica put up her balloon, the first sight which greeted the observers was a sleeping camp, neatly arranged in a dip in the ground, out of sight of Bacchante but within easy range of her guns. Through their excellent field glasses they could see an occasional dot moving about, but for the most part the camp was not yet astir. If there were sentries, they doubtless regarded the distant balloon hanging in the sky as a harmless form of amusement for jaded British officers, and saw no connection between it and the long guns of the Bacchante which were turning round towards them. But the boom of the cruiser's forward turret opened their eyes and a rude awakening followed when the top of a hillock some hundred yards beyond the camp was hurled into the air. No reveille ever blown commanded so instant a response. Every tent burst into life, and the ground was soon swarming with running specks. A second shot burst on the northernmost fringe of the camp, and a third right in the midst of the tents. Bacchante had the range to a nicety, and began to fire salvoes of 6-inch shells. A scene of indescribable confusion followed. Tents were rent to pieces and flung into the air, dust spouted in huge fans and columns, and brightly through the reek could be seen the flashes of bursting shells. Like ants from an overturned nest, the little brown dots swarmed and scattered. Across the plain galloped a few terrified mules, and in an incredibly short time the wreckage was complete. Of the once orderly camp, nothing remained but torn earth and twisted canvas, and when the smoke cleared away, no movement was to be seen. The trial was simple but convincing. *Manica* signalled "Cease Fire", and lumbered home behind her consort, metaphorically wagging her tail.'[27]

On Monday 19th April one aeroplane was spotting for HMS 'Talbot' using the W/T channel, when a second aeroplane was sent up to spot for HMS 'Agamemnon'. They could not use the W/T system so reverted to using a searchlight and Aldiss lamp, which did not work well at all and 'Agamemnon' did not get a shot off. A gun battery was also attacked by three aircraft carrying three 100lb bombs and six smaller 20lb bombs. One gun took a direct hit while a gun limber and a pile of ammunition was hit and set off. The date of the landings on Gallipoli was confirmed at a meeting on the 'Queen Elizabeth' as 23rd April, weather permitting.

Lord Kitchener received a shock when a report on the fighting in Basra landed on his desk on late on Monday 19th April. His belief that the Turk was not a good soldier was proved to be completely wrong. Kitchener wrote to Hamilton:

'The Turkish troops were well disciplined, well trained and brave. Their machine guns were well positioned and well concealed, and were used with great effect.'

The British and Indian troops had found that 'Johnny Turk' did not turn and run at the sound of gunfire. The Turkish soldiers stood and fought and had to be turned out of their trenches and other defences at the point of a bayonet, a far cry from what Kitchener had promised Hamilton at the start

---

[27] TNA: AIR 1/11/15/1/44

of the Gallipoli campaign. Turkey might well be seen as the sick man of Europe but her Army could fight. Yet again he had got it wrong and passed the buck onto Churchill.

The weather was not good on Tuesday 20th April, so only four flights were sent up that morning. All the pilots noticed that some of the Turkish tented encampments had moved or just plain disappeared. Lieutenant Isaac had a quiet afternoon as intelligence officer so he decided that he would walk into the town of Tenedos and get some wine and fresh fruit and vegetables to supplement the mess rations.

A storm was blowing on Wednesday 21st April and the rain was coming down in buckets. The weather did moderate later but far too late for any flying. There were rivers running across the airfield and the men collected the fresh rain water; many had a shave. So Isaac had another easy day. Samson called for him and told him that he would not be flying again until after the invasion because he was needed as the intelligence officer full-time. It was a job he came to love and held for all his time in the Dardanelles.

Early on Thursday 22nd April, orders were beginning to filter down to the lowest private for the coming invasion but the weather was still playing up and the planners were not happy. On Friday 23rd April Samson and 3 Squadron were ordered to attack the Turkish port of Maidos and every aeroplane that could carry a bomb was put into the air. The raid was a great success and all work in the docks was brought to a halt as a lot of damage was done to the piers and warehouses. Maidos itself was hit by a number of bombs.

The weather and the sea state was greatly improving and it looked far better for the invasion, and, as the day of the invasion approached, the aeroplanes were called upon to carry out far more duties. Samson and his Squadron were having to develop new tactics as every time the Turks heard an aircraft they stopped firing and camouflaged their position. However, he had trained his pilots well while they were in France and one of the things they learnt was how to dive-bomb. They would switch off their engines and dive down to 1,000ft, flare out and drop their bombs on the target, then switch the engine back on and climb for home. This system worked very well. Samson's men became very adept at this dive-bombing technique and took the skill with them to the Dardanelles. Until now, on hearing an aeroplane the Turks would stop firing their guns and camouflage them, hoping not to be seen but 3 Squadron's dive-bombing technique stopped the Turks hearing their approach and allowed them to attack the guns and camp fires with greater success, destroying a number of Turkish guns this way. They also worked out when the Turks had their breakfast and dinner and would attack the camp sites using the same system, letting the bombs go at about 1,000ft, but often well below that, and aiming for the centre of the cooking fires.

By now Butler and Isaac could see that the 29th Division was walking into a deadly ambush at Cape Helles. They could see from the photographs that it would be nothing but murder on the landing beaches and yet the senior officers of the Division could not see what was before their eyes as they did not know how to read the photographs. The ANZACS decided to solve this by sending a senior Intelligence Officer to take a look at what 3 Squadron had really got and very unexpectedly Samson insisted that he should go and take a look for himself. Marix took him up and flew him over the enemy positions and showed him exactly what they had seen in the photographs, he could now see with his own eyes. He was horrified.

The weather still did not look favourable for the morning of the 23rd and the attack was postponed for 24 hours. On the evening of 23rd April an apparently endless line of warships and transports assembled and moved towards the peninsula. It was difficult to hide that something was going to happen and very soon. But still the weather was not good for the landings so yet again they were postponed for another twenty-four hours. Later in the day, orders were issued postponing the invasion until 25th April.

Saturday 24th April was a good day at last and it would be the last full day that many men would see. At 0700hrs church parade was called on all the ships carrying the infantry for the assault. Samson ordered Butler to fly over the beaches and take a last set of photographs while others would carry out reconnaissance and bombing missions behind the beach line. At noon the battleships and other warships slowly weighed anchor and moved out to their assembly areas, quite a sight from the air. 'Manica' was working with HMS 'Queen Elizabeth' that day. The Gaba Tepe position was shelled and a Turkish barracks destroyed, killing and wounding many men.

The Rev Captain O Creighton was part of General Hunter-Weston's command and he, like others on the General's staff, could see from the intelligence reports and photographs that this invasion was not going to be easy. He wrote:

'Meanwhile the Turks, under German direction, have perfected their defences. It seems a perfectly desperate undertaking, to attack the Turkish positions. The aerial reconnaissance reports acres of barbed wire, labyrinths of trenches, concealed guns, Maxims, and howitzers everywhere. The ground is mined. In fact everything conceivable has been done. Our men have to be towed in little open rowing boats to land in the face of all this.'[28]

---

[28] Rev Captain O Creighton, *With the Twenty Ninth Division in Gallipoli, 1916*, page 42

Yet still the general himself could not see. He could not believe what was before his eyes. Before 1914 no senior officer, or any general who had fought a battle in the past, had ever had the advantage of aerial photography and this innovation would change the way war was fought for ever. General Hamilton grasped this new innovation but poor old Hunter-Weston could not. He saw this as black magic and even worse - the work of the devil that could not be trusted and so must be ignored. Because of this he would mindlessly send thousands of men to their deaths. This was very much a case of lions led by donkeys.

The overall plan of the invasion was described thus:

'The object of the expedition was to assist the fleet to force the Dardanelles by capturing the Kilid Bahr plateau and dominating the forts at the Narrows. The general plan to achieve this object was:-

1. A bombardment of the Bulair lines at daybreak, followed by a feint landing on the mainland north of Xeros Islands by the transports carrying the R N Division.

2. Simultaneously with the above bombardment of the heights commanding the beach between Kapa Tepe and Nebrunesi Point accompanied by a landing by the Australian and New Zealand Army Corps on the beach between Gaba Tepe and Fisherman's Hut.

3. At the same time a bombardment of the southern extremity of the peninsula, immediately followed by a landing of the 29th Division in the neighbourhood of Cape Helles.

4. Simultaneously with the foregoing, the French Fleet were to make a demonstration at Besika Bay, in combination with a landing to be effected by a portion of the French Expeditionary Force near Kum Kale. This landing would be a temporary one with the object of safeguarding the landing at Cape Helles from the fire of guns in the vicinity of Kum Kale. As soon as a secure footing was gained on the Peninsula the French were to re-embark from Kum Kale and land at Cape Helles.

The Australian and New Zealand Army Corps (ANZAC) the covering force, after overcoming any resistance at or near the shore, was to occupy the Sari Bair heights, and thus cover the left flank of the main Force. This body was then to advance some four miles east of the landing place and assault Mal Tepe, a hill overlooking the straights and three-quarters of a mile south of Boghali.

The Objectives of the 29th Division- after the covering force had overcome any resistance at or near the shore, it and the main body were to advance and occupy Krithia and Achi Baba.

In accordance with the general plan of operations the main landings were to take place at two widely separated positions of the peninsula:

A. About a mile north of Gaba Tepe

B. At three beaches at the southern extremity of the peninsula.

At the same time the French Division were to make a feint landing at Besika Bay and to land a small force to occupy Kum Kale on the Asiatic shore and its vicinity and the Naval Division were to make a feint at landing at the head of the Gulf of Xeros.'[29]

Hamilton laid down strict instructions for aerial co-operation during the landing.

'A. Aeroplanes from Tenedos, as directed by Commander C R Samson, DSO will work:- Some under Rear Admiral S Nicholson, MVO spotting for covering ships on the Gallipoli Peninsula. Others under General Officer Commanding land operations conducted by the 1st Squadron.

B. Ark Royal with seaplanes will be attached to Queen and act under the orders of the RA [Rear Admiral] commanding 2nd Squadron.

C. French aircraft including seaplanes and aeroplanes coming from Egypt will act under orders of Contre Amiral Guepratte and GOC the French Division. [The French land aeroplanes did not make it till after the landings.]

D. SS Manica with the kite balloon section will work under orders of RA Commanding 2nd Squadron unless required by Vice Admiral.

E. During forthcoming operations aircraft will not be fired at by the Navy or Army unless committing hostile acts or being obviously marked with a black cross they indicate their German Nationality.[30]

The one exception to the above is that any aircraft approaching the Kite balloon are to be fired on. Aircraft should avoid flying over transports.'

Detailed orders for aeroplanes at the landing were for two aeroplanes to be up continuously all day, one over Helles and the over the Asiatic side. Early each morning they were to overfly and keep a watch on the ships covering the landing, to signal the position of any Turkish batteries firing on the landings or the ships and to spot for the warships bringing shell fire on to

---

[29] TNA: AIR 1/681/21/13/2209
[30] TNA: AIR 1/681/21/13/2209

the target. After the landings, aeroplanes were to continue to spot ships onto the same batteries and on to reinforcements, to watch roads and to drop bombs on any troops seen. They were also to keep an eye out for any enemy aeroplanes. The job of spotting for the fleet was supposed to last until lunchtime by when the Army would have landed their own artillery and been in control of the beaches. But things ran late and the 'Ark Royal' and 3 Squadron were ordered to fly more spotting flights.

The night between Saturday and Sunday was beautiful, clear and quiet. Moonrise was at 1212hrs and set at 0257. As the British ships took up position off the beaches they could be seen by the Turks and a warning was raised. So much for a surprise landing! Sunday 25th April was a beautiful morning. First light was at 0525hrs and sunset would be at 1903hrs. The sea was like glass, the sun was shining and all was well, except for on the beaches.

The pilots of the 'Ark Royal' could not sleep and spent the night drinking and playing cards. The ship had a good day for once as most of her seaplanes managed to get up and support the ANZAC landings. The first flight was made by Captain Kilner who took off in No 161 at 0517hrs but had to return at 0525 with a broken oil pump. At 0543hrs Whitehead took off in No 176 with Lieutenant Strain as observer and patrolled over the eastern end of the landings near the village of Boghali, then Kershaw took off in No 1438, landing back again at 0652hrs. Whitehead returned at 0722hrs, then Bromet took off in No 172 at 0725hrs, followed by Garrett in No 1437 at 0743hrs, though engine problems brought him back at 0823hrs. Bromet landed back at 0900hrs. Whitehead's flight was the last before lunch; he took off at 1021hrs and landed an hour later. At 1300hrs seaplanes No 136 and No 1438 took off to carry out a reconnaissance.

Some 15 flights in all were made from the 'Ark Royal' during the day, which was by far their best flying day since being commissioned, each pilot making three flights. The first flights over the beaches were of no real value as the fleet ignored all W/T and Aldiss messages. This action at the Dardanelles was the first time the Mediterranean Fleet had used this system of aerial spotting and consequently at times of great excitement they forgot to keep a radio watch on the spotting frequency. Seaplanes from the 'Ark Royal' were also kept very busy at Angar. She would remain on this station for 14 days covering the ANZAC landings. Just to bring Clark-Hall's men back down to earth, the next day, 26th April, was the worst day for the 'Ark Royal' when all six aircraft failed to fly due to engine failure.

The 'Manica's balloon observed for ships covering the ANZAC landings on 25th April 1915. The balloon, with two observers, went up at 0521hrs and fourteen minutes later discovered the Turkish battleship 'Turgud Reis' in the Narrows. The position was reported to HMS 'Triumph', which opened fire causing the enemy battleship to retreat. This encounter was witnessed by the American reporter Raymond Swing, who noted that:

'The first salvo directed by the balloon struck at least 1000 yards away, the second 500 yards away. The third passed through the rigging and burst 50 feet away. She did not wait for any more.'

However, she returned at 0900hrs and began to pour fire onto the transport ships from which troops were being landed. This caused an interruption to the disembarkation, which was only resumed when HMS 'Triumph', again guided by 'Manica', drove the battleship out of range. The balloon was hauled down at 1405hrs, marking the end of nearly nine hours of close and effective co-operation with 'Triumph'.

Communications between the ship and the balloon were by telephone, with four wires running from the balloon to four parts of the ship: the Observation Hut, the bridge, the W/T cabin and the anti-aircraft gun position. The sound quality on the phone was good except when the ship used its W/T. As a backup system a W/T buzzer was fitted to the basket and this would be used to send Morse to the ship. An Aldiss lamp was also fitted to the basket for visual signalling and was the most satisfactory method of signalling the firing ship. The observers in the basket could see the fall of shot from the battleship and would have reported the result within 30 seconds so a good rate of fire could be kept up and a number of targets hit.[31] Every time the balloon went up it would receive a number of shells as the Turks tried desperately to shoot it down.

The Vice Admiral telegraphed the Admiralty on the 29th April, as follows:-

'Warships covered the advance and were instrumental in defeating several counter-attacks and silenced batteries. The kite balloon once more proved invaluable.'

The Helles landing was made by the 29th Division under the command of Major General Aylmer Hunter-Weston. The division landed on five beaches in an arc around the tip of the peninsula, named from east to west as 'S', 'V', 'W', 'X' and 'Y' Beaches. At 'Y' Beach the Allies were able to land unopposed and advance inland during the first engagement around the village of Krithia. There were only a small number of defenders there but lacking orders to exploit the position, the 'Y' Beach commander withdrew his force back to the beach. It was as close as they came to capturing the village.

The main landings were made at 'V' Beach, beneath the Seddülbahir fortress and at 'W' Beach, a short distance to the west on the other side of

---

[31] TNA: ADM 116/1352

the Helles headland. The covering force from the Royal Munster Fusiliers and the Hampshire's landed from a converted collier, SS 'River Clyde', which was run aground beneath the fortress so that the troops could disembark via ramps to the shore. Several machine guns were set up in sangars on the deck of the ship and were commanded by Lieutenant Commander J Wedgwood of the RNAS Armoured Car section. All the men were from the RNAS Armoured Car Division, who would remain at their posts all that day firing on the Turkish positions and supporting the men on the beach.

The Royal Dublin Fusiliers landed at 'V' Beach from open boats. At 'W' Beach, the Lancashire Fusiliers also landed in open boats on a shore overlooked by dunes and obstructed with barbed wire. On both beaches the Turkish defenders occupied very good, strong defensive positions and inflicted many casualties on the British infantry as they landed. Troops emerging one by one from sally ports on the 'River Clyde' were cut down by the Turkish machine-gunners in the Seddülbahir fortress. Of the first 200 soldiers to disembark, only 21 men reached the beach. At 'W' Beach, the Lancashire's were able to overwhelm the defences despite suffering 600 casualties from 1,000 men. The battalions that landed at 'V' Beach suffered about 70% casualties. Six awards of the Victoria Cross were made among the Lancashire's at 'W' Beach and a further six were awarded among the infantry and sailors at the 'V' Beach landing. Three more were awarded the following day as they fought their way off the beach. Five squads of Turkish infantry led by Sergeant Yahya distinguished themselves by repulsing several attacks on their hilltop position, the defenders eventually disengaging under cover of darkness. After the landings, so few remained from the Dublin and Munster Fusiliers that they were amalgamated into "The Dubsters". Only one Dubliner officer survived the landing, while of the 1,012 Dubliners who landed, just eleven survived the Gallipoli campaign unscathed.[32]

The Turkish defenders were too few to defeat the landing but they inflicted many casualties and contained the attack close to the shore until they started to run out of ammunition. By then they had halted and blunted the British and ANZAC spearhead. For all that the Turkish defending force was relatively weak, it performed remarkably well in holding back Hunter-Weston's force of 35,000 at Cape Helles. Of the five landing sites, two ('W' and 'V' Beaches) came under heavy Turkish machine-gun fire. The remaining three sites were quickly secured yet inexplicably Hunter-Weston chose not to press the attack but to dig in and hold the beach. He could however find recourse in Hamilton's vague directive stating that the actual landings were to be given highest priority rather than further advances inland.

---

[32] Cecil Aspinall-Oglander, *'Military Operations Gallipoli'*, Faber (1929).

At Ari Burnu, however, Birdwood and his ANZACs found the entire landing unopposed and took full advantage by pushing up in the direction of the Chunk Bair height which overlooked the entire peninsula. However, a resolute Turkish defence force hastily assembled by Colonel Kemal halted the ANZAC advance, eventually forcing Birdwood's men back to the beaches by the end of the day.

Samson could not sleep well the night before the attack. He got up and dressed for his morning flight, then sat under a tree having a cigarette and running over everything in his mind. Had he and his men done enough to support the attack? They had carried out 42 reconnaissance and 18 photographic flights and had dropped over 50 bombs, but his task this particular day was to help cover the Helles beaches. They were to be in position over the beaches before the first tows left the ships and then watch for Turkish guns firing on the little boats and direct the big guns of the fleet onto them. He started before first light, taking off at 0515hrs in a Maurice Farman with Osmond as his observer and, rather appropriately as he was a Lancashire man, covering the Lancashire Beach. Samson could see the fleet shelling various targets or what they thought were Turkish positions but they were actually hitting nothing, and he and his men were ignored when they tried to get them on target.

Samson saw the little boats with their tows leave the ships and make their way to the beaches but just before they slipped their tows, all hell erupted from the landing beach as the Turkish gunners opened fire. It seemed impossible for any of the boats to get through to the beach but they saw some of the men leap out of them and run onto the beach, only to fall dead, while a few others managed to run on and up the slope and engage the Turks. Samson could see one battery giving the men in the boats hell and dived on it, dropping his bombs from a low level but missing the guns. The beach was now covered in dead bodies but they could see reinforcements arriving on the beach. It was now time to head home and just then they spotted their relief. They passed over Sedd-el-Bahr and saw the 'River Clyde' and the carnage that surrounded it. They could see the small boats riding in the swell but they were full of dead and wounded. The 'River Clyde' was being hammered from stem to stern by machine-gun bullets. Samson and Osmond could see the sea all around the ship and for some 50 yards out had changed colour: it was now red and, knowing what it was, a horrible sight. They landed back at 0750hrs.

Flight Commander Marix and Major Hogg had taken off at 0530hrs and landed back three hours later at 0830hrs, while Butler and Midshipman John E Sissmore took off at 0630hrs in No 1241 and returned at 0830hrs. Their task was to carry out a reconnaissance of Turkish reserves getting into position behind the beaches and they spotted a group of troops moving south from Krithia. Sissmore tapped out his message in Morse on his W/T and this was in the hands of General Hamilton only a few minutes later on HMS 'Queen Elizabeth'. It was a major step in the speed of getting intelligence back to where it could be used very quickly. More than that, this was also a first in the world of aviation and intelligence and yet again the RNAS were leading the world. Thomson and Peirse took off at 0730hrs to spot for HMS 'Vengeance' and landed back at 1000hrs.[33]

Samson was on the ground for an hour on Tenedos being refuelled and having a spot of breakfast. He took off again at 0910hrs with Collet as his observer this time. They arrived over the fort and village of Sedd-el-Bahr just as the 'Queen Elizabeth' came in close and opened fire with her 6-inch batteries. Suddenly Samson had to turn and head back to Tenedos as his throttle cable snapped and the engine was running wide open on full power. This gave them a hairy flight at times but the landing was no problem as Samson switched off the engine and glided in, landing at 1030hrs. He and Collet got another aeroplane and headed back out to the landings. Bell Davies and Midshipman Erskine K H St Aubyn took off at 0920hrs and landed back at 1100hrs. They had been spotting for HMS 'Prince George'.

Marix and Hogg took off on their second flight at 1030hrs and landed at 1230hrs, having carried out a reconnaissance on Turkish positions and then bombed one of them. This, of course, was standard 3 Squadron operating procedure: whatever the mission, carry bombs and drop them on the enemy before you return. Lieutenant Newton-Clare and Captain Jenkins took off at 1050hrs and carried out a reconnaissance flight over Turkish positions behind Helles before landing back at 1250hrs. They too had flown over the 'River Clyde' and seen all the dead in the small boats and the colour of the sea and they too like Samson were horrified at the price of the invasion. Thomson and Peirse took off again at 1130hrs and carried out some spotting for one of the warships.

Samson took off at 1200hrs to spot for HMS 'Goliath' and HMS 'Swiftsure' who were firing on Krithia and Achi Baba. After the main mission was finished they flew over a Turkish position and dropped their two bombs. They came in low and could see a group of British soldiers trying to cut the Turkish wire; all four men fell and failed to cut the wire. They were shot at and picked up several bullet holes, even one in the propeller which caused a vibration to start up. All the way back to Tenedos the vibration got worse until even the fillings in their teeth rattled. In spite of this, they landed safely at 1430hrs.

Everybody in the squadron had been up, even their largest and heaviest pilot, Bill Wilson, who took with him one of the tallest men in the

---

[33] TNA: AIR 1/681/21/13/2209

squadron, Bill Samson. Together they climbed into one of the most underpowered aeroplanes on the airfield and somehow coaxed it into the air at 1000hrs and returned at 1200hrs, having carried out a reconnaissance. They flew over low over Helles and collected several bullet holes for their temerity. As each aircraft landed back on Tenedos, the crew were interviewed by Lieutenant Isaac, who then selected what was really important and sent it to the General on 'Queen Elizabeth' so that he could warn the commanders of his units or change orders. Bell Davies spotted some 2,000 Turkish troops heading south-east from Krithia, information that was in Hamilton's hands within a few minutes. The big problem was getting the information to the troops in the front line. That still took a long time.[34]

Flying continued non-stop that day. Butler took a solo flight at 1115hrs and returned at 1315hrs. Marix and St-Aubyn took off at 1315hrs and returned 1615hrs, having been spotting for two of the ships and finally attacking a Turkish gun battery with their bombs. Newton-Clare and Whittaker took off at 1330hrs and carried out a similar mission to Marix. Bell Davies and Osmond went out at 1600hrs on a spotting mission and returned at 1830hrs. Wilson and Jenkins took off at 1655 with a full load of 100lb bombs, returning 1833hrs. This was the last 3 Squadron flight of the day.

The men of the RNAS felt at first they had not really carried out any part in the invasion but as the day went on and more and more aeroplanes and seaplanes returned with bullet holes in them, they knew they had pulled their weight. They had clocked up some 292hrs of flying between them. Samson could not have been prouder of his Motor Bandits and along with the men of the 'Manica', the 'Ark Royal' and the RNASACD on the 'River Clyde', the RNAS had performed far beyond what was expected of them and proved to be a real thorn in the side of the Turk. Samson's squadron had worked very hard this day with most of them carrying out three flights. Nevertheless, the men of 3 Squadron were all rather depressed as it was more than obvious that the landings were a failure and they expected come the next day to discover the British forces had been pushed back into the sea.

The Allied position by the end of 25th April was not an encouraging one. Landings had been achieved at Cape Helles and Ari Burnu but advances had not been feasible at either. Turkish troops quickly halted the Allied force and in addition were in possession of the heights above the beachheads. Hamilton's force, finding itself short of the necessary ammunition, was further handicapped by the requirement to use its artillery sparingly, each gun being rationed to just a few shells per day. On the morning of 26th April the British troops on 'Y' beach were in real

---

[34] TNA: AIR 1/681/21/13/2209

trouble. They were being pushed back to the water's edge and an urgent shout went out for any spare lighters and steam launches to get the men off the beach. Samson was ordered to support the operation and keep the heads of the Turkish gunners down while what was left of the 'Y' beach force was pulled off the beach, leaving behind several hundred dead and wounded.

April 26th was a terrible day for the 'Ark Royal'. She could not get any seaplanes up in the morning; they all failed to fly due to engine failure. Kilner left in No 161 for just thirty minutes before returning to the ship. Kershaw took off at 1448hrs and returned at 1519. Not an impressive display by any standards! However, on 27th April the 'Ark Royal' had a good day and managed to get a number of seaplanes in the air. At 0631hrs Kilner took off in No 161 and landed back at the ship at 0705hrs, a very short flight that was followed by two short ones by Dunning in No 136 (0730hrs to 0831hrs) and Whitehead (0936hrs to 1016hrs). At 1146hrs Kilner took off again and this time remained out for some two hours, landing back at 1343hrs. However, this variable performance was little use to the Navy and reflected badly on seaplanes as war machines, certainly in the hands of Clark-Hall's men.

On 26th April 'Manica's balloon made seven ascents in support of the ANZAC operations, spotting again for HMS 'Triumph' and for HMS 'Queen Elizabeth'. During the afternoon shells from HMS 'Queen Elizabeth' blew up an ammunition store at Kojadere with spectacular results. On the following day, 'Queen Elizabeth' was directed onto two Turkish transports coming from Constantinople. One was the 'Scutari', a British steamer which had been detained in Constantinople at the outbreak of war. It was hit at a range of seven miles with the third shell and sank in just a few minutes. At first all observations from the 'Manica' were done from the height of 1,500ft-2,000ft and this gave good results, but when a longer winch cable arrived they could get up to 3,000ft and got a far greater distance for the firings. They tried to take aerial photographs from the balloon but these were a failure so this was left to the aeroplanes. The Fleet thought a great deal of the 'Manica' and her balloon, so when HMS 'Triumph' spotted a submarine approaching her, all other action stopped and any gun that could be brought to bear opened fire to protect her. They sank a tin bath.

Air activity from 26th April to the middle of May 1915 was intense as the flyers tried their best to help the Army that was still trapped on the beaches as they could not move 'Johnny Turk' from the high ground. During this period of twenty-two days, the RNAS would carry out some 284 missions. The balloon on the 'Manica' went up on thirteen of those days for eight hours per day on average. The 'Ark Royal's performance had slipped back and it was only capable of sending up on average two flights per day, which was a poor show compared to Samson and 3 Squadron's daily average of ten. 'Manica' and the 'Ark Royal' were assigned to looking after and supporting the ANZAC landing force, while Samson and 3 Squadron were to look after the five beaches at Cape Helles. Samson was also charged with carrying out long-range reconnaissance missions up over Bulair looking for Turkish reinforcements coming down the isthmus and for lines of support for the men at the front.

A few days before the invasion, the cable ship 'Levant II', belonging to the Eastern Telegraph Company, joined the Fleet off Tenedos, the ship and crew, including her Master, Harold G.E. Wightman, having been taken into the RNVR. 'Levant II' was a deep-sea trawler that had been bought by the Company so that they could lay telephone cables from all the various beaches and HQs to a central point, enabling General Hamilton to be in constant touch with all his units. More than that, the cable gave Hamilton excellent communications with London and the War Office. If the line was cleared, he could get a message to Horse Guards in an hour. On 26th April the 'Levant II' was still at Tenedos, a cable station for the Company as we have seen, and awaiting orders from the Admiral to lay cable from there to Cape Helles. Orders to do so were received late in the morning of the next day. They laid some nine miles of cable then dropped anchor off Kum Kale and waited for daylight.

At 0730hrs on the morning of 27th April, during the first Turkish counter-attack at Anzac Cove, twelve battalions of Mustafa Kemal's 19th Division, reinforced by six battalions from the 5th Division, attempted to drive the six Allied brigades at Anzac back to the beach. The Turkish 57th Regiment attacked in a close-knit mass, charging down the seaward slope of Battleship Hill within view of HMS 'Queen Elizabeth', which fired a salvo of six 15-in (380 mm) shrapnel shells, halting the attack completely and leaving many hundreds of wounded and dead Turks on the battlefield. Also on 27th April, the 'Manica' had spotted a Turkish transport ship moving near the Narrows. HMS 'Queen Elizabeth', stationed off Gaba Tepe, had fired across the peninsula at a range of over 10 miles and sank the transport with her third shot. For much of the campaign, the Turks transported troops by rail, though other supplies continued to be transported by ship on the Sea of Marmara and Dardanelles.

Samson now decided it was time to land at Helles and see if he could find room for a landing strip so that reconnaissance flights with important information could land straightaway and deliver it immediately into General Hamilton's hands. He found a suitable place near Hunter-Weston's redoubt about half a mile from the Lancashires' beach. They kept one or two aeroplanes working from there for a while but the airstrip was in plain sight of the Turkish positions and constantly under artillery fire. Having lost some five aeroplanes there in a few weeks, it was closed fairly quickly. This greatly pleased the Army, as they too were shelled when an aeroplane came in. As a parting gift, the men of 3 Squadron and the French squadron MF 98 T built a dummy aeroplane and placed on the end of the runway. The Turks fired some 150 shells at it before destroying it.

The Turkish defenders at Helles rallied on 28th April and despite the attentions of 'Manica' and 'Queen Elizabeth' on the right flank, brought up several batteries of field guns and began to shell the troops on the beach furiously. Nothing could be seen from sea level but to the observer at 3,000 feet all was revealed. The 'Queen Elizabeth's secondary armament was brought to bear on them and the six-inch guns soon knocked the batteries out. However, the Turkish guns were well-sited and continued firing in spite of some losses. The 15-inch guns were brought into action and in five minutes all Turkish firing had ceased as the whole area around the batteries was pulverised. The same day, near Y Beach landings, the 'Queen Elizabeth' was sighted on to a party of about one hundred Turks. One fifteen-in (380mm) shrapnel shell containing twenty-four thousand pellets was fired at short range and killed the entire party. For the rest of the campaign, the Turks were very wary of moving within sight of battleships and it gave them another reason to desperately try to sink the 'Manica' or destroy the balloon.

On 28th April the 'Levant II' finished laying the first cable then anchored about 140 yards from Cape Helles beach where three days ago such fierce and terrible slaughter had taken place. Having still got the cable end on board, two of the engineering crew were splicing the cable and testing it there, possibly because the camp on shore where the switchboard was going to be placed was being hit with shrapnel from time to time. The crew of 'Levant II' found the Straits a wonderful sight. About 200 vessels of all descriptions were anchored between Helles and Kum Kale. Battleships and cruisers, transports from huge Cunarders down to humble tramps, patrol vessels, trawlers and tug boats. The warships were continually firing over all the ships towards the Turks.

Lieutenant Commander Wedgwood and the machine gunners of No. 3 RNAS Armoured Car Section had been playing a strong role in supporting the men on the beaches at Helles. On the morning of 28th April, Wedgwood, without any orders, decided to take his men and machine-guns forwards towards the Turkish position. Once he had been found again that afternoon, he was ordered to take his guns forward to support the 29th Division. Yet again, as in France and Belgium, valuable time was lost looking for the man and his command. The 29th was very close to pulling out and retreating as they had run out of officers and did not know what to do. Wedgwood, Sub-Lieutenant C H Parkes and Chief Petty Officer Little rallied the men around them. In the end, they formed an adhoc unit of some 600 men that they got to stand. Chief Petty Officer Little moved from position to position encouraging, goading and just downright bullying the men to get a backbone and stand and fight with the machine-guns. He did expose himself to enemy fire as he moved around the position, but he ignored it and got on with the job. That evening orders came up for this unit to pull back and take up a new position.

On 29th April, the ship carrying the French squadron MF 98 T arrived off the island of Tenedos and with the help of some of 3 Squadron they got the French men and their camping equipment off the ship. Room was made for the French over the next few days and they then set about putting up their Bessonneau hangers. Like the men of 3 Squadron, the French lived in tents but soon set about converting the large packing cases their aircraft travelled in into workshops and sleeping accommodation. The first French aircraft, a Maurice Farman, was not ready until 11th May. Within days of the French setting up camp, a full working relationship between the two squadrons was developed and the two commanders, Samson and Captaine Césari, became good friends. The French came especially well equipped with the latest type of top quality aerial photographic equipment. They were shocked that Samson was using one little hand-held camera and gave him two full camera sets. This exchange of equipment became quite normal between the two squadrons and both sets of ground crew helped each other out every day.

On 29th April some of the crew of 'Levant II' went ashore to land the cable end. An office switchboard was fitted out that morning in a tent on the beach at Helles. Some of the crew walked up the hill to have a look at some of the old Turkish trenches. They could see the front line which was about two miles away. From time to time shrapnel would burst overhead making them feel it was not a bad idea to get back to the safety of the ship. On the 30th the 'Levant II' had been doing cable work all day between the shore and the ships, one of which hooked and broke the newly-laid cable. This did not go down well with either the crew of 'Levant II' or the Admiral.

On 30th April Samson sent out a reconnaissance flight north of Bulair, A good deal of information was brought back and some great photographs of new Turkish artillery positions. In all they spotted some 7,000 Turkish reinforcements and that a new camp had been set up near Boghali which could hold some 3,000 men. Samson could not resist such a tempting target. Every aeroplane that could fly and carry bombs was sent up but unfortunately this was only four as the others were out working with the Fleet. They carried six 100lb and nine 20lb bombs between them. On arriving over the target, they dived down on the camp engines off and let their bombs go, causing great confusion and terror among the Turks. A large number of fires and other explosions were seen. Many pack animals stampeded, disappearing off into the distance.

The RNAS had landplanes, seaplanes, an armoured car unit and a balloon ship working in theatre and had now been joined by an allied squadron with whom they could work well. It was too good to last. Just as the French aeroplane squadron landed on Tenedos the Turks received a couple of Albatross aircraft and other general aeroplane supplies and spares from the Germans. The Turks were back in the air war.

Chapter three
May 1915

General Hamilton had found an ingenious way of setting up a communications network with all his command posts and a number of the main warships by arranging for the Eastern Telegraph Company to come out to the Dardanelles and lay telephone cable between all the islands and Gallipoli. One telephone was placed in the intelligence tent on Tenedos as that was manned all day by Isaac, allowing him to be in constant contact with General Hunter-Weston of the 29th Division at Helles and to send him verbal reports. Updated map information, however, still had to go out each evening by boat to the 'Arcadian', moored in Kephalo Bay, for map overlays to be made in its print shop and distributed to all command centres. The main cable terminal was at Helles in a deep gully and was manned by men from the Eastern Telegraph Company, always dressed very smartly in their suits. They were there for the duration of the campaign and as the British and ANZAC forces pulled out, so the Eastern Telegraph Company salvaged their cable and other equipment and pulled out too.

The telephone system worked well and took the strain from the wireless system but a recurrent problem was that the ships did not keep a good watch for the cable buoy and dropped anchor on the cable, causing a break. The cable ship 'Levant II' became a common sight moving from island to island laying and repairing the cables. One of the Royal Navy's ships had snagged the cable from Tenedos and broken it soon after it was laid but this was fully repaired by 1st May.

That day an early reconnaissance flight had spotted a large Turkish supply column, made up of some 200 pack animals and a number of wagons, moving in the direction of Krithia. Samson got all his spare aircraft into the air, all of them carrying bombs, a total of six 100lb bombs and nine 20lb bombs between them. They attacked the column and camels and donkeys scattered in all directions. Yet another supply column never made it to the front line. They also spotted thousands of Turks moving forward, over 7,000 men moving towards the front lines.

When the Turks launched an attack at moonrise on the night of 1st/2nd May, the RNAS Armoured Car section helped hold the line. The British line was actually breached in two places but the centre, where the machine-guns were, held and all night the RNAS repelled the Turks. Come first light and then the dawn, they could see their handiwork and it was not a pretty sight. They were faced with hundreds of bodies in all forms of death. On the left of Wedgwood's position were the Hampshires. They too had fought a desperate battle in the darkness. At one stage a company of the Royal Scots came up to plug any gap and hunt down any Turk that had got through. It was a fierce and desperate night's fighting.

On 2nd May the 'Manica's balloon was up spotting for British battleships. Their main target for the day was a battery of 8-in Turkish guns that were being a real problem; these were shelled and three direct hits were confirmed. The same day Samson wrote to Commodore Murray Sueter:

'Dear Commodore Sueter

So far we have had wonderful luck. Up to today our mileage is 18,851 miles, which is pretty nearly a record as the average number of machines is six. Information from a prisoner states that one of our 100lb bombs killed 23 soldiers. I had the luck also to hit a big howitzer full and square with a 100lb bomb.[35]

We live in the air all day and it is taking it out of our machines. I am not too keen on the BE.2C as they climb rottenly carrying a passenger, and we have a lot of passenger work to do. Some more M Farmans, 100 Renaults or sister machines to No 1421 are urgently wanted. No 1241 engine has only about 10 hours to do now to beat the world record. She has not been taken out of the machine. The way it runs is due to the mechanic, Derroussors, whom I have frequently recommended for promotion to CPO but he has not been promoted.

A steady supply of 100 x 100lb bombs a month is essential. I can get rid of them as quickly as they are supplied. We generally do a before breakfast bomb attack. Lt Butler has taken wonderful photographs of the German positions which have proved of great value to the Army.

One of the Farmans that had been out on a shoot came back and reported that he had spotted with great success, that the '*Agamemnon*' completely destroyed 3 out of 4 howitzers in a battery that has been annoying the fleet and landing place. We did 2,400 miles the first day the army landed.'

The Commanding Officer of 3 Squadron was clearly the man of action needed in a position like this, if only he had enough aircraft and bombs to do all he wanted. On another occasion that Samson wrote to Murray Sueter, his letter was again a mixture of pleading for more equipment and genuine enthusiasm for the task in hand:

'I am still of the opinion that the only war machines are fast *Pushers* with good climb. The M Farman with 100 Renaults and 1241 are absolutely splendid. Other types of machines cannot compete at all. Avro's etc. are just so much waste of money. These M Farman's can do 75mph, carry wireless and 2 100lb bombs, therefore they can spot, reconnoitre or attack, whichever is wanted. They can also fight. Their only drawback is that they turn slowly and wallow about in the wind. It was rotten seeing the soldiers get hell at the landing places. Knowing the defences I did not believe they

---

[35] TNA: AIR 1/361/15/228/50

would be able to get ashore. These Turks are devils to the wounded. We are giving them no rest with bombs. One of our machines got two 100lb bombs in a divisional camp and blotted out over 18 tents and their occupants. They must have killed over 100 men. We also got a lot of good hits on Maidos and Chanak, the day before yesterday and the day before that a big camp near Bogheli. I have two very good Army Officer Observers and two Midshipmen. Everyone seems quite satisfied with the work we have done. One of the BE.2Cs chased the German today but we could not catch him.

We will soon shift to the mainland but it is not free from shells yet and it is not worth risking all our machines as they can reach our new landing ground quite easy. The German dropped bombs here and made good shots 12 days ago. I sent two units in return, and we laid him up for 10 days. He only escaped today by the skin of his teeth as an M Farman and myself in No.50 were just between him and home, and we never saw him as we were busy dropping bombs. He must have passed within a quarter mile of me, running away from Osmond on the BE.2C. The Breguet is now ready. I urgently require three or four more good carpenters. The kite balloon appears to be jolly useful only he has to be too far away. I got hit right along the propeller by a rifle bullet the other day. I think the job will be a great success soon, as although the Turks and Germans have got awfully strong positions our men have got their blood up, as the Turks are such devils to the wounded. Aeroplane spotting I really consider has helped a devil of a lot, as now we can get batteries silenced right away. Practically always now the batteries cease fire when an aeroplane gets over the top of them. I honestly believe that our aeroplanes have given the Turks a healthy feeling of dread.'[36]

On 2nd May 'Levant II' laid cable from Gaba Tepe (where the Australian troops landed) to Cape Helles, a distance of about 12 miles. Alfred Lawrence Spalding was one of the crew of the cable ship 'Levant II', and he kept a diary of his time at Gallipoli. The entry describing this day reads as follows:

'Gaba Tepe beach is almost continually swept by shrapnel. Had a yarn with Lieut. in charge of Signal Office while cable end was being landed. He said they have lost far more men by the shrapnel fire on the beach than in the actual fighting against the Turks. Our Troops apparently only hold the top of the ridge and are unable to advance. Our ship was hit several times by enemy's shrapnel fire. After landing the cable end we paid out to Cape Helles.

While we were at Gaba Tepe a Destroyer anchored close to us. She had made a raid higher up the coast and captured 18 Turks. The boat load of these prisoners being unable to make shore in a strong wind, tied up

---

[36] TNA: AIR 1/724/76/6

alongside of us. The Turks look a wild dishevelled lot. They had been treated like lords compared with the lot of our men captured by the Turks.'[37]

The men of the 5th Turkish Army were learning the hard way about hostile aircraft. During an early morning reconnaissance patrol, some 3,000 fresh troops were spotted being landed and making camp near Boghali. Yet again Samson got as many aeroplanes into the air as possible; they attacked this new battalion and caused a large number of casualties. As he and his pilots returned to base and flew over the Turkish lines, they could see that the Turks were massing for a large attack. On landing Samson made his report to Isaac, then tried to contact the General directly by using the new telephone but all he got was an engaged tone. Isaac typed up the report and sent it out by currier boat to the General. He then kept on trying to raise the General on the telephone but still only got the engaged tone. Finally, the report arrived before the telephone cleared and the General was not at all pleased that the phone had been tied up for several hours on what was actually unimportant business.

Mid-morning on the 2nd a Turkish seaplane was spotted heading towards Tenedos. Marix took off to intercept the enemy and caught it up near Kephez point. He managed to kill the Turkish observer and forced the seaplane down onto the water, following the aircraft down. Unfortunately he was now just 50ft above the water and only 300 yards from Chanak, whose defenders gave him a very hot reception with artillery and small-arms fire.

Colonel Eduard von Sodernstern planned an attack for the night of the 2nd/3rd of May, believing that Samson could not see or attack his forces during the night. This hit the British centre just at moon-set forcing a limited breakthrough but come daybreak the British forces pushed the Turks back to their own lines.

On 3rd May Samson started sending supply flights to the forward landing strip on Helles that he had scouted out on 27th April. He also managed to get three volunteers to man the trench there. They would service any aeroplane that landed while the observer took the reconnaissance report directly to 29th Division HQ. The landing procedure on Helles airfield, as it was called, was extremely risky. You landed on a slight downward slope and did not stop until you got to the bottom. Still at speed, you swung around the hill and out of sight of the Turks, having been followed down the runway by shells. Departure was equally hairy. As the aircraft ran up its engine, it would sprint out from behind the hillock, do a tail slide and align for take-off, manoeuvres that would bring down immediate Turkish

---

[37] atlantic-cable.com/CableStories/Spalding: A L Spalding's diary, 1915

artillery fire upon it. The aeroplane would then race up the runway with shells exploding behind it. It was not a good position but the three men who manned it, one of whom was Arthur Beeton, enjoyed it and their time with the Army. This could be explained in part at least by the facts that they got far better food from the Army than they did on Tenedos and that they were their own bosses. Samson offered to relieve the men but they wanted to stay and did, until Helles closed after the loss of a number of aeroplanes.

The cable ship was hard at work on the 3rd, laying three more short cables from Helles beach to SS 'Arcadian', the Headquarters of the General and his staff, which was anchored offshore among the numerous transports. The first one of these was broken by a trawler's anchor within an hour of its laying! 3 Squadron carried out 6 flights that day; two were reconnaissance flights, two were bombing attacks and two spotting flights. The 'Ark Royal' was anchored off Gaba Tepe and flying started early on the 3rd. The first seaplane was No 176 at 0457hrs, which should have been flown by Whitehead but he failed to take off. The next up was Kershaw in No 1438, taking off at 0520hrs and returning at 0635hrs. He took off again in the same aircraft at 0908hrs but returned twenty minutes later with an engine problem. Kilner went up at 1157hrs in No 161, returning at 1249hrs. Douglas took off at 1645hrs flying No 922 and had to return straightaway with engine problems. He took off again at 1741hrs, heading towards the 'Manica'. This was very unfortunate as at 1450hrs a Turkish aeroplane had dropped out of some cloud cover and bombed the balloon ship. Luckily all the bombs missed, because by the time a few AA guns opened fire, the enemy was gone before they could get the range. The Fleet had been caught napping once but now they thought the enemy were back and opened fire. 'Ark Royal' flashed immediately that this was a friendly seaplane but when Douglas landed back at 1821hrs he had a number of new holes in the fabric, whether British or Turkish is a question that cannot be answered. The 'Manica' was attacked again that day at Gaba Tepe by another Turkish aircraft. Luckily all three of the bombs it dropped missed. But it was very clear the 'Manica' and its balloon were beginning to hurt the Turks and they now went out of their way to try destroy the balloon.

'Ark Royal' did not start flying until 1055hrs on 4th May when Douglas took off in No 922, with all its holes patched, returning at 1220hrs. Kershaw went up in No 1438 at 1300hrs and returned at 1400hrs. Whitehead tried to take off at 1646hrs but failed due to engine problems. 3 Squadron, on the other hand, had a busy day yet again. Several reconnaissance flights were made including photographic flights, as updates were required for the intelligence map. Samson also put up four spotting flights. Naval gunnery officers on the battleships now noticed that whenever an aeroplane or seaplane passed over, the Turkish gunners would cease fire.

May 4th was a very quiet day for the cable ship as she remained anchored off Helles but at about 2100hrs on the evening of 4th/5th May, there was an urgent shout from ANZAC (as it was now called) that their phone line was down. Spalding was sent ashore with Cottrell and they did a rough test showing the break was at the far end. They returned to the ship and steamed down to the break on the 'Levant'. Next morning at day-break Cottrell, Jordan and Spalding were taken to ANZAC with boat-load of cable, arriving there at 0700hrs and finishing the repair by 0930hrs. The men working on the joint and splice in the boat were subjected to rifle fire from the Turks, either stray bullets coming over the cliffs or direct sniping. If it was the latter, it was not very successful as no one was hurt. Samson and his men were in great demand gathering intelligence and carrying out bombing raids on tented encampments. They also carried out four spotting flights and a photographic mission that day while the 'Ark Royal' put up two flights in all. The first was Douglas in No 922 at 0810hrs, landing back at 0840hrs and the second was Kilner, taking off in No 161 at 1157hrs and returning at 1410hrs.

On 5th May the rest of 3 Squadron RNAS Armoured Car Section landed from the 'Inkosi' while No 4 Squadron RNAS Armoured Car Section, who had come on the 'Inkonka' and had been held at sea, were also landed. General Hunter-Weston placed Wedgwood in command of the RND's twelve Vickers machine-guns, plus his own four. After having had dinner with the General that evening, Wedgwood returned to his men at midnight. He had no idea what they were to do, they had no specific target or objective, they were just to attack the Turks. Wedgwood did not know any of his new men and they had no idea of what they were supposed to shoot at. In the morning all the guns advanced 500yds and then dug in. Once the 29th Division's attack started, Wedgwood started running in the open from machine-gun to machine-gun directing their fire, as CPO Little had done a week before, but as he ran, he was followed by artillery shells. He was very effectively showing the Turkish gunners the position of his own machine-guns, which were then knocked out. His unit was taking heavy casualties. Lieutenant Coke was killed, Lieutenant Illingworth was wounded and Wedgwood himself was hit and wounded in the groin.

General Hunter-Weston's attack plan for 6th May lacked any subtlety - it was heads down and charge! The Allied advance began at 1100hrs that day and was swiftly halted by strong Turkish resistance. The 88th Brigade, 29th Division, advanced on Fir Tree Spur and managed to capture Fir Tree Wood. The 6th (Hood) Battalion of the Royal Naval Division advanced strongly along Kanli Dere but the gains were never more than 400yds at all points along the line and at no point were the Turkish trenches reached. The attack was resumed on 7th May, using the same plan and producing largely the same results, with an even greater loss of life.

On the morning of 8th May, the 88th Brigade on Fir Tree Spur in front of Krithia was relieved by the New Zealanders, who made yet another attempt to breach the Turkish lines which failed with a huge loss of life. The Wellington, Canterbury and Auckland Battalions gained another 400yds through Fir Tree Wood to a place called the 'Daisy Patch' before they became pinned down by enfiladed fire on the left from Turkish machine-guns in a ravine. They could neither advance nor withdraw and still had no sight of the Turkish positions. Despite the morning's failure, Hunter-Weston ordered the New Zealanders to resume their attack at 1730hrs. The brigade commander, Colonel Francis Johnston, protested but Hunter-Weston insisted the attack proceed. However, General Hamilton, the overall commander, came ashore at Helles to oversee the battle. He ordered a general advance to be made at 1730hrs along the entire front with the aim of capturing Krithia and Achi Baba. At 1800hrs the French beat their drums and sounded their bugles as they went over the top and attacked the Turks. The sea of blue coats and scarlet trousers rushed towards the Turkish lines, getting nearer and nearer, and it looked as if the Allies would take the position but suddenly the Turkish gunners opened fire which dropped amongst the French, decimating them. As the smoke cleared the Allied commanders could see the ground was now covered with dead Frenchmen. At 1900hrs Hamilton issued the order for all troops to dig in and hold.

Samson and 3 Squadron were very busy during this four day battle, flying some ten spotting missions and twelve reconnaissance missions. On 6th May at the very start of this battle work had started on the repair of Helles-Tenedos telephone cable as once again a ship had damaged the cable. The work was finished on the 7th. While the telephone was vital for passing information from Isaac's intelligence tent to the General and his staff, the squadron's aircraft passed messages in the air in Morse from the wirelesses they carried. This worked fine when spotting for the Navy but the Army had not got the right crystals for their radios to pick up 3 Squadron's signals. In great frustration Samson, Bell Davies, Marix and others took to landing at Helles Point, running into Hunter-Weston's redoubt, banging on the map table to get the attention of the master gunner to show him where his shells should be landing and also pointing out to him the position of the Turkish guns. They then ran out back to their aeroplanes, took off through the barrage of Turkish artillery shells and climbed back into the sky to carry on with the reconnaissance flight. Others in the squadron were meanwhile directing the naval ships onto various targets without the need for risky landings, gross subordination and hair-raising take-offs.

Wireless sets were new form of signalling which the Royal Navy had taken up with great gusto and became very skilled at using during World War One. The Army on the other hand had failed to come to terms with wireless. Admittedly the early sets had their failings. They were heavy and not particularly portable, and transmissions remained relatively unreliable. The transmission range also varied wildly depending upon atmospheric conditions, skill of the operator and many other factors. The British Army did not take any wireless sets with them to Gallipoli, deciding instead to rely on telephones and on visual signals using flags. The ANZAC Corps, however, had a full signals section and the Australian Light Horse were equipped with Marconi 500-watt pack W/T sets. As they had a number of these, four were put on board the 'Arcadian' along with a number of wireless operators, which allowed GHQ to talk directly to the ANZAC HQ. The Australians also set up a signals tent on Helles beach so the 29th Division could talk to GHQ[38].

The Royal Navy were tasked with supplying signalling for the British Army, while afloat and from ship to shore and all long-distance communications. It would also set up and man the beach signal offices. The British Army laid telephone cable in the trenches that linked all positions, as did the ANZACs, and was to set up WS/T stations at Helles and ANZAC to communicate with the ships supporting the landing with gun fire and with the RNAS aeroplanes and seaplanes directing the guns onto targets. However, it was discovered while the British Army was in Egypt that they had not brought any radios with them, so a number of men were selected and went through a crash course in naval signalling and using naval W/T sets. The courses were short and to the point. Differences in methods of the two services were reconciled as far as possible and naval W/T procedure was adopted on all joint channels.[39] There were a number of problems with the air to ground communications and the men manning the sets could not at times hear the signals. The Army struggled with the naval system of codes and procedures and until the navy took over all W/T stations, there were a number of lost signals. Spare naval wireless operators were brought out from Malta to man the Army communications and improve the passing of messages.

The 'Manica' and its balloon had a great day while spotting for British battleships on 8th May, zeroing in on four batteries and silencing them. Meanwhile the ANZACs put in a formal complaint to the Red Cross that the Turks were shelling their hospital. The Turks replied that the hospital was too close to other military targets.

Yet again on 9th May the ANZAC telephone cable had to be replaced as yet another naval ship had damaged the cable beyond repair. The admiral was far from pleased. This was becoming a problem and ships' captains were warned of the possibilities of breaking the cable and its consequences. Two flights were made from 'Ark Royal': the first was Douglas in No 922 from

---

[38] R F H Nalder, *'The Royal Corps of Signals'*, page 157
[39] ibidem

0612hrs to 0833hrs and the second later in the day when Whitehead took off in No 176 at 1450hrs and landed back at 1605hrs. The 'Ark Royal' upped anchor and sailed into Kephalo Bay on the island of Imbros, where she would now remain as a static workshop in this safe anchorage until she left the area. There was no flying from the 'Ark Royal' on 10th May, or for the next four days as the weather was not great. At 0940hrs a Survey Party left the ship to find and lay out a new camp and airfield for the seaplanes of the Ark Royal, returning to the ship at 1955hrs.

Samson and 3 Squadron had made several reconnaissance flights each day since the attacks started on the 6th but were not allowed to carry out any bombing attacks on the enemy in support of the British attack. By 9th May the Navy felt that Samson and his men had really got the hang of spotting as the target was usually destroyed with only a few shells. The kite balloon was also found to be very efficient and often only had to rise for the Turkish gunners to stop firing. During the lull in fighting which now followed, 3 Squadron carried out an in-depth reconnaissance of the Turkish positions for the 29th Division and a load of proclamations were dropped over the Turkish lines to encourage the Turkish soldier to desert his post and come over to the British as a prisoner.

A brief period of consolidation followed amongst the units of the 29th Division after the disastrous attacks. Allied stocks of ammunition were almost expended, particularly for artillery, and both sides paused to bring in extra stores and expand their trench systems. The Turks relieved a number of units opposite the Australian line, which was reinforced by the Australian Light Horse operating as infantry. Sporadic fighting continued, with sniping, grenade attacks and raids, just like the Western Front with opposing trenches separated in places by only a few yards. The cable ship 'Levant II' lay alongside the SS 'Arcadian' at Helles as its technicians were working on board the GHQ ship to improve the switchboard.

3 Squadron were now joined on their Tenedos aerodrome by the French unit L'escadrille MF 98 T (T for Tenedos). Their commander, Capitaine Antoine Césari, a veteran of the Battle of the Marne, was known to Samson by his reputation as was Samson to him: Commander Samson, the Hero of Douai. There was a mutually cordial understanding between them that full co-operation was essential for both units on this small Greek island, a situation that was not new to 3 Squadron, who had shared their airfield at Dunkirk with a French unit only a few months before. The French squadron had eight pilots, S/Lt Marcel Saint André, Warrant Officer Pierre Beausire Seyssel, sergeants Louis Garsonnin, Grosourdy Guy Saint-Pierre, Dumas, Jules Lecompte, Dubois and Brigadier quartermaster Célestin Boar, and eight Maurice Farman MF XI aircraft that were much more reliable and powerful than the British version.

Besides exchanging expertise, the two squadrons also exchanged equipment and one of the first things Samson got was two sets of French photographic equipment and cameras. These new cameras fitted to the aircraft, making the taking of pictures so much easier than with the hand-held camera that Butler and Thomson had been using. A joint intelligence centre was set up so that Isaac could use both English and French pictures on his map. They also shared their rations and established a central kitchen area, while the fitters and riggers helped each other out on a regular basis. All in all, life was not too bad at all on Tenedos.

The one thing that the French did not have were bombs so they set up their own bomb factory on the edge of the airfield. Césari acquired a number of shells from the French Navy, unloaded them onto the beach and brought them up through the airfield using a horse and cart. At their processing plant, they would weld fins onto the live shells and then make a crude delayed-action fuse. A few days into this operation there was a large explosion and one of the French pilots was killed. After this Samson increased his bomb supply orders so he could give some to the French - it was better for the health of the airfield.

On 11th May the men of MF T 98 and 3 Squadron lined up either side of the first French Farman and gave it a big send-off as it hurtled down the runway and up into the clear blue sky, carrying four 20lb bombs. It was a great day and a party was held that evening with the French inviting 3 Squadron to join them. This was the start of a great relationship and many joint operations. No seaplanes took off from the 'Ark Royal'. The Survey Party left the ship at 0715hrs and remained on the island until 1955hrs, keeping this timetable up daily until 17th May. After this they had a large working party with them.

As a result of the new arrivals, second telephone line to the airfield on Tenedos was required so on 12th May the cable ship started laying a new cable from Tenedos to Cape Helles. During the paying-out they received a wire from Tenedos reporting that a submarine had been sighted off Doro channel at 0900hrs but continued their work, finishing laying the cable at 1800hrs. Once the cable was laid there was not much to do so 'Levant II' anchored off Helles beach and awaited instructions. While spotting for a British battleships that day, the 'Manica' was directed to find a house that was believed to be the Turkish HQ. The building was razed to the ground. The 'Ark Royal' sent up Douglas in No 922 at 0450hrs to carry out a morning patrol over ANZAC and he returned at 1040hrs. Two new and large Turkish camps were spotted by 3 Squadron on the west bank of the Kereves Dere, but the Army howitzers were unable to hit them as they were out of range while Naval gun fire was also tried without success as the camp was in ravine.

There was reason to believe that the Germans would soon have some new and very powerful units ready to join its North Sea fleet and for this reason the Admiralty had decided to recall the 'Queen Elizabeth'. She was required to head the line with her sister, the 'Warspite'. An order was therefore sent to Admiral de Robeck on May 12th, instructing him that she was to sail for home at once with all despatch and secrecy, and that the 'Venerable' was being taken to replace her. With her was to go the 'Exmouth', and at the end of the month they would be followed by the first of two new monitors, 'Abercrombie' and 'Roberts', each of which was armed with a pair of 14-in guns and provided with bulges against mines and torpedoes.

Since the Turkish Army had no long-range cannons, the British and French battleships with large calibre armament like 'Queen Elizabeth' were able to remain out of range and had caused extensive casualties on the Turkish side. Though it seemed impossible, the Turkish General Staff decided to sink one of these ships. HMS 'Goliath' was chosen due to her position. On the night of 12th–13th May, 'Goliath' was anchored in Morto Bay off Cape Helles, along with HMS 'Cornwallis' and a screen of five destroyers. The weather was not good and a thick fog had made visibility bad. Around 0100hrs on 13th May, the Turkish torpedo boat destroyer 'Muâvenet-i Millîye' eluded the Allied destroyers and closed on the battleships. The 'Muâvenet-i Millîye' had reversed down the Dardanelles, moving slowly, stern first, and was mistaken by officers on watch for a British vessel. It fired two torpedoes which struck 'Goliath' almost simultaneously abreast her fore-turret and abeam the fore-funnel, causing a massive explosion. 'Goliath' began to capsize almost immediately, and was lying on her beam ends when a third torpedo struck near her after-turret. She then rolled over completely and began to sink by the bows, taking 570 of the 700-strong crew to the bottom, including her commanding officer, Captain Thomas Lawrie Shelford. Although sighted and fired on after the first torpedo hit, 'Muâvenet-i Millîye' escaped unscathed. 'Goliath' was the fourth British pre-dreadnought battleship to be sunk in the Dardanelles. After her loss the flagship 'Queen Elizabeth' was sent back to England with all haste to join the Home Fleet and a number of the other ships left in the Dardanelles were pulled back to safer anchorages behind anti-torpedo nets.

On 13th May, Whitehead left 'Ark Royal' in No 176, taking off at 0510hrs and returning with an engine problem at 0525hrs. Kilner took off in No 161 at 1055hrs, circled and landed immediately as he had damaged his float on take-off. The seaplane was taken aboard and repaired and at 1655hrs he took off again to carry out a two-hour patrol over ANZAC, landing back at 1855hrs. On 14th May, there were only two flights from 'Ark Royal', both by Whitehead, both in No 176, and both fairly short. He took off at 0500hrs and returned an hour later at 0600hrs. Then he went up again at 1110hrs and carried out a patrol, landing at 1155hrs. There was no more flying from the ship until 16th May.

On 15th May, Bell Davies was up spotting for HMS 'Agamemnon'. The target was a large howitzer mounted in the mouth of a valley and they had almost got the ship on target when what Bell Davies thought would be a last round hit the top of a hill half a mile away. The target could not be hit as the trajectory of the ship's guns' was just too flat for it. Just as they were about to give up on the spotting, Bell Davies spotted a long column of men marching along in the shadows of the hills. His observer was Warrant Electrician McLeod, an excellent Morse man but still very new at the role of observer. They followed the men up the valley and spotted two very large camouflaged camps. They brought 'Agamemnon' onto the new target and after just two rounds, they gave the 'fire for effect' signal. The camp ceased to be there, being replaced with fire, dust, smoke and flame, and men and animals running in all directions. They moved the ship's guns onto the next target and again very quickly got the ship on target, but then had to leave as the fuel situation was a little critical.

On 16th May, MF 98 T was reduced to seven aeroplanes after an accident in which an aircraft was lost at sea. Two aircraft were earmarked for observation and artillery spotting, but as this squadron's aeroplanes did not have radio they had to land or drop messages at Helles Point GHQ or land on the perilous Cape Helles runway. Two other aeroplanes were fitted with cameras and used for photographic work and two were reserved for long-range reconnaissance and for bombing. This latter activity would soon play a major part in the squadron's daily activity to harass the Turkish supply columns. The French, like their British comrades, took at least one bomb on each mission and they let go at everything that moved. Bombing in these early days of the war was very dangerous and it was yet to become a science. Samson and his men were full of enthusiasm and whenever possible would take the fight to the enemy. Their bomb racks in the Dardanelles were homemade and as for a bombsight, it was a case of seat of the pants aiming, so any unexpected problems like a spot of corrosion was just added to the problem list.

Césari was about to fly a bombing mission to Soghanli Dere but he had no observer and none was available, so he went off on his own in a two-seat Maurice Farman with a primed homemade bomb under the aeroplane. Now this type of Farman required a pilot to be at the controls at all times, holding the stick, in the rear of the nacelle but the release lever for the bomb was operated by the observer in the front of the nacelle. He had not worked out before take-off exactly how he was going to drop the bomb when the time came and was *en route* to Helles when he noticed that somehow the fuse had started to burn, the primer had been pressed and he only had a few seconds to drop the bomb! He tried to reach the lever from the rear cockpit but could not make it. He then stood up and reached over into the forward cockpit but could still not make it. He had to let go of the controls, step over into the observer's position and pull the lever to drop the bomb. By now the Farman had nosed down and entered a dive but he fought his way back into the pilot's seat just in time to pull it up. The bomb exploded harmlessly below. He returned and collected another bomb but this time tied a bit of string to the bomb release so he could operate it from the pilot's seat. He then set off and bombed Soghanli Dere. When Samson said to Césari that he must have been scared, his reply was:

'Mon commandant, I was all muckoo sweato'[40]

Samson had a similar experience when a bomb hung up during a raid. On the way back to Tenedos he threw the aeroplane around the sky trying to shake it loose. This failed, so he came into the airfield to make the softest landing of his career and as the aircraft touched the ground, he jumped out and rolled away just as the propeller passed over him. His men thought he had gone mad. The bomb had in fact dropped off with the others. Such experiences seem to have been reasonably common at the time. Lieutenant Peirse had a 'hang up' but he had an observer with him who climbed out of the aeroplane, kicked the bomb free, then got back in. The closest Samson came to killing himself on take-off was when flying a single-seater Nieuport, carrying his normal load of three 20lb bombs. He had just cleared the end of the runway and the drop down to the beach when he heard a loud explosion and his aeroplane was tossed up into the air like a feather. Bits of it flew around and his petrol tank emptied itself all over him. There was very little fabric left on the aircraft so Samson turned what was left of his machine very gently back to the airfield. He pulled the bomb release and heard the welcome sound of two explosions. He kept expecting the aeroplane to burst into flames but he made it and as the wheels touched the complete tail unit of the aeroplane fell off. Samson stepped out of the pile of debris with a smile.

On 16th May, Whitehead took off at 0900hrs in No 176 and returned to 'Ark Royal' at 1035hrs under tow from HMS 'Ribble', a River-class destroyer, which was acting as an escort for one of the battleships off ANZAC Cove. Fortunately for Whitehead, he had managed to land near it when he suffered engine failure.

The cable laying ship 'Levant II' spent much of the next three (16th-19th) days working on the cables between Helles beach, 'Arcadian' and ANZAC cove repairing minor breaks and improving the quality of the signal in general. The Eastern Telegraph office (ETO) was moved from its position in the middle of the beach to back against the cliff face, which gave the staff some better protection.

On 17th May Samson returned a number of aeroplanes that were unsuitable for active service in the Dardanelles to England. The weather was good so

---

[40] Charles Rumney Samson. *'Flights and Fights'*. Battery Press, Nashville, page 251

he and Marix took off at 0750hrs in the large Breguet. They had great plans for this aeroplane, the most important one being to bomb the main arsenal in Constantinople. The flight on this day was to test the aeroplane and its engine, which unluckily tended to misfire a great deal. It was loaded up with one 100lb bomb and fourteen 20lb bombs, and a Lewis gun was mounted in the front of the nacelle, this being the maximum load for this aeroplane. They took off and headed for Ak Bashi Liman, a small port that was being used as a supply depot. There was a lot of activity when they arrived as a new batch of reinforcements was being unloaded and they dropped all of their bombs into the middle of it. A great panic took hold of men and animals and they all ran for the hills; it took two full days to round up all the missing pack animals. They later discovered that they had done a lot of damage and killed or wounded 57 men.

They flew on and discovered another huge new Turkish camp near the ANZAC position: it looked like the Turks were massing for an attack. As soon as they landed they reported into Isaac and he sent an urgent message to the ANZAC HQ by telephone, then followed up with a written report detailing what had been seen. On getting this new information the ANZAC commander requested that 3 Squadron should carry out aerial reconnaissance over the area of the villages of Boghali, Kojadere and Biyuk, which were thought to be staging posts for the Turkish Army. From now until the Turkish attack was launched, 3 Squadron undertook five reconnaissance missions over the requested area, one a photographic reconnaissance. The Breguet's engine had misfired all the way back but the mechanic Derroussors said he could sort it out and then they could carry out more testing.[41]

Later this day Collet carried out a long-distance reconnaissance for the Australians lasting some 4 hours 20 minutes in which he collected a lot of information. The Australians were becoming very exasperated with the air support from the 'Ark Royal'. No wonder! On 17th May, for example, 'Ark Royal' put in less than two hours flying for the ANZACs. The first seaplane up was Sub-Lieutenant Dunning in No 136 at 1615hrs. He landed back at 1652hrs. At 1745hrs Garnett left in No 857 and returned at 1830hrs. The last flight of the day was Kilner in No 857 who took off at 1920hrs and returned at 1935hrs. This was nothing compared with what 3 Squadron were achieving and the ANZACs did not want to settle for second best.

On 18th May Rear-Admiral Thursby claimed that:

'No proper reconnaissance had been carried out around the ANZAC positions since they had landed' while the kite balloon was too far away to be of any service.

---

[41] John Lea, *'Reggie, The Life of Air Vice-Marshal R L G Marix CB DSO'*. Durham: Pentland Press, 1994, page 48.

The problem was that 'Ark Royal' and its seaplanes had been assigned to the ANZACs as 3 Squadron was required to cover the British beaches at Helles, so he had not seen many aeroplanes. When the weather got bad, as it did now for some four days, 'Ark Royal' could not get any seaplanes up but 3 Squadron could still fly and did. But now Samson's men and machines were getting tired as by 19th May they had covered 30,000 miles.

On 17th May, the SS 'Joshua Nicholson' steamed into Imbros bay with her cargo of supplies and Airship Expeditionary Force No 1, RNAS. This unit had only existed since 14th April when two Sea Scout Airships No 3 and No 19 were assigned to it. It was a totally new unit with a totally new weapon: the officers only had some 20 hours flying time in airships between them and only a couple of those were in the Sea Scout! Airship Expeditionary Force No 1 had a strength of six officers, 12 NCOs and 50 ratings. It landed all its equipment on the 18th and started to set up camp. Their airfield was on Imbros, close to the sea, and later in the year they would be joined by 3 Squadron (Wing) and 2 Squadron (Wing) RNAS. They set to and started to build their airfield, putting up their tents, offices and messes before turning to the construction of the very large airship hangar, a monstrous building of wood and canvas. On 19th May, the two airships took to the sky and carried out their first active service patrols. They then carried out several weeks of training and installed the wireless set which had to be tuned to the ANZAC Army artillery command. In the meantime, 3 Squadron did its best to fill the gap.

On the morning of 18th May Lieutenant Osmond carried out a 3-hour reconnaissance in front of the ANZAC position and later that day Major Hogg did a 4-hour and 45 minute reconnaissance in the same area. Looking at the reports and the new photographs, Isaac came to the conclusion that a Turkish attack was imminent so warned General Birdwood and sent over hard-copies of the proof. The Generals at GHQ agreed with him and all ANZAC forces were put on alert that day and the night of the 18th/19th so that when the Turkish infantry rose up and out of their trenches they were met by a withering fire.

The Turkish guns had been uncharacteristically quiet on 18th May but at 1826hrs, as a result of 3 Squadron's intelligence reports, an order was sent to each Brigade telling them to make ready to repulse an enemy attack and at 1850hrs the 2nd Infantry Brigade was ordered to deploy forward piquets. At 1900hrs reports started to come in of Turkish shelling of the Australian trenches then a steady rain of shells fell for five hours until just before midnight. At 2145hrs the 1st and 3rd Brigades threw out loose barbed wire in front of their trenches and what reserves were available were put into position to support the main front line. By 0053hrs on 19th May all battalions reported that they were taking heavy fire but all was well. An intense half-hour bombardment began at 0300hrs, followed by the advance of 42,000 Turkish infantry against a defending force of just 17,000 Australians and New Zealanders in an effort to push them back into the sea.

Lacking sufficient artillery and ammunition, the Turks relied on surprise and weight of numbers for success but as their preparations had been seen by 3 Squadron and reported to the ANZACs, yet again the Australians were ready and waiting for the Turks. What follows was a textbook stand by the Australians. The Turkish plan was simple: every man in the Turkish lines would charge the ANZAC lines like a great human wave which would crest on the parapet of the ANZAC trenches with bayonets fixed. In all, only about six Turks reached the Australian lines. The rest lay out in No Man's Land dead and dying. At the end of the day's debacle, the Allied forces had fired nearly a million rounds of ammunition. The last Turks pulled back at 0500hrs, trying to gather what men they could, and the Turkish commanders ordered another assault. The Turkish 2nd and 5th Divisions attacked again and again until almost 1000hrs, when the troops would no longer leave their trenches. Each wave had been cut down by the Australians.

The Turks would try again but they never managed to take the ANZAC's positions and force them back into the sea. General Birdwood was quick to thank Samson and 3 Squadron for their work, in particular the intelligence reports which he felt help save his command. General Hamilton also thanked 3 Squadron and all in all it was a good day for Samson and his men. But Hamilton did not put 3 Squadron's reconnaissance work into the official dispatches, all he mentioned was the bombing of enemy positions. His continued omission of 3 Squadron's reconnaissance role and the photographic maps made it appear to the Admiralty back in London that the RNAS were failing the Army on Gallipoli in its most basic duty. Samson, however, did not get involved with the politics and just continued supporting the Army, even continuing to support Hamilton's 29th Division.

Meanwhile, the Red Cross and the Red Crescent had struck up a local and very informal truce to collect up the wounded and bury the dead laying in front of the Australian lines. In the evening twilight an Australian unit mistakenly believed the Turks were gathering behind the casualty clearing operation and opened fire, thus bringing this truce to an end. But the stink from all the dead was unbearable and by 22nd May the ANZACS had started to talk to the Turks about a temporary armistice as there were now so many corpses piled up in No-Man's Land that it could become a health problem. The Turks were pleased with this as their men did not like to attack through their own dead. There was an official cease-fire on 23rd May from 0730hrs to 1630hrs in which time Turkish and Anzac dead were collected up and buried. This greatly helped with the smell.

'Ark Royal' put up no seaplanes on 18th and 19th May but the main part of the crew were sent ashore on the 19th to start erecting the tents and other buildings required by the fliers in their new base at Aliki Bay, Imbros. The working day was from 0745hrs until 1945hrs, except Sundays, which started an hour later. The weather took a turn for the worse and was not great over the next two days but 3 Squadron still put up several flights each day. On the 20th, Kilner left the 'Ark Royal' at 1840hrs in No 161, and returned at 1940hrs. Garnett had also taken off at 1935hrs in No 857, returning at 1955hrs after just twenty minutes in the air.

On the 18th No 3 RNAS Armoured Car Section was pulled out of the front line due to heavy losses, followed three days later by No 4 RNAS Armoured Car Section.[42] The next time they went into action was in June. Things were beginning to settle down in the ground war so all the intelligence officers wanted to know each morning if there had been any overnight changes to the Turkish positions. 3 Squadron started to mount a first-light patrol and it became a standing order that these patrols would carry bombs The breakfast cooking fires could be seen and made a very tempting target, knowing that men were gathered around them making breakfast. The pilot flying the patrol would cut his engine and dive down on one of these fires, release the bombs, restart the engine, and pull away. As the light improved, the pilot would then compare yesterday's photograph with what he could see on the ground. If there were no changes he would move on to the next photograph area.

There had been many rumours and supposed sightings of a German U-Boat but as of yet no real confirmed attacks or sightings. The German U-Boat U-21 left Kiel on 25th April and the voyage to Austria-Hungary took eighteen days. The U-Boat had to run on the surface to conserve fuel, which increased the risk of detection by Allied forces. U-21 finally arrived in Cattaro on 13th May, with only 1.8t of fuel left in her tanks, and arrived in her operational area off Gallipoli on 25th May. On their first day on station, she encountered the British pre-dreadnought battleship HMS 'Triumph', and the 'Manica'. A torpedo was seen approaching the 'Manica' amidships but it passed under the shallow-draught 'Manica' and continued on to strike the 'Triumph', which capsized and sank quickly. U-21 then dived under the sinking battleship to escape the destroyers hunting her. The captain took his boat to the bottom and sat on the sea floor until the Allied forces had abandoned the search for him. With the air in the boat very foul after twenty-eight hours on the sea floor, U-21 surfaced to recharge her batteries and bring in fresh air.

This attack changed the whole position of the Fleet. There was now a very real U-Boat threat. Henceforth the Fleet was kept in the harbours of

---

[42] H A Jones, *'The War in the Air'*, Vol II., 1928, page 51

Mudros and Imbros, protected by torpedo nets, only venturing out for specific operations and returning as soon as the shooting was completed. On 27th May, the U21 attacked and sank a second battleship, HMS 'Majestic'. This time, the Royal Navy had attempted to protect her with torpedo nets and had several small ships screening her, but the German was able to aim a torpedo through the defences. HMS 'Majestic' sank in just four minutes. These two successes brought significant dividends: all Allied capital ships were withdrawn into a protected area off Mudros and only came out from behind their nets when the big naval guns were required to support a ground attack on the peninsula. They were thus unable to bombard Turkish positions there at will any more.[43]

Flying from 'Ark Royal' carried on in its usual desultory fashion. On Friday 21st May Garnett left the 'Ark Royal' at 0635hrs in No 857, returning just twenty minutes later. At 1400hrs Douglas left the ship in No 922 to join the cruiser HMS 'Minerva'. The next day Kilner left the 'Ark Royal' in No 857 at 1320hrs and returned at 1655hrs. Bromet left in No 860 at 1750hrs and returned at 1930hrs, while Dunning left in No 136 at 1900hrs and returned 45 minutes later at 1945hrs. On Sunday 23rd and Monday 24th May there was no flying from the ship. On the 25th, the first flight was Kilner in No 161 at 0950hrs, returning at 1220hrs. Dunning was up next at 1448hrs in No 136 and Douglas returned in No 922 from his detachment to 'Minerva' at 1505hrs, followed down by Dunning who landed at 1510hrs. Whitehead went up in No 176 at 1748hrs and returned some 30 minutes later. There was no flying from the ship on 26th May. On 27th May Dunning was first up. He took off at 0500hrs in No 136, had engine trouble and returned to the ship at 0520hrs. At 0600hrs Bromet left the ship in No 176 and returned at 0645hrs. There was no more flying from the Ark Royal until Saturday 29th May. Eight days (four without flying) and only ten flights, not counting Douglas' return to the ship. It seems a remarkably poor showing from such a huge investment of money and men.

Meanwhile, it was very clear to all commanders in the Dardanelles/Gallipoli that a stalemate had been reached. The morale of the Army was low among the men owing to the prevalence of dysentery and other diseases. But the factor which had the most important bearing on the operation was the shortage of artillery, artillery ammunition, trench mortars and hand grenades.[44] The difference of opinion between the Navy and the Army proved as strong as ever. The Admiralty had informed Admiral de Robeck:

'That all idea of the fleet breaking through must be given up. They had always regarded the plan as a measure of necessity, and had they known

---

[43] Edwyn A Gray, *"The U-Boat War 1914–1918'*, 1994. page 124
[44] TNA: AIR 1/681/21/13/2209

that in three months an army of 100,000 men would have been available, they would never have undertaken a purely naval attack. In view of the new factors, the submarines, the Italian Convention and the needs of the Grand Fleet a revival of the idea was out of the question. The campaign had become, and must continue to be, mainly military, in other words, instead of a military force to assist the fleet, it was now a question of a naval force to assist the army, and for this purpose the naval force they were now organising was in their estimation as good as, and even better than the original one.'

De Robeck felt this was a real slap in the face and that his command was now purely one of support of the Army.

Lord Kitchener and Churchill had convinced Lord Fisher, the First Sea Lord, that the Dardanelles campaign was a good plan with no problems. As it progressed, or rather failed to, Lord Fisher felt more and more justified in his fears and hardened his opposition to the operation. To those who decided policy, three courses now seemed to be open: to withdraw at once, to push on for a quick decision, or to settle down to a long siege. Immediate withdrawal could scarcely be contemplated, a rapid decision was equally out of the question, and as to the third alternative, it was agreed that no conclusion could be come to until it was known what force would be required to ensure the success of the siege.

The meeting of the War Council on May 14th had made it very clear that the battle on Gallipoli could not be abandoned and must be continued as a military operation which could now only be of a prolonged nature. The same evening Fisher's apprehensions were confirmed. In order to meet the military objection and the ill-effects of the withdrawal of the 'Queen Elizabeth', Churchill, the First Lord of the Admiralty, drafted orders for an increase of the naval part of the Eastern Mediterranean expedition. This involved the absorption of all the new monitors that had been developed as an essential element in the North Sea plans for bombarding Belgium and Germany. Without them, the offensive could not be pushed into German home waters, and in view of the determination of the Government and the War Office to press on with the Dardanelles operation and feeling unable any longer to be responsible for the conduct of the war at sea, Lord Fisher resigned the next morning, 15th May.

To the country at large, Lord Fisher was the embodiment of the old fighting spirit of the Royal Navy, the man to whom we owed the organisation and strategical disposition which rendered the German fleet impotent. The loss of Fisher at this point in time was not good as he was held in such high esteem by the general public and it could only add to the general depression about the state of the war. But his loss proved to be only the first step in a far-reaching process of disintegration in the Admiralty. In a few days Churchill, whose untiring energy had perfected Fisher's plans for expansion in the last days of peace, also left the Admiralty - and the RNAS lost its greatest supporter. Samson had a lot of time for both men and both men liked Samson and his attitude towards the war.

The general uneasiness about the conduct of the war, which had been vaguely displaying itself for some time with the public, received a deeper and more restless impetus. The confidence in the Government was waning. The people of Britain wanted a success, a great victory, but this was a long way away. The Government's grasp and handling of the initial problems of the war had been inspired but this had gradually faded away as more and more failures appeared. The shortage of shells was only one example of this. The changes at the Admiralty delivered the final shock and within five days of Lord Fisher's departure, the leaders of the great political parties were sitting in council to form a Coalition Government.

Kitchener's role in the Cabinet was threefold at the start of the war. Firstly, he was to manage national recruiting. His second task was to oversee the management of the UK's industries that now needed to be on a war footing, and his third role was to be responsible for military strategy. It was a huge workload for a man who did not like to delegate and who had no staff to delegate to. Kitchener was especially against being, as he saw it, harried by politicians. He believed that politicians had little if any idea on how to manage anything remotely concerned with warfare and it soon became obvious that he and some members of the Cabinet would clash. On a number of occasions he threatened to resign because of what he saw as interfering politicians hounding him about his job. However, Asquith could not afford to lose Kitchener from his Cabinet as his status among the public was that of a great military leader, a hero of Great Britain. But his cabinet colleagues did not share the public worship of Kitchener; they saw the man as an interfering old fool and who should have been put out to pasture years ago. He was gradually relieved of his responsibilities. His support for the disastrous Dardanelles operation, combined with the 'shell crisis' of 1915, eroded his reputation further.

The Cabinet was in agreement over a withdrawal from the Dardanelles – all except Kitchener. He considered withdrawals to be a sign of weakness that would encourage the enemy. Many in the Cabinet felt that Kitchener had served his purpose but now had to go. They pressed Asquith to either sack him or push him into resigning from the Cabinet. Asquith was in a difficult position because Kitchener was still something of a talisman to the public and a sacking would not be greeted well. He spared Asquith this problem when he offered to resign in November 1915 but although Asquith refused to accept his resignation, believing that his public aura far outweighed the doubts expressed by some in his Cabinet and the military, he did remove more of his responsibilities. By the end of 1915, Kitchener was only in charge of administering the War Office. He finally resigned from the Cabinet when senior army commanders were given free access to it. Previously they had to go through him, which to some extent gave him control over who in the army met with the Cabinet and who did not.

Samson had packed up all his useless aeroplanes and returned them to Britain on 19th May and a request, made with the backing of Admiral de Robeck, was put in for more Farman-type aeroplanes with the larger engine. On 25th May de Robeck put in a formal complaint to the Air Department, run by Murray Sueter, and the First Lord of the Admiralty, that:

'Our Aeroplanes are getting very worn, and it is occasionally impossible to obtain one when required.'

He obviously hit a nerve as Sueter replied the same day, sending de Robeck a telegram announcing that six new Voisin 140hp Canton Unné aeroplanes were at last on route to Samson.[45] The next day they actually arrived, and one was quickly put together and flown. These new aircraft did not have an airspeed indicator or a compass fitted, both of which Samson felt were essential. The Canton-Unné engines were very reliable but a little underpowered when two men and a bombload were on board. They found that it could lift two 100lb bombs but it took some 30 minutes to get to 4,000ft[46] and the engine had to be run full out to make them climb. Still, beggars can't be choosers and they were a great improvement on the little Henri Farmans.[47]

Early on the morning of 26th May the 'Levant II' proceeded to Anzac where the cable had been broken as the 'Triumph' had gone down on it the day before. The crew quickly found the break, which was only about 150 yards from Anzac Beach but during the attempt to repair the shore end of the cable, the ship was subject to heavy shrapnel fall-out. The Turks from Gaba Tepe suddenly opened fire on the 'Levant', three shells in quick succession bursting over the ship. Two men were slightly injured. 'Levant's crew cut the cable and cleared out as quickly as possible. They were, after all, civilians and not used to being on the wrong end of artillery fire. They then found the ship was holed above the waterline. Two lumps of shrapnel had entered the testing room, one passing through the inkstand and the other striking the wooden bulkhead. Fortunately for Spalding, he was at the Morse instrument and not at the table when the vessel was hit.

A doctor from one of the minesweepers attended to the injured men but luckily they had just sustained flesh wounds. The ship moved further out. They had lunch at anchor and considered how the new end could best be

---

[45] TNA: AIR 1/361/15/228/50
[46] ibidem
[47] Richard Bell Davies, op. cit., page 123

laid. After lunch they scrounged a pinnace, coiled the end of the cable in her stern and steamed in close to the beach. One of the crew, Jordan, jumped into the water and carried the cable end to the beach by himself in just a few minutes. The men on shore took the end and put it in place. The ship had drifted in shore and they were spotted again by the enemy who again opened fire just as ship got turned round. They paid out the rest of the new cable quickly and got away with no more damage than riddled decks and awnings, which were pieced in many places. The repair was finished without further mishaps though rifle bullets from time to time struck the water around the ship and buried themselves in the deck. The binnacle top had been smashed and the saloon sky-light scored. The final splice was made about half a mile off the beach. After the repair they anchored off the beach and the crew began a general hunt for curios on board.

Samson explained to Sueter and the Admiralty that the Army could not get enough of his photographs and that more pilots should be trained in the art of aerial photography. He also explained that the aerodrome was as good as Eastchurch and was now fitted with electric light. However, as a number of the cruisers and battleships had now moved away from Tenedos, they felt a little unprotected and had started to build bunkers and mount Vickers guns in them.

On Saturday 29th May the first seaplane up from the 'Ark Royal' was No 176 flown by Lieutenant Bromet, taking off at 0840hrs and returning at 0925hrs. Kilner then took off in No 161 at 0930hrs and returned at 1155hrs. In the afternoon Bromet went up again in No 176, making a 30-minute flight between 1320hrs and 1350hrs. At 1415hrs Douglas took off in No 922, landing back at 1605hrs. The last seaplane up was No 1438 flown by Kershaw: he took off at 1722hrs and landed back at 1830hrs. On 31st May Kershaw left the ship in No 857 at 1355hrs and returned at 1520hrs. This would be the final flight from 'Ark Royal' itself as the beach airfield at Aliki Bay, Imbros, was now fully up and running. When Kershaw took off again at 1655hrs, he left this time from the beach and returned at 1835hrs to the new facility. That night and from then on, the seaplanes were pulled up onto the beach and did not return to the 'Ark Royal'. At night, or if a seaplane was not required during the day, it was parked on the salt lake behind the main beach, a distance of only about 100 yards. At first the seaplanes were mounted on trollies on a wooden causeway but this was soon replaced by a narrow gauge railway to move them from the beach to the lake and back again. From now on 'Ark Royal' would act as a tender for all RNAS flying units, supplying fresh water and bathing facilities, which helped greatly to cut down the problems with lice.

'Ark Royal' had arrived in Kephalo Bay on 10th May. From 9th May until June she only launched 37 seaplane flights and a number of them were very short due to mechanical problems, meaning in effect that the seaplane did not carry out its mission. In the same period Samson and 3 Squadron made 170 flights over enemy territory. The men of 3 Squadron alone were able to carry out on average seven flights per day. This was a mix of reconnaissance, spotting and bombing missions and it put a terrible toll on their aeroplanes and on the pilots themselves and ground crew. As the seaplanes of 'Ark Royal' could not get the height over land to be safe from Turkish guns, they were switched to anti-submarine patrols, as were any spare 3 Squadron aircraft. One German submarine was spotted in the Dardanelles and attacked unsuccessfully with bombs.

The weather and the state of the sea cannot be blamed for the very poor showing from the 'Ark Royal'. She had some six seaplanes (and two landplanes) in her hold so should have performed a lot better. Her captain, Clark-Hall, was not a combat commander but he was a great trainer. He was good at passing on knowledge to young officers, especially in gunnery, but as for commanding the 'Ark Royal' in the Dardanelles, he had no enthusiasm or interest in the job and as such was a failure at it. Hence why the ship was such a failure during the operations in the Eastern Mediterranean. While some may argue that comparing seaplanes to landplanes is not fair at this time in this theatre, look at the comparison between the work done in a 20-day period by the 'Ark Royal' - six seaplanes, 37 seaplane take-offs - and that done in a similar period of time in the Dardanelles by the 'Ben-My-Chree', a seaplane carrier like Ark Royal, with only four seaplanes but 51 take-offs.

Commander Cecil J L'Estrange Malone was in command of HMS 'Ben-my-Chree' in June 1915. Having commanded the aircraft for the Cuxhaven Raid of 25th December 1914, he served in the Dardanelles Campaign and was mentioned in dispatches, largely due to his pioneering work in equipping aeroplanes to carry torpedoes and successfully torpedoing three enemy vessels. He, like Samson, trained his men and pilots well. He was a pilot himself and led by example and, just like Samson, his men responded well and followed his orders. All of the ship's company of the 'Ben-my-Chree' were full of fighting spirit and would follow their commander without hesitation.

It was noted by many of the captains of warships that the sheer sound and then the sight of an aircraft would make the Turkish gunners cease firing and retreat under cover. The same with the 'Manica's balloon: as soon as it went up, Turkish guns stopped firing. However, Samson and 3 Squadron were in poor health having been on active service without a break for nearly a year now. Yes, they had just taken delivery of six new machines but their other aeroplanes were falling apart as many had flown in France in 1914, and were still flying, but only just. They had flown over 30,000 miles, and 303 missions alone during May. Spare parts were very difficult to find so any rubbish tip was being scrounged and any aircraft that was beyond repair was being torn apart to give up spare parts.

The Turkish Air Force was reinforced by a new Albatros which arrived on 2nd May and it now conducted almost daily reconnaissance flights over the Allied frontline, fleet and airfields. During May, the 1st Aircraft Company of the Turkish Air Force was brought into being, comprised of two flights of two aircraft each. Despite repeated bombing attacks against the airfield at Chanak by 3 Squadron, the Turks also made regular flights (usually twice-weekly) over the main British bases on Tenedos and Imbros to count the ships in harbour. A load of handmade bombs were carried and dropped as they passed over the airfield on Tenedos during these missions. Over the Allied lines, they dropped quantities of steel darts that were thrown over the side as an anti-personnel weapon. The British, it should be mentioned, also used these flechettes, although the darts which Samson and his men had to deliver reportedly wobbled so violently in descent that they had no effect whatever, and even bounced harmlessly off tents. Anecdotal evidence suggests that the Turkish versions were more lethal and hence more psychologically effective. On 27th May the Turks also used their aircraft to notch up a first by conducting a propaganda mission against the Allies. Pamphlets written in Urdu were dropped over ANZAC and the French lines at Helles, appealing to Moslem Indians and French colonial troops not to fight fellow Moslems. The tactic was promptly copied by the Allies, who responded with a pamphlet drop over Turkish lines four days later. This return attempt to undermine enemy morale was essentially misguided since most Turkish officers and troops were illiterate.

Chapter four
June and July 1915

There were hardly any flies on Gallipoli in May; the weather was warming up and it was quite pleasant. On Tenedos daily swimming was encouraged after work for all ranks. During the summer, however, the temperature soared and remained high even through the night, preventing the soldiers, sailors and airmen from being able to rest or sleep. Now the British, French, ANZACs and Turks had to contend with swarms of flies. June came and the bloated flies arrived in droves. They were so thick in July that they carpeted the men and the land, a big problem even as far as the island of Tenedos. They could choke a man by getting into his throat, blocking his nose and infecting his eyes. Not only were they annoying, they were quickly spreading disease by spending some of their time on the rotten left-over food that littered No-Man's-Land and the human excrement that littered the trench system of both sides. The other half of the flies' time was spent on decaying corpses in No-Man's-Land, bringing about infestations of maggots and lice. The flies and maggots could strip a corpse to the bone in just eight days, though this greatly helped with the smell. Dysentery and other diseases raged as a result of the inadequate sanitation, the poor diet and the impure water. There was no rain, or at best very little, so there was no fresh water. The earth turned to very fine dust and this dust got into the men's food.

The ANZAC commanders had yet another problem to contend with: 'Ark Royal's failure to supply regular aerial surveillance. They took a quick and effective way to deal with their problems. As they had not seen a seaplane for many a day, on 2nd June 3 Squadron was asked by the ANZACs to fly over ANZAC Cove and carry out a full reconnaissance. Samson himself carried this out and he also brought along a 100lb bomb to use on a target of opportunity, which he duly dropped on the Turks' front trench line. However, another RNAS seaplane carrier was already on its way out east and while out there, this ship and her seaplanes would make history. In Harwich docks, England, on 1st June 1915, a ship was making ready to go to sea. HMS 'Ben-My-Chree', a brand new seaplane carrier, was short of a few crew but otherwise she was ready to sail. At last the missing crew members turned up and at 1301hrs the 'Ben-My-Chree' reported she was ready for sea and at 1307hrs she let go all lines and headed out. Her orders were to join the Eastern Mediterranean Fleet off the Dardanelles.

'Ben-My-Chree' had started her life as a steamer for the Isle of Man Steam Packet Company but was chartered by the Royal Navy on 1st January 1915. She began her conversion into a seaplane carrier at the Cammell Laird shipyard in Birkenhead on the 2nd. Part of her aft superstructure was removed and replaced by a large hangar, aft of her rear funnel, which housed four to six seaplanes. The aircraft were lifted in and out of the water by derricks mounted fore and aft on the ship. A dismountable 60-foot-long flying-off platform was installed forward of her superstructure, equipped with a trolley and rails to allow a seaplane to take off while the ship was underway. In Royal Navy service, she displaced 3,888 tons (3,950 t), was 387 feet long overall, with a draught of 16 feet (4.9 m). 'Ben-My-Chree' was credited with a speed of 24.5 knots (28.2 mph), although that speed was often exceeded in service, and to provide this propulsion she could carry 502 tons (510 t) of coal. Her armament consisted of four quick-firing 12-pounder guns, and two Vickers three-pounder AA guns, carrying 130 rounds per 12-pounder and 64 rounds for each three-pounder. When 'Ben-My-Chree' emerged from her conversion in January 1915 she was the fastest of the seaplane carriers then in service, with a crew of approximately 250 officers and enlisted men. Her air group comprised four Short Type 184 seaplane torpedo bombers, the most advanced type then in service with the Navy. A more useful ship than some of the earlier conversions like the 'Ark Royal', she was initially attached to the Harwich Force and participated in some of the abortive raids on the north German coast.

HMS 'Ben-My-Chree' was under the command of Commander Cecil L'Estrange Malone, a man cut from the same cloth as Samson. They knew each other already and would get on very well. L'Estrange Malone joined the Royal Navy in 1905 and attended the Royal Naval College at Dartmouth. In 1911 he was chosen to undergo a flying course at Eastchurch, where one of his instructors would have been Samson, and qualified as a pilot with Royal Aero Club certificate No 195. He therefore became one of the founder members of the RNAS, which was established in July 1912. Following the outbreak of World War I, he was placed in command of the RNAS units that took part in the raid on Cuxhaven on 25th December 1914, the first combined sea and air operation undertaken by the Royal Navy, and was mentioned in dispatches. Placed in command of HMS 'Ben-my-Chree' in March 1915, he served in the Dardanelles Campaign and was again mentioned in dispatches, largely due to his pioneering work in equipping aeroplanes to carry torpedoes and successfully torpedoing three enemy vessels.

Not content with just sending a second seaplane carrier to reinforce her aerial component, the Royal Navy now sent another RNAS kite balloon ship to back up the very successful original, HMS 'Manica'. Kite balloon ship HMS 'Hector', under the command of Commander Geoffrey M R Rayne, left Birkenhead on 2nd June after her refit and transformation into a balloon ship and set sail for the Dardanelles. After a poor voyage through the Channel and the Bay of Biscay when all the RNAS men were sick, the 'Hector' arrived at Gibraltar on 7th June at 1400hrs. A wireless expert, Flight Lieutenant B S Benning, was in charge of the 'Hector's RNAS balloon section. He had worked for Marconi before joining the RNAS at the beginning of the war. The ship still had its problems. A number of Pierce

Arrow lorries, now known as 'Samson Trucks', she carried were causing problems in the hold. All the electrical wiring had to be replaced and the crew had tried and failed to scrounge a 6pdr gun that could be mounted on the stern for self-protection. She was also missing several crew members.

The 'Hector' left Gibraltar and headed to Malta where she acquired the missing crew, leaving Malta at 0700hrs on 12th June and heading for Imbros. At 0400hrs on the 14th she was met by HMS 'Cornwall' and escorted into the anchorage at Lemnos. At long last she dropped anchor off Mudros at 0430hrs on 15th June, where for the next three weeks the ship carried out a number of drills and practice launches of her kite balloon. There was no peace for the wicked: the average working day was from 0615hrs to 1900hrs. However, before training could start the 'Hector' went over to Tenedos and unloaded a large consignment of bombs and the lorries for Samson and 3 Squadron, freeing up valuable space below.

Though not identical, the balloon carriers shared some common features. They had a capacious forward hold, lined with wood, into which an inflated balloon would fit. This was covered with a split hatch so that when open each half formed a windbreak down the side of the ship. When no heavy seas were expected the balloon might be carried with its top half-proud of the hatchway but protected by the hatch halves. However in any sea the balloon had to be part deflated to allow the hatches to be shut. The winch was located at the bottom of the hold and the observers could get in and out of the basket in the hold. Each ship was fitted with a gas generator and a compressor for filling the cylinders used to top up the balloons' lifting gas.

On the equally successful cable-laying front, it was merely a case of replacing like with like as the 'Levant II' headed to Mudros Bay on 2nd June, where she was about to be relieved by the 'Levant I', another cable-laying ship. This probably delighted the crew of the 'Levant II', who had been working flat out since their arrival in theatre in April.

From the beginning of June the tempo of air operations seemed to pick up with bombing raids by both sides becoming more frequent. Clashes between aircraft also began to take place. In the Helles sector, which had been extensively entrenched by both sides, the Allies launched another attack on Krithia and Achi Baba in the Third Battle of Krithia on 4th June, with the 29th Division, Royal Naval Division, 42nd Division and two French divisions. Major-General Aylmer Hunter-Weston, the butcher of the 29th Division, had been removed and Major-General Henry de Beauvoir de Lisle was placed in command of the 29th on 24th May 1915. He would remain in command of the division until the end of the war.

3 Squadron carried out many reconnaissance and artillery spotting flights over the Turkish lines on the days up to the attack on 4th June. They also

took a large number of photographs of the area, as the Turkish trench system was now very complicated. Lieutenant Butler got some very good pictures and made a brand new map of the area, which was flown over to Helles and delivered to General Hamilton with the aircraft landing on the airstrip there coming under fire from the Turks as usual. The forward base was used a lot on the run up to the attack on the 4th but it was becoming very dangerous. On the day of the attack itself, Samson had four aeroplanes there carrying out constant standing patrols.

General Hunter-Weston's previous battle plans had lacked subtlety or sense. They had been straightforward suicidal frontal attacks that turned out to be consistent failures. Some elements of refinement had begun to appear in the plans for the latest attempt on Krithia. For one, General Sir Ian Hamilton, the commander of the Mediterranean Expeditionary Force, insisted that the objectives should be limited to an advance of 800yd. This was to be made in two steps: the first step was to capture the Turkish trenches; the second was to advance a further 500yd and then establish a new trench line. An innovation was the use, for the first time, of eight armoured cars of the Royal Naval Air Service, which were to advance along the main Krithia road in support of the Royal Naval Division's advance.

The usual morning dust storm of 4th June obscured everything and so the naval bombardment was not very accurate. The ships were not allowed to stop in the water as they had to maintain headway due to the U-Boat threat, even with the new Sea Scout Airships[48] overhead looking for the U-Boat. At first light Samson had one of his aeroplanes over the battlefield spotting for the artillery and attacking the morning cooking fires. The main artillery attack was to start at 1120hrs with a feint then stopped after a few rounds. At 1130hrs the main bombardment would start and more aeroplanes from 3 Squadron arrived over the battlefield to help spot for the artillery.

Once the bombardment stopped the main attacks would go in starting at mid-day. On the left of the attack was the Indian Brigade. They were quickly halted except along the Aegean shore where the Gurkha Rifles managed to advance. The 14th Battalion of King George's Own Ferozepur Sikhs Regiment, advancing along the floor of Gully Ravine, were almost wiped out, losing 380 men out of 514 and nearly all of their officers. The 2nd Battalion of the Hampshire Regiment from the 29th Division, advancing along Fir Tree Spur alongside Gully Ravine, managed to advance but having lost contact with the Sikhs on their left, were forced to defend along the bank of the ravine as well as to their front. Elsewhere, the 29th Division advance was held up with heavy casualties by Turkish strongpoints that

---

[48] See Chapter five for their invention and introduction into service. Also known as 'Submarine Scouts'

had survived the bombardment unscathed. The advance of the 42nd Division was, by Gallipoli standards, very successful, quickly reaching the first objective of the Turkish trenches and moving beyond to advance a total of 1,000yd. This attack was made by the 127th (Manchester) Brigade which broke through the Turkish 9th Division's defences and captured 217 prisoners.

The Royal Naval Division's (RND) advance was led by the 2nd Naval Brigade. They were to be supported by the eight RNAS Rolls-Royce armoured cars, now under the command of Lieutenant Commander Arthur Drummond Borton. Three roadways, which were no better than dirt tracks, were to be cleared and bridged so the armoured cars could use them as they went in during the attack. This meant bridging parts of the British trench system and other gullies during the night so the Turks could not see what was going on. Some of the cars had been modified. They were equipped with grappling hooks on long poles that could be dropped into the Turkish wire by the reversing armoured cars, then they would floor the accelerator and pull away, tearing large gaps in the Turkish wire for the men to charge through. That was the plan, anyway. There was a great cheer from the RND as the armoured cars went forward but it was a short-lived triumph. One car came off the track and flipped over, another went over a bump at speed and its turret bounced off while the other cars came under intense machine-gun fire and were shot to bits. The tyres were shredded and the wheels damaged but then, this was a job for a tank not a light armoured car. It was the only time they were used in battle during the campaign. In spite of this setback, the RND managed to reach and capture the Turkish trenches. When the second wave attempted to continue the advance, they were caught in enfilade fire from Kereves Dere to the right where the French advance had failed. The battalion, one of the newly-arrived reinforcements, was utterly annihilated and was never reformed. Further attempts to reach the second objective were successful but the position was untenable, so within a couple of hours the RND units had retreated to their starting positions.

Samson was to complain that if the armoured cars had been used sooner and more aggressively, far better results could have been obtained, and that one or two self-propelled guns could have made a great difference. This led to some people claiming post-war that it was just sour grapes on Samson's part as he was not consulted about the use of the armoured cars or how to command them in battle and was restricted to flying from Tenedos. Nevertheless, it is an indisputable fact that he and a number of 3 Squadron personnel had a lot of combat experience in fighting the Germans from their armoured cars and knew how to do it, while most of the men of 3 and 4 Squadron RNASAC section had very little training and no combat experience at all before arriving in Gallipoli. A bit of advice from someone who had had experience in action may not have been altogether wasted. After the attack on 4th June General Hamilton decided that there was no requirement for the armoured cars so he kept three officers and 34 men with their Vickers guns and shipped the cars and the rest of the men out to Alexandria once transport was available.

At 1600hrs, the troops were ordered to dig in and consolidate their positions. However, this coincided with the Turkish reserves counter-attacking against the Manchester Brigade in the centre. Within an hour, the brigade was under attack from three sides and was eventually ordered to withdraw. By the end of the battle, their new front line was a mere 200–250yds in front of their start line, passing through a patch of vines that earned the area the name of 'The Vineyard' which was to be the site of heavy fighting in August. Although the British broke through the Turkish lines towards Krithia, this advantage was not followed up and the enemy line held. The British suffered more than 4,500 casualties, the French more than 2,000 and the Turks more than 9,000 dead and wounded.

During the battle, one of Samson's pilots landed at Helles and reported that he had spotted a U-Boat near Rabbit Island. Samson was on the airfield on Tenedos when the news came through and, having had a 100lb bomb fitted to his aeroplane, went off in search of the submarine. He found the U-Boat in the entrance to the Dardanelles heading for a stationery French cruiser that was supporting the attack. Samson dived on his target and let go his bomb which hit the surface of the water and exploded and the submarine passed under the cruiser without attacking it. Later that evening Samson spotted the U-Boat on the surface when he was returning from a long reconnaissance flight but with no bombs on board, he attacked the sub using his rifle. [49]

Due to the U-Boat threat and her very poor speed, 'Ark Royal' was no longer allowed to move around and was brought into Kephalo Bay, Imbros, and anchored up behind anti-submarine nets. Here she became a depot ship for all the RNAS, with one special advantage: she had a large bathroom so the men of all the squadrons did not suffer the lice problem that the Army did. Her seaplanes flew from Aliki Bay and carried out as much support as they could for the ANZACs, mainly reconnaissance missions, and a large number of anti-submarine patrols.

As Samson found out in the Dardanelles, life is very interesting when you have multiple bosses. While Admiral Sir John de Robeck, and Admirals Nicholson and Thursby were always trying to help and support the RNAS, other admirals felt their orders were more important and should be carried out first. Their rank *must* be higher than the last officer to give Samson an order, especially if he was an Army General! They felt, or at least some of them did, that as Samson was Navy and the Navy was the senior service

---

[49] TNA: AIR 1/681/21/13/2209

then naval orders should take precedence. By now Samson had a limited number of aeroplanes and a limited number of pilots, all of whom were showing the strain of having been in action with no rest since August 1914. No other unit in the British armed forces had been asked or ordered to remain in action for some ten months like this. Samson made a point of talking to all the admirals and generals and putting his side and explaining what he could do under the circumstances.

3 Squadron carried several long-range reconnaissance missions on 5th June looking for reinforcements coming down the road to bolster the Turkish front line. However, all the roads to the rear of Krithia were empty of troops; the only thing moving were a few supply wagons, which were duly attacked. By now the average Turkish soldier was asking: 'where are our aeroplanes? We are constantly attacked and our animals scared off.' Even some of the officers felt this way and so the price on Samson's head and those of his men was raised. One Australian remarked 'we have the best English and French flyers here. One named Samson, the Germans have offered £6000 pounds (for) dead or alive'.

Some six reconnaissance missions were flown by 3 Squadron on 7th June. The first thing to be spotted was that there were several new gun positions and the trenches at Magram were now repaired and full of fresh troops. As the day progressed it became far more difficult to see things on the ground due to a dense heat haze. It was also very clear the Turks were very quickly repairing the damage done to their trench system along the Helles front. On the 9th fifty large trucks were spotted moving along a dried-up river bed towards Magram and all the trenches in the area seemed to be full of men. The Turks were quickly getting back on their feet.[50] Rumours were beginning to filter back that they were not treating their prisoners well and that a number had been shot out of hand. Samson now issued an order that all aircrew were to carry a pistol, and at least one rifle per aeroplane, and that the men should expend all but their last round. That they could use as they saw fit.[51]

On 10th June Major Hogg, one of Samson's spotters, sent in a report to the Vice Admiral and the Assistant Director of the RFC. Hogg seemed to think that he and the other Army spotters were supposed to be working for the Army and carrying out their requests for reconnaissance and spotting. He went on to say:

'The position is a somewhat anomalous one as we are practically absorbed into No 3 aeroplane squadron, the OC [Samson] of which, though directly under the orders of the Admiral meets the requirements of the C.R.A as far as possible........The military observers are myself and Captain

---

[50] TNA: AIR 1/681/21/13/2209
[51] TNA: AIR 1/7/6/172

Jenkins…..At present one or two machines go over daily the first is a HF which is of little value, the other is a B.E. with observer and wireless which does all the work for the day, generally 5 to 6 hours in the air. Latterly two of us have done the work on alternate days.'[52]

He went on to explain that the Turkish AA gunners were now doing a much better job and had scored a number of hits, pushing Samson's men up from 4,000ft to 7,000ft, a height that would have been unimaginable for general reconnaissance a year before.

In his book 'The fight in the Dardanelles', a German major who was adjutant to General L Von Sanders stated that they, the Turks, had insufficient aeroplanes to attack the British forces in any really threatening way. He also pointed out that 3 Squadron had been engrossed in reconnaissance work up until now, but now that things had settled down they were free to carry out a large number of bombing raids.[53] 3 Squadron and the French squadron MF 98 T were causing real concern amongst the Turks with their random bombing attacks, enough to cause the Red Crescent to protest that one of their hospitals was bombed on 11th June but both Samson and Césari put in strong rebuffs that this was a false claim.

On 12th June, three new pilots arrived on Tenedos to join 3 Squadron. All three of them, Sub-Lieutenant Harold Spencer Kerby and Lieutenants Barr and Dawson, had only passed their flying exam in early May. By the time they joined Samson they had very few hours under their belts and none on the types of aeroplanes that 3 Squadron flew. He was angry with this situation – such inexperienced pilots were not able to do the work required, were a danger to themselves and risked a valuable aeroplane - and wrote to Murray Sueter about the state of supply of machines and pilots. On one occasion he even returned a group of so-called pilots to Eastchurch.

HMS 'Ben-my-Chree' joined the Eastern Mediterranean fleet on 12th June but for her own protection she was sent south to Iero Bay, Mitylene, seventy miles south of the Dardanelles, where she would remain till the end of the month training her pilots in the use of the aerial torpedo. Her Schneider floatplane No 1445 would fly daily reconnaissance flights in support of ships patrolling off Smyrna and always found some enemy target for her four small bombs. Like the aeroplanes of 3 Squadron, the seaplanes of 'Ben-My-Chree' carried bombs whenever they went off on a reconnaissance flight. On 14th June the 'Ben-My-Chree' started her training at 0530hrs when her seaplanes were swung out. She could carry six but at this time only had four on board, Nos 821, 841, 1841 and 1445. Commander L'Estrange Malone, the captain of the 'Ben-my-Chree', took the training

---

[52] TNA: AIR 1/361/15/228/50
[53] TNA: AIR 1/681/21/13/2209

and fitness of his men very seriously and even the sailing crew of the ship were subjected to route marches and rifle drill. At 0800hrs on 18th June all navigating party and the small arms company went for a route march for three hours.

All pilots, including Samson, now reported a great increase in anti-aircraft fire as the Turks shipped in more guns to cope with 3 Squadron and MF 98T. On 14th June some new big guns were spotted being moved into new positions. The information was taken back and marked up on the intelligence map and later that week they were bombed by 3 Squadron and the French. Eight new Henri Farmans arrived, which in Samson own words, 'were perfectly useless'. Later that day Admiral de Robeck arrived in his ship HMS 'Triad' to visit and talk to Samson. He often dropped in to see the men of 3 Squadron and to offer lunch or dinner to their commanding officer. Samson took the opportunity to talk to Sir John about the aeroplanes and asked what could be done:

'If we keep them the Admiralty will credit me with eight new aeroplanes, and we will not get any good ones; therefore I would suggest, sir that you send them home again somehow.'

The eight aeroplanes vanished into the blue, never to be seen again. The Air Department kept on harassing Samson about the aircraft but he could honestly say, hand-on-heart, he had not got the aeroplanes and he did not know where they were (and did not care). To this day they are still listed as missing.

The British and French battleships were now corralled behind anti-torpedo nets and when they did come out they were not allowed to stop and bombard the Turkish positions. Only small ships like destroyers and the new monitors were allowed to do this, so the number of spotting missions for 3 Squadron had dropped dramatically. Instead, attacks on gatherings of Turkish troops, whether with bombs or darts, increased and now became a daily task. When the battleships did come out, they were very slow to respond to the 'ready' signal from the aeroplane. Some aeroplanes had to wait for up two hours for the first shell to arrive in the target area because the battleship would not move until the aeroplane was on the target but by then the aeroplane would be short of fuel and have to break off and return to base.

As well as Helles and the Fleet, 3 Squadron were now given the ANZAC area to look after as the 'Ark Royal' seaplanes were unreliable. They did a lot of heavy battery registering on to the Turkish gun positions. Some of these took a lot of finding and then registering, especially the long-range guns that were firing from over a mile away from the Australian position. Captain A H Keith-Jopp, Royal Australian Field Artillery, who first flew with the RNAS on 18th June, was to become the ANZAC spotter specialist as a member of 3 Squadron. He flew his first reconnaissance mission as an observer on 18th July and he had carried out some fourteen by 1st August. Jopp had eyes like a hawk and a very good eye for detail; he had soon spotted and plotted all the Turkish guns that were giving the ANZACs problems. Samson put him in charge of ANZAC reconnaissance and spotting, a very good choice as he made a point of going over to see the Australians in person and talk to them about what they wanted and needed. His biggest problem was the shortage of artillery ammunition. He would get the ANZAC gun on target only to be told there was no more ammunition and this he found very difficult to take.

For the first few weeks of June, Marix and Samson had been getting the Breguet ready for the long flight to Constantinople that they were planning on carrying out on the 21st. Samson went up with Marix three times and each time he took the Breguet up, Marix would load it with 200lb of bombs, then take anyone who was free as an observer. On one of the flights with Samson as observer, they spotted a very large body of Turks who were either being paid or drawing rations. On this occasion they only had a 100lb bomb with them that they let go onto the tempting target. Samson followed the flight of the bomb which exploded right in the middle of this mass gathering of about 400 men. The loss of life was tremendous. On 21st June, Marix and Derroussors, the Breguet's engineer, spent the morning getting the large aeroplane ready and fine-tuning the engine. One large and 13 small bombs were loaded onto the aircraft and all was well. At 1330hrs Samson and Marix took off. It climbed away well and they settled into the flight. Then the engine started to misfire and the further north they went, the worse the engine missed. They were level with ANZAC when they were forced to turn back, dropping their bombs on several targets to lighten the aeroplane. The closer they got to Tenedos the weaker the engine was getting and the pair of them thought they were going to get their feet wet but they just made it. The engine died as they landed and the aeroplane rolled to a stop, Derroussors rushed up to the machine and started taking the plugs out of it. He got three plugs out and threw his tools down exclaiming:

'Commandant what this pig of an engine wants is not a mechanician but one ammer'[54]

He then burst into tears and had to be led away. He had worked like a slave on the engine although suffering from dysentery and if Derroussors could not get the engine to go, then no-one could. Basically, it was a bad engine.

In the middle of June it was decided to close the Helles airfield as it was becoming far too dangerous. Samson had lost one aeroplane and the French two, both French pilots being killed. The other problem with the site was the sandy soil, which got into the oil filter and other parts of the

---

[54] Charles Rumney Samson, op. cit., page 251

aeroplane engines, causing engine failures and increasing the amount of serving required.

Lieutenant Tom Warner had not been a happy man since he left France, when he had had to leave behind his precious gun that had been mounted on a truck. Now due to the increased enemy air activity he had managed to get himself what he felt was a bigger and better gun, a 12-pdr. Samson never worked out how he got the gun or from what ship, but get it he did and with no-one screaming that they had lost one or foul play. The next problem was what to mount it on. There was a large Turkish mooring buoy down on the beach so Warner and a few Turkish prisoners got the buoy on a wagon and brought it up the airfield. It was dug in and the gun mounted on the top but the weapon slid down the side of the buoy when it was fired. A new mount was required.

On 21st June 3 Squadron flew eight missions, six of which were bombing attacks on Turkish positions in which they dropped six 100lb and four 20lb bombs, while the other two were reconnaissance flights with cameras. The French squadron MF 98 T were also very active, as they were covering the French attack on the Turks at Haricot Redoubt and Kereves Dere. They had aeroplanes over the battlefield all day spotting for army guns and naval ships, carrying out several bombing attacks and two photographic reconnaissance missions, one at the start of the battle and one towards the end.[55] However, the French made little progress but suffered more than 2,500 casualties while the Turks lost more than 6,000 killed and wounded.

On 22nd June Collet was flying a Voisin with Major Hogg as his observer. Hogg was a very good shot and always carried a rifle in case he got a chance to have a go at an enemy machine - and today he did. They spotted the enemy machine below them and dived down and behind the Etrich-Rumpler Taube. For the first few minutes of the fight the enemy pilot did not see them and Hogg had a clear shot at the underside of the aeroplane and at the engine. The Turkish pilot then realised he was being shot at and tried to get out of the way of Collet's aeroplane but after 20 minutes, Hogg hit the engine with his bullets and did some serious damage. Smoke was coming from the engine and all the way down the Turkish aeroplane was dropping bombs on its own men. The pilot managed to put his aeroplane down near Achi Baba and Collet turned his aircraft back to Tenedos to get some bombs to finish the job. They refuelled, bombed up and returned but could not find the aeroplane, which had been dragged into cover. Later that day a French aeroplane spotted the machine and called in some artillery fire from the French lines that hit and destroyed the aircraft.

On June 22nd 'Levant II' left Imbros early for Gaba Tepe to test the Anzac

---

[55] http://albindenis.free.fr/Site_escadrille/escadrille524.htm

cable which had again broken down. They proceeded to Anzac Cove to deal with the fault which was close to beach but on passing Gaba Tepe point, a Turkish battery opened fire on the ship. The shots fell wide though close enough to make them change their course to seaward to get out of range of the Turkish guns. They anchored about 3½ miles from shore and waited for night fall as it was impossible to work in daylight owing to the enemy's gun fire. After dark they moved closer in and carried out the repair, leaving Anzac about midnight and steaming towards Helles. While moving off with lights out, the ship collided with a trawler, smashing up a cutter and doing some damage to boat davits and to plates on 'Levant II's port side. They anchored off Helles about 0100hrs. The damage it had sustained must have been quite extensive as it took from 25th June to 17th July to get it repaired and the rest of the ship made good. They then left for Syra to replenish their stock of cable and, after spending three days there, returned to Mudros fully-stocked with provisions and cable, arriving back on 20th July. When 'Levant II' returned, the crew found that things had not changed. It was a case of carrying out repairs and laying any new cable when required, like when the French decided they wanted their own phone line, but on the whole the month was very quiet.

On 23rd June a ship arrived off Tenedos for MF 98 T. Césari was delighted as he was short of pilots having had several killed and two wounded. On board were seven new pilots and seven new aeroplanes, four 80hp Farmans and three Morane Parasol fighters. Samson was a little jealous as Césari had taken delivery of some good aeroplanes. In all fairness, however, any new aeroplane with a decent engine was a good aeroplane in Samson's eyes. The three Parasol aircraft were to be used as fighters. At first it had been intended to base them on Helles advanced airfield but as this had now closed as it was far too dangerous, they stayed put on Tenedos and one of them was kept at the end of the runway in a constant state of readiness to take off and chase any enemy aeroplanes.

No new aircraft were forthcoming for the RNAS units right now but 'Ark Royal' had managed to repair one of its broken seaplanes. By 23rd June the 'Type 807 folder' No 807 had been rebuilt after using parts from several cannibalised seaplanes for No 922 and was now operating from the new seaplane base on the shores of Aliki Bay, Imbros, along with a wingless Schneider (awaiting wings from England) and 200hp Wight pusher floatplane No 176.

24th June was not a good day for Samson. Firstly, he lost two Canton Unné engines to add to the two he had lost the previous day. As he put it to Murray Sueter, he had lost all faith in these engines and desperately needed new ones. Murray Sueter's reply was:

'It is a little difficult to know what to do about this......I have heard of no trouble with the Canton Unné engines at Dunkirk, but I am verifying on this.'[56]

Samson's frustration must have reached boiling point. Whether or not the wretched engines worked at Dunkirk, they were certainly not working in the Dardanelles!

Secondly, Samson got a message that his brother Bill had been badly hurt in a crash. He had been ordered by Admiral de Robeck to send an aeroplane and crew to Mytilene on the island of Imbros to carry out some reconnaissance work, all part of a ruse to fool the Turks that a second attack was going to come from this island. The aircraft sent on the mission had Lieutenant Bill Wilson as pilot and Lieutenant Bill Samson as observer. On the outward leg their engine suddenly cut out and they had to make a forced landing in the water. The landing was not good and both Wilson and Bill were injured in the crash, Bill breaking his leg when the machine hit the water. He still managed to remain afloat for some four hours with the help of Wilson, a good swimmer. He gave Bill his life vest to help keep him afloat until they were rescued when a British patrol boat came along and fished them out of the water. One of the boat crew trying to salvage the aeroplane picked up a bomb and started to fiddle with it. Fortunately Bill spotted what he was doing and took the bomb away from him, ditching it over the side before it could explode and explaining to the sailor what he had been playing with. The sailor went very white! Wilson and Bill were shipped back to hospital in Malta from where Wilson was sent home. Bill, however, was seen by the medical board on 27th July and asked to return to his unit, which was granted on 28th August. Wilson's resourcefulness and bravery were recognised when he got a medal for keeping Bill Samson alive.[57]

Trouble comes in threes. June 24th saw the arrival at Mudros Bay, Lemnos Island, on board the destroyer HMS 'Agamemnon', of one of Samson's bêtes-noir, Brevet Lieutenant Colonel Frederick Sykes. Sykes had served as RFC Chief of Staff until 26th May. His departure from this corps was not without controversy as he had clashed with those who believed that RFC units should be placed directly under the control of the corps or divisional Army commanders in the field. The fact was that his services were now no longer required by the RFC because he had fallen out with all the senior officers in both the RFC and Army, quite an achievement in anyone's books. He had also started to empire-build, a habit that wins no friends.

On 26th May he was released by the RFC at the request of the First Lord of the Admiralty and the War Minister and placed at the disposal of the Lords

---

[56] TNA: AIR 1/361/15/228/50
[57] TNA: AIR 1/726/137/2

Commissioners of the Admiralty. Commodore Murray Sueter had convinced the Admiralty that they needed Sykes' expertise to inspect the naval air units in the Dardanelles, to sort out their problems and pull all the RNAS units together. This was his way of putting Samson in his place, as Sueter felt Samson was demanding too much and causing him problems at the Admiralty. Sykes was officially informed of his new appointment by Murray Sueter on 12th June. His move to Gallipoli was a promotion.

Sykes' private papers contain many letters from friends and family that mention his friendliness, his valuable advice, and his fatherly image within organisations. He was kind and helpful and had an 'aura' of calmness and a statesmanlike quality about him which inspired others. The papers in London liked the man, one describing Lieutenant Colonel Sykes as 'an extremely popular officer' who performed 'in a masterly manner.'[58] Yet by the time of the Gallipoli evacuation, Sykes was disliked by most of the senior Army, Navy and RNAS officers in theatre. Sir Philip Joubert de la Ferte had called Sykes 'a deep thinker and most competent staff officer, but lacking in strength, far too cold to secure men's affection and too calculating to inspire enthusiasm and trust.'[59] For a senior officer to produce such a widespread reaction amongst those who came into contact with him professionally, he must have had a very different persona there to that in his private life.

When Sykes went out to the Dardanelles, the senior RNAS commander on the scene was Samson, a man noted for his sharp tongue who did not suffer fools gladly, but whose men would walk over burning coals for him if asked. He was only in command of 3 Squadron and did not superintend or command the other RNAS units in the Dardanelles: the Armoured Car sections at Helles, HMS 'Ark Royal', HMS 'Manica', HMS 'Hector' and HMS 'Ben-my-Chree'. Each of these units had a separate commander and each carried out the orders given to them by the Navy but Sykes could not grasp that all these individual commands were standalone units.

Now Samson and Sykes had already crossed swords in France over the winter of 1914-15. Then Sykes had lost no opportunity to try to get him and his squadron sent home, or at least to severely limit their activities, as they showed the RFC in a very poor light. There had been talk in early December 1914 of putting No 3 Squadron directly under Sir John French, which Samson was quite happy about as he would not be under Sykes, who was actually junior in rank to him. Perhaps he laid himself open when he added, in correspondence with Murray Sueter:

'Although if the service demands, I am ready to work under Colonel Sykes'

---

[58] Daily Telegraph, 3rd July 1914
[59] TNA: AIR 1/669/17/122/788

orders, I feel that it would be rather unfair to me to put me under a man whose experience is not half mine, and is also junior to me.'[60]

Well now the service, in the shape of Murray Sueter, did demand it!

Between 24th and 30th June four big-gun monitors left British waters and headed towards the Dardanelles: HMS 'Abercrombie', 'Roberts', 'Raglan' and 'Havelock'. The 'Abercrombie' was the flagship of this small flotilla. The four monitors of the 'Abercrombie' class were built to take advantage of four twin 14-in turrets, offered to Great Britain by Charles M Schwab, president of the American steel company, Bethlehem Steel. This was a breach of American neutrality early in the First World War and the deal would result in a protest from the US State Department, but Winston Churchill, the First Lord of the Admiralty, gladly accepted the guns. The four ships were all of the same design and each one took just four months to build. While they were very basic and had no crew comforts, more alarmingly, they were not good sailing ships, as they had a top speed of only between 6-7 knots and in bad weather made very little headway and were awash with water. They had to be given a tow from other warships to get them to the Dardanelles. They were very distinctive ships, with few structures visible on the main deck other than a tripod mast, the funnel and of course a massive battleship turret. The secondary guns were hidden below hinged bulwarks, below and in front of the main turret.

The 'Ark Royal' sent two seaplanes to the monitors, one going to the 'Abercrombie' and the other to the 'Roberts', but both were returned as they became damaged by the blast from the big guns. All four ships gave great support to the Army and would remain in the Eastern Mediterranean until the end of the First World War. They were very difficult to sink by torpedo due to the blisters on their sides and so helped make up for the loss of the 'Queen Elizabeth' and the corralling of the other battleships. The 'Roberts' would remain at Rabbit Island for the whole of the campaign, bombarding the Turkish guns on the Asiatic side of the Dardanelles.

On 25th June the 'Ben-My-Chree' launched Schneider floatplane No 1445 to bomb Smyrna but it suffered an engine failure on the way back to the ship. The seaplane had to put down in the sea and was towed back to its mother ship by the torpedo destroyer HMS 'Weir'. Also on the 25th at 1340hrs Lieutenant Garnett left in 1437 for the new seaplane base at Aliki Bay, Imbros. There were several seaplane types there. Short Nos 161, 163, 164, 165 and 166 had all arrived in theatre in June and there were also two Sopwith Schneiders. No 164 would be placed on loan to HMS 'Roberts' on 28th September but only made ten flights before returning due to fabric damage to the seaplane caused by the blast from its main guns.

---

[60] See John Oliver, *'Samson and the Dunkirk Circus'*, 2017, page 145

In a report written to Murray Sueter on 27th June Samson spelt out what had been happening to his squadron for the last few weeks. His report goes on about the shortage of aeroplanes, engines, rations, and another wireless set that was required as one had been lost in the sea when an aeroplane crashed.[61] They were still having problems with the Canton Unné engines. The problem was the valve springs and valve stalks were breaking and when they broke, the engine died and the aeroplane crashed. One crew almost crashed in the water but just managed to limp onto the water's edge on Rabbit Island. The Australian Corps had been very pleased with 3 Squadron bombing as they had put the fear of God into the Turks opposite them. One bomb hit their front line trench and killed a lot of enemy soldiers; the rest came out and the Australians got them all with a Maxim. There were, however, several Turkish guns and emplacements that were dug into ravines and other deep places tricky to bomb or hit with a naval gun so Samson thought they would try and burn them out. He instructed Warner and some others to build a super petrol bomb. The bomb container was a fuel tank from 1241, the tail was a 20lb Hales bomb, the body of the bomb was packed with cotton waste, cordite and Verey lights while the tank was filled with 20 gallons of petrol and 4 gallons of paraffin!

By late June 1915 agreement had been reached between the government in London, in the form of the War Minister, Lord Kitchener, and the Commander-in-Chief, Mediterranean Expeditionary Force, Sir Ian Hamilton, to despatch sizeable reinforcements to the Gallipoli peninsula to facilitate a renewed offensive in August in the north. During June and July a series of small attacks were mounted from Helles on the southern tip of the peninsula. Prominent among these was the Battle of Gully Ravine, fought on 28th June along the Aegean spine of the peninsula in the wake of a moderate French success a week earlier. The newly-appointed commander of the British 29th Division, Major-General Henry de Beauvoir de Lisle, proposed a limited objective attack - in accordance with Hamilton's strict enjoinder that no sweeping breakthrough be henceforth attempted - along the Gully Ravine Spur. The advance went well, five lines of Turkish trenches were won that day. Samson and 3 Squadron carried out a total of 17 daylight missions, 31 hours of flying over the Turkish lines in Helles. Most of them were bombing attacks in support of the ground attack.

A few reconnaissance missions were flown later on the day of 28th June. One of those was by Lieutenant Charles Butler, who was wounded in the right foot while taking photographs but managed to get his aeroplane back to Tenedos and land it. The landing was good with no damage to the aeroplane – or, more importantly, the camera. In many ways it was surprising that Butler wasn't wounded earlier in the operation as they had

---

[61] See John Oliver, *'Samson and the Dunkirk Circus'*, 2017, page 145

to fly low to get good quality photographs and he would often bring his aeroplane back with many bullet holes in it. By the time he was wounded, the Maurice Farman he was using could not climb above 4,000ft. He carried out some 57 photographic missions over the Turkish lines and would pick up a DSC for his work but remained a very sick man for several years due to the dysentery he had picked up in the Dardanelles.

The first camera that was used was owned by Butler himself but this was soon replaced by the borrowed unit from the French which worked well and gave excellent results. The bulk of the photographic work was now going to fall on Lieutenant George Thomson, RN, who, working on his own, managed to make 900 exposures and produced 3,600 prints. In spite of all this, while all the other commanders were praising the work carried out by Samson and 3 Squadron, in particular the quality of the intelligence provided, General Hamilton did not make any mention of them in his reports to London.

HMS 'Ark Royal' continued on its unlucky way. On 28th June No 922 yet again suffered an undercarriage collapse when Flight Lieutenant Sholto Douglas hit the water hard landing it in Kephalo Bay. The seaplane bounced, the floats broke away and it began to sink when he next hit the water. He was pulled alongside the 'Ark Royal' and retrieved by one of her steam cranes, the floats still attached and dangling as the seaplane was placed with care on the deck. At this time 'Ark Royal's Commander, Clark-Hall, reported that Sopwith Folders were satisfactory but not recommended, as the spring of the floats made them bounce and the floats broke too easily. He added that Sopwith and Short 225hp machines were bedevilled with troubles in their Sunbeam engine whilst single-seat Schneiders were fine-weather machines, useful only when there was no need for detailed reconnaissance information as they could not carry an observer. He might well have had a point in some or all of these complaints but it is hard to find much sympathy when his general results were so poor.

Since the Ark Royal arrived in the Dardanelles her seaplanes had suffered a total of 91 engine failures. They were due to carry out a total of 270 missions of various types, but had to date only managed to carry out 139.[62] In June her seaplanes were due to carry out some 44 missions but they only carried out 14, due to engine failures. The following table demonstrates the flying hours and flights of her various machines that month. The disastrous figures speak for themselves:

---

[62] TNA: AIR 1/726/137/2

Machine	Flights	Useful service	Flight time	Engine failures
No 136	8	4	8hrs 53min	3
No 161	7	2	3hrs 8min	4
No 176	4	2	2hrs 48min	-
No 807	6	2	4hrs 1min	1
No 922	8	2	4hrs 26min	2
No 1437	5	1	1hr 35min	1
No 857	2	1	1hr 20min	2
No 860	4	-	1hr 38min	4

The night of the 28th saw Samson bring back night bombing when he himself and four pilots went off to bomb the Turkish camp fires. Missions like this fell on the old hands of 3 Squadron as he felt the newer pilots just did not have the hours or the experience. None of them had flown at night yet, let alone landed in the dark, and as aeroplanes were very scarce he could not risk one in these unexperienced hands. Osmond had the best result that night, landing his bombs amongst a large group of men queuing up for their evening meal.

With the bulk of the Squadron covering the Helles attack there were only a couple of aeroplanes left to cover the ANZAC position but their reconnaissance flights brought back important information about the Turkish forces that were massing for an attack in the ANZAC region. On 29th/30th June the Turks threw in a last desperate attack to move the Australians off the peninsula but it failed. 3 Squadron yet again help fight off the attack by dropping bombs on the Turkish positions. One 100lb bomb landed square in a Turkish trench - the second time 3 Squadron had managed this - killing a large number of Turks but also chasing out a large number of men who were cut down by the Australian machine gunners.

General fatigue, dysentery and other illnesses were becoming a common problem for the whole squadron. On seeing Samson and his men, Vice Admiral de Robeck decided that they needed a rest and it was decided that a few at a time would go to Alexandria for a spot of leave. Patterson, the squadron's medical officer, was in full agreement. These breaks in Egypt would be the first leave that most of the men had had since the war started in August the previous year.

In spite of the no-stop nature of their deployment, they did find some time on Tenedos for relaxation. Near the airfield was a fair-sized hill and the men of 3 Squadron would carry out timed races up and down it for fun, even challenging the French squadron to try their luck. The starting post was about 400 yards from the base of the hill and the course was up and back to the starting point. Doctor Williams got the men to carry out the timed races and would give very good odds on certain times. Needless to say, he won almost all of the time. Bill Samson and Keith-Jopp were the best performers but Keith-Jopp had been sand-bagging unknown to the doctor, who one day gave Keith-Jopp odds of 10-1 that he could not get up and down in 32 minutes. The race was on and its outcome was inevitable. Right from the start, Williams realised he had been had. Felix Samson was not going to be outdone by his elder brother and one day turned up at the start line with a motor bike. The going was not good but Felix was not perturbed. He shot up the hill but the higher he got, the slower he became until the bike hit a large stone and Felix was thrown up in the air. He landed back on the bike but was now going downhill, hanging on for grim death and legs all over the place, bouncing down the hill much faster than he went up!

Another pastime was to walk into Tenedos town, have a drink at the café, sit and talk to the locals or, on the odd special occasion, watch a local getting married. The French did not walk: they had a beaten-up old car that would take four of them into town. One day Marix made a very rash challenge to Samson: he reckoned that with a five-minute head start he could beat Samson on Nigger, his captured German horse, into town. Samson took him up on it. Unbeknown to Marix, on the day of the challenge Samson sent a Marine ahead to clear a path through the brush for him and his horse and mark the way with white-washed stones. Off went Marix, very confident he would win. Five minutes later, off went Samson and very quickly caught up with him. At first he made it look as if he was having problems but with a touch of spur to his flanks, Nigger shot past Marix leaving him to eat dust. Samson pulled up a little way along the trail and the three of them walked into town for a coffee. Marix, of course, was one of the squadron stalwarts and on 1st July Samson lost two of his best men, Flight Lieutenant Peirse and Flight Lieutenant Osmond, who were both re-called home to become instructors. They had been with the squadron a long time and had both fought on the ground and in the air. The inevitable breakup of 3 Squadron had started.

Come the end of June the General Head Quarters was really fed up with the lack of air support but it is good to see that they recognised that the squadrons themselves were not always to blame.

'Aeroplane service appears to have broken down. An average of one aeroplane daily is available for work with the Army at ANZAC and Helles. [This referred to Artillery spotting] The pilots and observers are worn out from long sustained and continuous effort without relief. The machines themselves are worn out, and the new ones from England are machines rapidly constructed with inferior workmanship which makes their running uncertain.'

General Sir Ian Hamilton wrote of the RNAS in letter to the Admiralty:

'Much might be written on the exploits of the Royal Naval Air Service, but these bold flyers are laconic, and their feats will mostly pass unrecorded. Yet let me here thank them, for the nonchalance with which they appear to affront danger and death, when and where they can. So doing, they quicken the hearts of their friends on land and sea - an asset of greater military value even than their bombs or aerial reconnaissances, admirable in all respects as these were.'

However, it is a shame that he did not think to emphasise the importance of their reconnaissance work at the same time as praising their undoubted bravery.

Training had been going well for the crew of the 'Ben-My-Chree' until 25th June, when a torpedo was accidentally released while hoisting a seaplane over the side. It hit the water and sank. A dive boat was sent out for the next few days but failed to find the missing torpedo. Commander L'Estrange Malone was not at all pleased, to put it mildly! On 30th June training started very early and the seaplanes were out by 0255hrs. At 0315hrs seaplane No 184 flown by Flight Lieutenant George Dacre left the ship for a morning patrol, returning at 0423hrs. Flight Commander Charles Edmonds had been carrying out practice manoeuvring and take-offs in seaplane No 841 with a torpedo slung underneath but as he carried out his manoeuvrings, he burst a float and the torpedo was launched by accident. It dived to its pre-set depth and shot off in a dead straight line for the 'Ben-My-Chree'. Seeing the torpedo heading for the rear of the ship, a number of the crew moved rapidly to the forecastle, along with a fair amount of shouting, but it passed harmlessly under the ship just below the after-magazine, to a general sigh of relief amongst the ship's crew.

Between 28th June and 5th July, Turkish forces at Helles attacked the British positions at Gully Ravine which the Turks had previously lost. In eight days the Turks suffered over 16,000 casualties, more than 10,000 of whom had been killed. The stench of the battlefield was beyond description and the flies were now a seething, buzzing mass that could be walked on. Every time the men took a drink or a mouthful of food, down would go a couple of flies. Intelligence had noted from prisoner interrogations that the Turks did not like crossing No-Man's Land and attacking over the bodies of the dead, so when the Turks asked for a ceasefire after this battle Sir Ian Hamilton turned it down.

On 2nd July the kite balloon ship HMS 'Hector' left Lemnos heading up towards the fleet. She would now spot for the fleet with the 'Manica', taking a lot of strain off 3 Squadron. The next day 'Hector' and HMS 'Venerable' moved into the Gulf of Saros. The balloon went up at 0930hrs and remained up for the rest of the morning. Several salvos were fired into the town of Gallipoli and set the docks on fire. The Turks were not slow in responding and quickly got a few guns into action, trying to bring down the balloon or hit the ship. They even had a go at attacking 'Manica' and her balloon using one of their aeroplanes.

Samson and Césari had become very fed up with the few Turkish aeroplanes in the area and decided to destroy them and their airfield in one large raid. One particularly annoying thing the Turks were doing, though this was the ground forces not the aircraft, was increasing the amount of wireless interference so much so that the pilots were all reporting bad communications with both the Fleet and the Army, a very serious matter. Both the French and British ground crews worked through the night of 4th July. Come the morning of the 5th, all aeroplanes were serviced and made ready, even ones that were a bit dodgy; a total of 14 French and eight British aircraft all lined up and bombed up ready for the off. This was going to be the largest single raid of the campaign. The plan was that the slowest would go first followed by the others so that they would all arrive over the target at the same time and shower the airfield and its buildings with bombs.

The Turkish airfield in question, at Canakkale on the Asian side of the Dardanelles, had been found by Samson on a reconnaissance flight back in April. Every aeroplanes made it over the target and they let them have it. All the buildings were destroyed, either set on fire or just blown up, the main hangar was hit and all three aeroplanes were destroyed. It must have been quite a sight as the 22 aeroplanes turned and flew back to Tenedos. Many of the Turks must have been shaking in their trenches as they had never seen so many aeroplanes at one time, coupled with the fact that the Allied aircraft had brought so much death and destruction amongst their ranks over the past weeks. That for now was the end of the Turkish air force in the Dardanelles. However, the very same day a small naval aviation unit consisting of GOTHA seaplanes arrived from Germany. A week later four new aircraft commanded by Lieutenant Ludwig Preussner, a German aviator, reinforced the first squadron. Samson meanwhile had had some intelligence reports that the Turks had taken delivery of some new seaplanes so on the 5th he attacked the seaplane base hoping to catch the aircraft in their shed but he missed and none were damaged.

On 6th July the 'Ben-My-Chree' hoisted out seaplane No 1445 at 1800hrs. It took off with no problem carrying four bombs and about two hours' worth of fuel but there was great concern on the ship when by 2100hrs the seaplane had not returned. Then just before midnight an aeroplane could be heard approaching the ship. Using a signal lamp, No 1445 called up the ship to report its return as they did not want to be shot down, well aware that the captain had been drilling the gun crews and these men were now very good at their job. It turned out they had suffered an engine failure and put down on the sea, carried out the repair and returned to the ship. While the ship was in training mood, Commander L'Estrange Malone felt that all of his crew should be able to swim and so started up a 'New swimmers class'. This was, of course, also another way of keeping his men fit and the morale of his crew high with races and other competitions.

HMS 'Hector' had spent most of the month so far in Mudros getting ready to move up and take her place alongside the 'Manica', her sister balloon ship. Her last training day was 2nd July when she put to sea then had a practice with the balloon. Finally on the 9th the 'Hector' left Mudros harbour and made her way to Kephalo harbour, which she entered at 1525hrs, dropping anchor at 1625hrs.

Sykes meanwhile had wasted no time in making his mark. On 9th July he sent his report into the Admiralty, his assessment being that the RNAS needed to be reorganised, relocated, and strengthened. He went on to report that the need for aerial reconnaissance was 'very real and urgent,' and he implied that, with adequate support, the RNAS at Gallipoli could help turn the campaign into a success. This assessment was biased by two influences: his army background and his Western Front experiences. He requested RFC-type aircraft rather than naval types, which was a problem as the Army did not have any seaplanes, and predictably also aroused immediate animosity from Samson and other RNAS officers who thought that their aerial service and machines were superior to anything in the RFC[63]. Sykes stated openly that he based his reorganisation ideas on what he had seen in France specifically and that the RNAS needed a HQ located as close as possible to the main Army GHQ, which was at Imbros. He spent six days talking with Army and Navy commanders, inspecting aerial operations, and participating in aerial reconnaissance in a kite balloon flown off HMS 'Manica' to support the gunnery attacks of Chanak by HMS 'Lord Nelson'. He visited the Army at Helles and Anzac and discussed their predicament with his friend, Lieutenant General William R Birdwood, GOC ANZAC Corps.

Sykes' investigations had been short, superficial and conducted mostly at senior officer level. He did not know that the 'Ark Royal' was the first RNAS unit on station in the Dardanelles; he believed it was Samson and 3 Squadron. He thought that Samson had been tasked to support the ANZACs and did not know that Sir Ian Hamilton and Vice Admiral de Robeck had given orders that the 'Ark Royal' would carry out the ANZAC support missions. General Birdwood had had to phone Samson for help because it had fully and completely failed to do this. Sykes talked to the senior officers of the various Army and Navy units in the Dardanelles but did not visit the intelligence tents or offices where he would have seen the large photographic maps made by Lieutenant Isaac of 3 Squadron. During

---

[63] Eric Ash, *'Sir Frederick Sykes and the Air Revolution 1912-1918'*, Frank Cass, 2005, page 77

his six days of fact-finding he never once visited Samson and 3 Squadron on Tenedos, so he never saw the Intelligence Office or the hundreds of glass negatives taken by 3 Squadron. Blinded by his dislike of Samson, who had come off the better when they had crossed swords before, Sykes now felt the failure of the Dardanelles/Gallipoli air campaign was Samson's fault. In addition, his transfer from France had done nothing to curb his enthusiasm for self-aggrandisement. Sykes was trying to find himself a job and he could see that by taking over the RNAS in the Eastern Mediterranean he could build his own little empire. He returned to London and the Admiralty on 12th July and was then able to put before their Lordships everything that he saw was wrong and to lay the blame on Samson and 3 Squadron for the failures of air support, a good part of which was actually the failure of the 'Ark Royal'.

The madness of the Gallipoli Campaign continued on the peninsula. On 12th July, one of the hottest days of the campaign, the British and French launched an attack on the Turks. The men were wearing their heavy serge uniforms and had not slept well due to the heat and flies. They were overhot and dehydrated before they even started. The attack went in at 0730hrs and was a glorious failure.

3 Squadron flew some twelve missions on 12th July and on all of these the aeroplanes carried bombs. Samson alone flew three spotting missions for the British guns. On that morning Lieutenant Harold Kerby was to fly his first long-range mission so he wanted it to go well. He was to pilot Voisin No 9 with Major Miles as his observer; they were to drop their bombs on the Turkish camp fires at Sogun Dere. They took off at 0215 hours, heading for Gallipoli. As they passed over Krithia, Kerby spotted a Turkish supply column on the road, flew over it and released one bomb. It was a near miss but had the desired effect as animals shot off in all directions. They then moved on to Sogun Dere and dropped their last bomb on a storage building which took a direct hit. They then moved on and, flying a figure-eight over the Turkish positions, started to spot for the British guns. Miles spotted for the guns for an hour until they were relieved by another aeroplane. They had drawn some AA fire but it was not too bad. Now they turned and headed back to Tenedos.

HMS 'Hector' now had three busy spotting days on the run. On Sunday 11th July she put to sea in the afternoon and joined HMS 'Talbot' at 1658hrs. The balloon was put up at 1845hrs and brought down at 1930hrs after a very successful operation, the ship returning to Kephalo harbour where she dropped anchor at 2035hrs. The next day she left harbour at 0545hrs in the company of HMS 'Prince George'. Conditions were good for spotting that day as the wind was only a gentle force 2, and there were two separate shoots, morning from 0700hrs to 0740hrs and in the afternoon from 1600hrs to 1730hrs, on both occasions with the 'Prince George'. 'Hector' returned to harbour and dropped anchor at 1900hrs. On the 13th 'Hector' went into action spotting for HMS 'Chatham', putting up her balloon at 1720hrs. The spotting went very well, 'Chatham' shelling a number of Turkish batteries at Krithia and Achi Baba. The 'Hector' returned to harbour at 1955hrs.

Now the Turks were trying to get back into the air war. On July 13th they took delivery of four Rumpler B1 aeroplanes and set up their new main aerodrome at Gatala. Samson swiftly retaliated. On the evening of 15th July during a clear night with a partial moon, two aeroplanes attacked the seaplane shed with 100lb bombs but yet again missed.

The French squadron's attempt to make an incendiary bomb (with the help of some men from 3 Squadron) finished on 14th July. Their great incendiary bomb was made up of four two-gallon petrol cans welded to a 20lb bomb, then totally enclosed in thin sheet metal with some crude tail fins on the rear. The French made several of these bombs. Some worked and some failed. Some did not go off at first but they certainly exploded once the Turks shot at them!

HMS 'Hector' finished an active week with two more days spotting. On Thursday the 15th she was spotting for HMS 'Chatham' again off Gabas Tepe, sending up her balloon between 1540hrs and 1700hrs with just a short break of a few minutes when there was a problem with the phone. She returned to harbour relatively early, dropping anchor at 1804hrs. The next afternoon she spent spotting for HMS 'Yarmouth'. The balloon went up at 1700hrs and came down at 1825hrs, when both ships moved to a new position and target, going up at 1900hrs and coming down again at 2000hrs. On 17th July the 'Hector' put back into Kephalo Bay for stores. She attempted to leave again on the 19th but was forced to put back into the anchorage due to the weather

On 18th July Samson received the first of a number of telegrams from Sykes informing him that new aeroplanes were on the way. By the end of the stream of telegrams, Sykes was promising 45 new aeroplanes and a large amount of spares. The date of arrival for 33 of these aircraft was 9th August and they couldn't come too soon. Samson was now down to just three aeroplanes and was in danger of not being able to help and support the Army in its new push. He went to Tenedos and over a good meal with Césari, the French commander, asked him if he could borrow a few aircraft from him if push came to shove. Césari was only too pleased to help out.

By mid-July a captured German aerial camera had been sent from France out to the 'Ark Royal'. It worked very well and some good pictures were taken but the success was short-lived. On 28th July the seaplane carrying it flipped over while taking off from the beach and was destroyed along with the camera. HMS 'Ark Royal' seemed to be truly jinxed. By now some very nasty reports were coming back about the way the Turks treated their prisoners, so Samson reminded all flying crews yet again that they had to carry small arms for their own protection.

Throughout July Samson had made reconnaissance a main priority of 3 Squadron and a closer working relationship was forged between it and the Army. More and more staff officers were taken for flights over the Turkish lines so that they could see for themselves that photographic reconnaissance was real and not, as some of them had thought, the work of the devil. All artillery officers and intelligence officers were also taken for flights so they could get a better lay of the land, including Samson's own intelligence officer, Bernard Isaac, who carried out five flights over Turkish lines but the novelty wore very thin after the second. Yet none of this was in Sykes report!

The weather was not good from 20th to 22nd July. All the balloons were grounded and their place was taken, when it could be, by seaplanes from the 'Ark Royal' but a lot of the time they failed to take off. Under cover of this bad weather the Turks moved up a large number of men and artillery. These long columns were too tempting a target for 3 Squadron and every aeroplane that could fly was put into the air regardless of the weather. The information was passed on to the French squadron on Tenedos who gladly took part in the attacks.

The Australians had put in an urgent request for new trench maps of the Turkish positions on Plateau 400 and Lone Pine. Lieutenant Thomson, who had taken over from Butler when he was wounded, flew two photographic reconnaissance missions undercover of the poor weather on 20th July. It was discovered from his pictures that the Turks had started to cover their trenches with logs to help protect their men from artillery fire and bombing. It was clear something was brewing. However, Samson knew he would soon be off on leave and felt Bell Davies and Marix could cope, a decision he had cleared with Admiral de Robeck.

The 'Ben-My-Chree' had now finished her working up and was ready to join the main fleet off the Dardanelles. She set off at 1900hrs on 22nd July, arriving off Rabbit Island at 0430hrs on the 23rd where joined up with the monitor HMS 'Roberts', better known by the fleet as 'Big Willie'. Two wireless sets were waiting for the ship on arrival at Rabbit Island, to be fitted to Shorts No 184 and No 841. They had arrived not a moment too soon. On 23rd July a wonderful target was spotted: a column of 250 wagons. This was attacked by all available aeroplanes and some naval ships were also 'spotted' onto the column. The 'Hector' and HMS 'Abercrombie' were ordered to the site. 'Hector' hove to at 1540hrs and put her balloon up as soon as possible. Just as the convoy was collecting itself together after the first attack, the 'Abercrombie' started to drop 14-inch shells amongst the animals, which not surprisingly all stampeded and headed for the hills. 23rd July was a day of ship movements. The 'Levant II' was in action again after her repairs and steamed into Kephalo Bay, starting to lay a cable the next day from 'Ark Royal' to ANZAC, and the 'Ben-my-Chree' was ordered to move up to Rabbit Island and support HMS 'Roberts' and the monitor 'M.19'.

Sykes had recommended in his July report for the Admiralty that the airfield on Tenedos should be moved to Imbros. This would cut down the flying time to Gallipoli and also cut down on the amount of open-water flying that had to be done. Open-water flying was one thing that did not worry the pilots of the RNAS. They were Navy after all and it was the Army pilots of the RFC who were more concerned about flying over the sea. Sykes was oblivious to this. He had chosen a spot on the island overlooking Cape Kephalo harbour which was surrounded on three sides by water with very erratic air currents. Trying to land an aeroplane here was very difficult. Samson looked at the so-called air strip and even tried to land on it on a visit to the airship squadron but failed as the weather was too rough. It did not bode well for the others.

The advance party for the move to Imbros was made up of most of the pilots, most of the ground staff and all serviceable aeroplanes but Samson arranged for the repair section to remain on Tenedos until things were settled. The men of 3 Squadron set to and put up tents and a Bessonneau hangar and in general tried to make the airfield operational. A group of Turkish prisoners were used to smooth and sort out the runway in general. They also built some stone buildings, one of which would be used as the darkroom for the photographic unit, but until this was complete the intelligence unit would remain on Tenedos. The squadron was not fully moved to Imbros until the end of August when the last of the spares and other equipment were moved over.

As the squadron was now shut down for a few days as they moved from Tenedos to Imbros, the repair crews had time to fix some of the rather poor aeroplanes. Samson left Bell Davies in charge of the move and Marix carrying out a lot of the flying while he and Collet went on two weeks leave. They were the first of the squadron to be sent down to Egypt for a spot of rest and recuperation and were selected by the doctor on medical grounds as the most run-down. Admiral de Robeck picked them up in his yacht 'Triad' and took them to Imbros where they waited on the SS 'Aragon' for their leave transport, the 'Argyllshire', which took them to Alexandria. There Samson met up with his brother Felix, who was looking after the squadron's transport and other vehicles. The men were all fit and very well and were in the best of spirits. Felix had had Samson's Rolls-Royce polished and tuned up and the two of them had a ball - good food and lots of wine and women - as the one thing Samson was not short of was money. He had a pocketful of back pay as on Tenedos there was nothing for him to spend his money on. On the way back Samson was in good spirits but poor Collet was very depressed and very quiet. The spot of leave had done him a lot of good but he was very thin (down to nine stone) and still not at all in good health.

On 24th July 1915 Sykes was appointed Officer Commanding the Royal Naval Air Service Eastern Mediterranean Station with the rank of Colonel Commandant in the Royal Marines as well as the rank of Wing Captain in the Royal Naval Air Service, making him the air commander for the Dardanelles Campaign. He kept his Army rank of Colonel. The appointment of Sykes did not lead to more pilots and men or more aeroplanes being sent out to the squadrons. Nothing changed at all. All the RNAS units ignored Sykes and got on with the job at hand. Samson did carry out the paperwork requests he received from Sykes until he left the squadron in November 1915. Apart from that, he continued supporting the fleet and the Army units on Helles just as he and his squadron had done since the first day they arrived in the Dardanelles and sending his reports to Admiral de Robeck and not to Sykes.

Sykes was not due back in theatre until early August and in fact returned on the 6th. He sent orders from London that his new HQ was to be built next to the Army GHQ on Imbros. It would be like a small village with a hospital, messing areas, sleeping accommodation and various huts and buildings for Intelligence, stores and other services that he thought might be required, but his real interest lay in his new kingdom rather than in his men or the units of the RNAS. His plan for 3 Squadron was that it should become 3 Wing and should grow in size to have three squadrons. Each squadron was going to have three flights and a flight of seaplanes, making a total of 38 aeroplanes [Sykes figures]. There would also be 18 airframes in reserve, plus 18 spare engines. Where all this was to come from I have no idea.

On 26th July Marix led an attack on the new Turkish airfield at Chanak. The results could be seen for miles as several buildings were hit and the fuel dump was set alight. The same day General Hamilton's office contacted 3 Squadron and asked if an aeroplane and pilot could be put on standby to take the General up. He duly turned up on the 27th and was first taken to Isaac's Intelligence tent to have the lay of the land explained to him and to ask if he wanted to view a specific area. After the briefing, Bell Davies gave him a safety talk and explained everything that could go wrong and he was then taken up by Marix in a Maurice Farman, taking off at 1015hrs and returning at 1235hrs. They flew over the peninsula from Anzac Cove to Suvla Bay, allowing him to see that the salt lake was dry and the thinly-held Turkish trenches at Lala Baba and Chocolate Hill. It was trips such as this, before a major attack took place, which could make all the difference between a total massacre and some success. Major successes were not a feature of the ground war in Gallipoli.

On Tuesday 27th July the 'Hector' was out early, meeting with HMS 'Endymion' at 0428hrs. They stopped near Gaba Tepe at 0545hrs and sent the balloon up at 0550hrs, but nothing was spotted so the balloon was taken down after forty minutes. At 0855hrs the balloon went up again and a Turkish battery opened fire on the 'Hector'. While it is easy to understand the frustration of the Turkish gunners at the balloon ship's presence, this was not a wise move. HMS 'Endymion' opened fire at 0915hrs and silenced the battery in fifteen minutes, ceasing fire at 0930hrs. The balloon was brought down and the 'Hector' returned to port and dropped anchor at 1107hrs, having had another successful day.

On 'Ark Royal' things were rather different. Her old bad luck was holding. On 28th July Schneider seaplane No 1438 was hoisted out after undergoing some repairs to its fabric. As it began to taxi in the choppy water for take-off, it was noted from the ship that the seaplane was getting lower in the water and was, in fact, beginning to submerge. The pilot realised there was something amiss and tried to turn back to the ship but the aircraft rolled over and sank. It was salvaged but the damage was too great for any repairs and it was deleted from service. On Thursday 29th July, Seaplane 922 took off from Aliki Bay with Captain Kilner as pilot and Lieutenant Strain as observer. This seaplane had been built from several cannibalised airframes of the 807 type. It was not only Samson who was desperate for new aeroplanes!

In the afternoon of the 29th, the 'Hector' set out and joined up with the monitor 'M.32' at 1500hrs. At 1650hrs the balloon went up and remained up for 40 minutes before being brought down. The balloon went up again at 1810hrs, but was only up a short time until being brought down at 1835hrs. On Friday the 30th the 'Hector' was out again in the company of 'M32'. The balloon went up first of all at 1600hrs and was up for just 35 minutes, then again at 1800hrs and came down an hour later at 1900hrs, with the ship returning to harbour at 1950hrs.

At the end of July, all naval air units in the Aegean were being centralised at Kephalo on the island of Imbros, 10 miles off the coast of the peninsula, in readiness for the imminent new Army offensive of 6th August on Gallipoli. An airfield was established on Kephalo Point on the east side of the harbour and Samson's mixed bag of landplanes, including his two little-used SS Tabloid scouts Nos 1205 and 1206, were moved over from Tenedos. Samson's long-established airfield there was now officially handed over to the French. Some of 'Ark Royal's Air Service men dragged one of the Sopwith SS3 Tabloid aeroplanes (Serial No 1202) out from the depths of her hold and put it together at Aliki Bay. The aircraft had been put into the ship back in January 1915 but nevertheless, it was found to be sound when reassembled. It was slowly towed over to 3Squadron who were desperate for aeroplanes.

Samson had been sending requests to Murray Sueter almost on a weekly basis demanding pilots, aeroplanes, new engines, food, bombs and ammunition; in short, all the essentials for running an air campaign. He had also started to complain about the pilots he was sent as they had very few flying hours and could not fly the aeroplanes at Tenedos. They were fresh from 'school' machines and he needed experienced men who could jump into any aircraft and fly it, as his stock of aeroplanes was about as mixed as you could get. All Samson wanted was equipment for his men who could then give better support to the Fleet and the Army. But Sueter was finding the RNAS far too difficult and far too big for him to run on a daily basis. It was beyond his capabilities and required a more senior officer at the helm with a far bigger organisation. In the midst of his struggles to keep on top of things, Sueter felt Samson was being unrealistic and unreasonable and should be put in his place. He felt he was being made a fool of by a junior officer and he didn't like it.

It seems very likely that this was behind the letter Murray Sueter wrote on 31st July to Admiral Keyes in the Dardanelles:

'I am writing a line to you to ask a favour and that it is to do your best to make our efforts with air units under Col. Sykes a success. We are very lucky indeed to obtain his services, as the navy cannot spare us any officers with organizing powers. Commander Samson is I think our bravest flyer, but isn't much good at organizing anything big. Therefore may I suggest that you send for Samson and inform him that he has got to make the show run under Col. Sykes. We do not want any rows in the air service, all we want is to try and make ourselves useful to the fleet and the Army.'

There were still a lot of 3 Squadron personnel in residence besides the French squadron when the Turks attacked the airfield at Tenedos at 0445hrs on 31st July. Luckily no injuries were recorded although the aerodrome was hit by a couple of bombs and 2,500 metal darts. Marix was on the airfield near his Nieuport which was armed with a Lewis gun while the French aeroplane on standby was a Morane Parasol, also armed with a Lewis gun. He and one of the French pilots jumped into their aircraft and shot off down the runway chasing the two Turkish seaplanes, which they quickly caught even from a standing start. Marix got under and alongside a Gotha seaplane and sent a burst of machine gun-fire into the engine. The seaplane stuttered in the air then headed out of control down to the peninsula, crashing on Soghan Dere. However, the Turks claimed that the aeroplane had dived steeply to the beach for safety and that none of the crew were hurt.[64]

On 31st July Bell Davies received a message from Admiral de Robeck, ordering him to fly to Imbros, land at the airship station and make his way

---

[64] TNA: AIR 1/681/21/13/2209

to the beach where a boat would pick him up and take him out to the 'Triad', the admiral's command ship. When Bell Davies arrived on board, he was given the outline of the Suvla Bay operation and a full brief of his squadron's duties. It was to be turned over to Sir Ian Hamilton for the duration of the operation. The Admiral asked about the state of the aeroplanes and Bell Davies did not mince words: he knew there were new aircraft *en route* but they were being held up. De Robeck immediately wrote an order out to the Vice Admiral, Malta:

'That first priority was to be given to all aircraft, aircraft stores and were to be sent forward at once any that reach Malta'[65].

Bell Davies then moved on to the Army and met up with General Braithwaite, the Chief of Staff, and Colonel Aspinall, who would be issuing the orders. The Army undertook to send tents and to arrange that they would be issued with rations and water. Bell Davies explained the aeroplane situation and that as soon aircraft were repaired they would be quickly sent forward to Imbros. The Army was happy with this though Bell Davies was only too aware of how thin their resources were.

July was still not a good month for the 'Ark Royal', as this log of its activities shows. No 860 had taken its last flight on 27th June due to its poor engine and had been taken out of service.

Machine	Flights	Useful service	Flight time	Engine failure
No 136	1	-	0hrs 57mins	-
No 161	12	8	11hrs 46mins	1
No 176	3	1	1hrs 50mins	-
No 807	7	4	6hrs 22mins	1
No 922	6	-	1hrs 24mins	2
No 1437	1	-	0hrs 15mins	-
No 1438	3	1	1hr 25mins	-
No 857	8	3	7hrs 37min	2
Totals:	**41**	**17**	**31hrs 36mins**	**6**

To put this into context, 3 Squadron flew 188 missions in July compared to the 'Ark Royal's 17. It is no wonder that at times the Army felt they were not getting any air support, particularly the ANZACs who were supposed to be entirely supported by the 'Ark Royal' and had to almost beg for air support.

---

[65] Richard Bell Davies, op. cit., page 125

Chapter five
August 1915

August was less than a week old when the Allies made yet another major assault on Turkish lines. The days preceding this were used by the various RNAS units in preparation for the coming attack as well as for undertaking their usual tasks. At long last on 1st August a ship dropped anchor off Tenedos beach and set to unloading a number of very large wooden packing cases containing the 100hp Henri Farman aeroplanes and some Nieuports that Samson had been asking for months. August was going to be a logistical nightmare for Bell Davies: these six new aeroplanes had to be put together and tested as quickly as possible as they were urgently required for the new offensive. Before any of this could happen, all the aeroplanes had to be dragged in their crates up from the beach, unloaded and checked.

However, the biggest problem facing 3 Squadron was the move to Imbros. They had been given only one small steam lighter to move all their gear and they were short of manpower but a request was put to a group of Turkish prisoners of war who were only too happy to help out. A new pier was built by the navy for the squadron to use during their unloading and the 'Ark Royal' moved into position to help with the unloading of vehicles using her deck cranes. It was soon apparent that one lighter was not enough and one by one more were assigned until they had some four ships plying between Tenedos and Imbros. Even though they were in the middle of a move to a new base, work had still to go on and a number of reconnaissance missions were flown that day. One was photographic. It was noted from this that the Turks were increasing the amount of trench that was roofed over using logs but little notice seems to have been taken of this intelligence by the Army in the field.

The island of Imbros has a Mediterranean climate with warm and dry summers and wet and cool winters. Although summer is the driest season, some rainfall does occur then. Snow and ground frost are not uncommon in winter. Minor and noticeable earthquakes are common. The main town is known as Panaghia Balomeni but it has had several name changes through time as the island has changed from Greek to Turkish. It boasted a few taverns selling local beer and wine and the main inn in the town always displayed a bush over the door. The necessity for the bush was apparent in the quality of the wine.[66] The island was not ideal for building an airfield, as the wind currents coming over and down the volcanic mountains made landings very difficult at times. The site of the new aerodrome on Imbros was selected by the Army and whoever chose it had no idea about flying.

---

[66] TNA: AIR 1/2301/212/7

The choice resulted in several crashes and would cause the death of at least one pilot.

If 1st August gave Bell Davies a headache, it gave Flight Lieutenant George Dacre on the 'Ben-my-Chree' two migraines in one morning. He had gone back to bed with the second when orders came down at 1410hrs from Commander L'Estrange Malone, the captain, that he was to get all his kit packed as he was going to join the 'Roberts' with his seaplane, Midshipman Sissmore and three air mechanics at 1420hrs. L'Estrange Malone obviously felt he could spot a malingerer a mile off! Shortly after the seaplane and its crew were dropped off at the 'Roberts', it was discovered that the compressed air starting bottles for the aircraft had been left on the 'Ben-my-Chree'. A wireless message was duly sent, the 'Ben–my-Chree' came back and the missing parts were handed over. By now Dacre was in two captains' bad books, not one! To compensate L'Estrange Malone for his annoyance, the 'Ben-my-Chree' took delivery the same day of a brand new Shorts seaplane, No 842, which was then put together and tested before going on the strength of the 'Ben-my-Chree' on the 10th.[67]

On Monday 2nd August the 'Hector' was ordered to spot for the cruiser HMS 'Theseus'. The balloon was raised at 1600hrs and brought down again at 1730hrs after the successful bombardment of a Turkish position. The next day the balloon was up again at 1530hrs and came down at 1800hrs, spotting once again for the 'Theseus'. On Friday 6th August, 'Hector' spotted for the monitor 'M.32' between 1415hrs and 1730hrs, when the balloon was brought down and the ship returned to Kephalo and anchored up for the night.

On 3rd August the 'Ben-my-Chree' joined a French naval force bombarding Port Sighajik near Smirna, some 150 miles south of the Dardanelles, hoping to convince the Turks that this was to be the location of a new Allied landing. As the French ships were not yet versed in gunnery direction from the air, 'Ben-my-Chree's "Schneider" seaplanes were sent out to bomb key targets, each aeroplane carrying two 20lb bombs. No 1560 returned safely but No 1445 overturned on landing when a gust of wind caught it, though luckily the pilot escaped unhurt. The seaplane was completely wrecked but the engine and the instruments were recovered. After lunch on 3rd August, Dacre was ordered up to spot for the 'Roberts' and 'M.19', a successful shoot as at least one battery was put out of action. They had just finished when an aeroplane swooped down on them and chased them. It turned out to be one of Samson's pilots who had been briefed that no other aeroplane or seaplane would be in the area.

---

[67] Ian M Burns, *'Ben-my-Chree'*, Colin Huston, Leicester, 2008, page 71

Meanwhile, Commander Robert Clark-Hall, the captain of the 'Ark Royal', was informed his ship would be a static support ship for the squadrons on Imbros so he volunteered to captain one of the new armoured 'Beetles'. These were the first specially-designed armoured landing craft and had a front ramp allowing troops and equipment to be quickly disembarked directly onto a beach. It was the lack of this sort of craft that caused so many of the terrible casualties as troops landed on the peninsula in the early stages of the campaign.

The Royal Navy had yet another new invention preparing to go into action in the area: the Sea Scout or Submarine Scout (SS) airship, soon to be known affectionately as 'Blimps'. The SS craft were designed and built at RNAS Kingsnorth and were effectively a standard kite balloon, as used for the balloon ships like 'Manica', teamed with a BE 2c aeroplane fuselage that acted as a gondola. The fuselage was stripped of its wings, tailfin and elevators, then slung below the balloon and attached to it by wires. An engine, but not the original aero engine, was fitted to the front to supply air to the balloon in flight and steering was done by wires attached to the balloon. It had a crew of two men, a pilot and an observer, and carried a small wireless with a range of only 30 miles. A camera could be fitted to the gondola along with a Lewis gun and it could carry 160lb of bombs. Its top speed was originally 50mph and it could remain in the air for eight hours. However, due to some improvements made by one of the pilots, Lieutenant Jack Wheelwright, its flight time was increased to some twelve hours.

Two Submarine Scout airships had arrived in theatre back in May but their crews had very little flying time and no training could be done *en route* out to the Dardanelles as the ship they travelled out on was too small to inflate the balloons. A lot of flying training was carried out during June and July but before this a lot of construction had to be done. First a large airship shed had to be built and a hydrogen plant established and running so a supply of hydrogen gas was available for the two balloons.

The airship hangar, a Dalacombe Merechal and Hervieu Ltd pattern, was a portable type, formed from a wooden skeleton 50ft wide and 60ft tall covered with canvas. It was held in place by steel wire rope and proved to be totally unsuitable for its purpose. It had only been finished for three weeks when it showed signs of the canvas wearing through due to chafing, because of the constant strong winds, and many of the cross bracings were also damaged. The two airships hangered in it had to be tightly tethered to the ground to prevent them moving about, and only one could be inflated at a time due to the poor state of the shed. There was a second portable airship hangar but because of the difficulties with the first shed it was never erected.[68]

---

[68] TNA: AIR 1/681/21/13/2209

Since landing, Wheelwright had carried out a number of improvements to both the SS3 and the SS19. He fitted additional air anchors, small parachutes that slowed and help to stabilise the balloon in turbulent winds. He also fitted extra levers and wires to SS3 so the pilot had better control over the engine. The SS19 had an extra anchor cable fitted to her to help steady her in the strong winds on Imbros. Wheelwright also increased the flying time on each airship to 12 hours by fitting two fuel tanks instead of one large tank. These fuel tanks were fitted to the sides of the balloon providing a gravity feed so there was no need for fuel pumps, which again cut down on weight. On 9th August Flight Lieutenant Scarlett was placed in command of the airship station.

It was 4th August before 3 Squadron finished the move to Imbros, just in time for the return of Samson, who was coming back early from leave in just a few days as he had been told about the imminent attack by Admiral Robeck. To Bell Davies' annoyance, yet again the Army had not lived up to its promises, this time to provide food and water on Imbros for the squadron, plus a large number of tents. None of these were to be found. The next morning, after spending the night on 'Ark Royal' with the men, Bell Davies set off like a battleship in full sail, intent on giving a broadside to someone as senior as possible in the Army. General Sir Ian Hamilton's aide heard he was coming and headed him off. By mid-afternoon a section of soldiers had appeared with food and water, and with tents that they started to put up.

On 5th August Bell Davies was given two sets of orders. The first came from the Army and contained an extensive list of targets to be bombed and reconnaissance flights to be carried out, along with spotting for the artillery. With the number of aeroplanes that the squadron now had it could be done. Then a set of orders arrived from Rear-Admiral Nicholson, in charge of the monitor force that was going to support the landing, who required the aeroplanes to spot for his ships. 3 Squadron could do one or the other but could not carry out both sets of orders. Bell Davies went to see Admiral de Robeck to get clarification from the Admiral on which orders he was to follow. After few threats from Bell Davies about not following orders, Commodore Roger Keyes, the Admiral's chief of staff, sorted him out and it was agreed that he would follow the Army's orders first and he would do what he could for the navy second.

He returned to Imbros still very anxious about whether the squadron was ready for action, but as he landed he was greeted by the others all reporting that as many aeroplanes as could be got ready were ready and most of them were bombed up and ready to go along with the photographic machine. Samson's men had done it again and pulled off the impossible. With a great sigh of relief, Bell Davies went off to clean up and go have dinner with General Hamilton. It was about this time that a small boat edged up to the pier on Imbros and set down Samson and Colle. Samson bounced along the pier like a new man and was more than ready for the next phase of action, just the opposite of Collet, who was still very down.

The aeroplane operations in connection with the Suvla landings entailed a lot of work for just one under-strength squadron. Between 4th-10th August 3 Squadron carried out 28 reconnaissance missions over the Suvla region, a number of which were extended to cover between Suvla and Bulair. Many long range reconnaissance flights, both photographic and plain-sight, were carried out between 4th-6th August and, as usual, bombs were carried every time. These flights were mainly confined to Helles but included one to the Dardanelles when Lieutenant-Commander Martin Nasmith of the E11 was taken for a flight up the Dardanelles before his second mission.

The bulk of operations at this time were in support of the Army. A number of large of new Turkish camps at ANZAC Cove were spotted and marked but were not attacked in case the troops moved towards Suvla. On 4th August all the Turkish trenches and gun positions around the landing beaches were spotted, and photographed. On the 5th Chocolate Hill was photographed in detail. A reconnaissance over the Suvla area also on the 5th discovered that all the Turkish gun positions were empty and no troops could be seen in the trenches. A new trench was spotted down by the Salt Lake, facing the sea but empty. On 6th August some 800 Turkish infantry were seen marching along the road from Kum Keui towards Boghali. All these flights had to be carried out at high altitude and with speed so as not to give the landing site away.[69]

The Suvla landing on 6th August was to be made by the newly-formed British IX Corps, initially comprising two brigades of the 10th (Irish) Division and the entire 11th (Northern) Division. Some of these men were from Kitchener's New Army and command of IX Corps had been given to Lieutenant-General Sir Frederick Stopford. An officer nearing retirement, whose previous service was limited to a ceremonial post in London, it was said of him that he had no conception of what generalship meant. He was not appointed on his experience, as he had seen little combat and had never commanded men in battle. When Stopford was first shown the plan on 22nd July, he declared:

'It is a good plan. I am sure it will succeed and I congratulate whoever has been responsible for framing it.'

Stopford's chief-of-staff, Brigadier-General Hamilton Reed, who had great doubts about the coming attack, was not so supportive. Reed was an artillery officer who had won the Victoria Cross during the Boer War and, having served on the Western Front, believed no assault on entrenched positions could be made without artillery support, which was one thing the

---

[69] TNA: AIR 1/681/21/13/2209

army was particularly deficient in. Reconnaissance had revealed no prepared fortifications at Suvla but Stopford found it hard to believe in photographic intelligence and proceeded to limit the objectives of the landing. General Hamilton failed to stop him. The final orders issued by Stopford and the 11th Division commander, Major-General Frederick Hammersley, were imprecise, requiring only that the high ground be taken 'if possible'.

There were strong rumours amongst the new men arriving for this attack that Gallipoli was a death sentence and if they were even wounded, they would not survive, not surprising considering the results for the campaign so far. The Surgeon-General, W A Birrell, the Army's chief medical officer, had made arrangements for some 30,000 casualties in the next battle but Hamilton over-ruled him, reducing the figures for expected casualties to 20,000. The Navy was beginning to feel that the Army's attitude to this attack lacked any grasp on reality and that the Army was not taking care of naval personnel. It decided to bring in more medical help in the shape of Surgeon-Admiral Sir James Porter and extra medical staff but this only led to greater confusion in the medical chain of command. As it turned out, Birrell was spot-on with his guess of 30,000 casualties, and yet again there was a shortage of water and small craft to move the wounded from the beach to the hospital ships.

The offensive was to open on 6th August 1915 with diversions at Helles, the Battle of the Vineyard, and at Anzac, the Battle of Lone Pine. The landing at Suvla was to commence at 1000hrs, an hour after the two assaulting columns had broken out of Anzac beachhead heading for the Sari Bair heights. The objective of this attack was the capture of the dominating feature of the formidable Sari Bair Ridge. On the days leading up to this attack the RNAS were not allowed to swamp the area with aeroplanes; if they did overfly the area it had to be *en route* to another mission. Only two reconnaissance missions were carried out before 4th August and in both cases it was noted that it seemed that the Turkish trenches were empty. One of these missions was carried out by Bell Davies as pilot and Captain A A Walser as observer. They were both hanging out over the edge of the cockpit as they flew over the Turkish lines and discovered there were empty (and very overgrown) trenches everywhere and there were no guns in the artillery positions. The next mission was flown by Marix and Second Lieutenant the Hon M H R Knatchbull-Hugessen, who flew around the Salt Lake and the trenches on Chocolate Hill. They too found all the trenches empty and the only Turks they spotted were moving away from these trenches to the rear.[70] On landing Bell Davies found the skipper of E11 waiting for him. He wanted a flight up the Dardanelles to the Narrows, so Bell Davies refuelled, bombed up and took off again.

---

[70] Richard Bell Davies, op. cit., page 129

August 6th was chosen as the day of the attack, as the moon would be in its last quarter and would not rise until 2230hrs. Hamilton was insistent that the men landing at Suvla Bay were to be landed before the moon came up. The 10th and 11th Divisions were to land at Suvla and the 13th Division would land in secret at ANZAC and remain hidden until the breakout. At Suvla Bay, British troops of the 10th and 11th Divisions were under the command of General Stopford, who had chosen to direct operations from the sloop HMS 'Jonquil', which was anchored offshore, where he slept as the landing was in progress.

The landings were in chaos, having been made in pitch darkness. This resulted in great confusion within units, many becoming mixed up and officers unable to locate their position or their men, due to being put down in the wrong place. Having once found their men they then had to try and find their objectives. Moonrise made it easier to sort themselves out but in the morning it was still chaos. It took many hours to sort the units out and where they were supposed to be going. The 34th Brigade attempted to land at A Beach within Suvla Bay but the landing went awry from the start. The destroyers conveying the brigade anchored 1,000 yards too far south, facing shoal water and on the wrong side of the channel that drained the salt lake into the bay. Two lighters grounded on reefs and the men had to wade ashore up to their necks in water. The 9th Battalion Lancashire Fusiliers waded ashore in darkness and were pinned down between the beach and the salt lake by sniper fire and shelling. Basically it was very poor planning and training and, to make things worse, officers still could not use the information from aerial reconnaissance.

Lieutenants Jack Wheelwright and Henry Laing were the pilots of the two SS airships, SS3 and SS19, and 6th August marked the start of their flying over Gallipoli. Laing was picked to make the first flight with a Petty Officer as the observer. Each blimp spent some seven hours over the battlefield and could see very little progress around Suvla Bay yet there was a lot of fighting at Anzac and Helles. Wheelwright and PO Turner were over the Australians as the attack on Lone Pine went in at 1730hrs. The first wave of 1,800 men of the Australian 1st Infantry Brigade threw themselves forward to open the attack. Half the force crossed the exposed ground between the trench lines. Dubbed the Daisy Patch, it was a distance of about 100yd and it was raked with Turkish artillery and small arms fire. Casualties among the first wave of attackers were 'relatively light' as the defenders in the front line of Turkish trenches were still sheltering from the preliminary bombardment and had not had time to return to their fire steps. When the Australians reached the Turkish trenches they found them roofed with pine logs with no easy entrance just as the commanders had been warned by the aerial intelligence they had received. To Wheelwright in the blimp it looked like the Australians were being mowed down and he began to shout at Turner to use the wireless:

'Send a message for God's sake. Tell them their men are advancing straight into a hail of gunfire.'[71]

Neither man had seen an infantry attack go in before, so it came as a great shock to them to see all these men being cut down by machine-gun fire and yet in the official reports of the day: 'casualties were light'.

There is some sort of bitter satisfaction in the knowledge that General Stopford, the commanding officer who believed at such a terrible cost to his men that the RNAS could be of little help in the attack, was relieved of his command on August 15th. His failure was the fault of Secretary of State for War, Lord Kitchener, who had appointed this elderly and inexperienced general to an active corps command, and also of Sir Ian Hamilton, who had accepted Stopford's appointment.

The kite balloon sections on the 'Hector' and 'Manica' were doing the best they could to support the Navy but they were not able to get in close due to the increased accuracy of the Turkish guns, therefore their own spotting was not as accurate. Turkish air attacks on the two ships were increasing but this luckily was still very inaccurate. The risk of submarine attack was also increasing, so the stress on the crews was constantly growing. Saturday 7th August saw 'Hector' spotting for the cruiser HMS 'Edgar'; the balloon went up in the morning at 0810hrs and came down an hour later at 0910hrs. In the early evening the balloon went up at 1805hrs and came down at 1850hrs, after which the ship returned to its anchorage.

E11 had just started her second tour when, on 6th August it successfully torpedoed the Turkish torpedo cruiser 'Peyk-i Şevket', causing serious damage. Two days later on 8th August as the new British landing was underway at Suvla, E11 torpedoed the antiquated Turkish pre-dreadnought battleship 'Barbaros Hayreddin' off Bulair at the northern entrance to the Dardanelles. The ship sank with the loss of 21 officers and 237 men, one of two Turkish battleships sunk during the campaign. Visiting Constantinople again, E11 sank a Black Sea collier. The 'Isfahan' had just tied up and was preparing to unload when a torpedo stuck the ship and it exploded. It was a significant blow as coal was the main fuel source and supplies were scarce. Moving into the Gulf of Izmir on the night of 20th August, E11's first officer, Lieutenant Guy D'Oyly-Hughes, swam ashore and blew up a section of the Constantinople–Baghdad railway line, a feat for which he was awarded the Distinguished Service Cross. Navigating Officer Lieutenant Robert Brown was also awarded the Distinguished Service Cross.

Meanwhile, things were changing in the senior ranks of the RNAS. It had been clear for some time that its growing role in the war and the hugely increased number of personnel in the Air Service was far beyond the old

---

[71] S J Plummer, *'A Man of Invention'*, Cloth Wrap Publishing, 2010, page 25.

administrative structure's powers to organise, control and supply. In personnel alone it had grown from 140 officers and 708 men on 15th August 1914 to 1,346 officers and 9,370 men on 15th August 1915. It needed a more senior officer than Captain Sueter in command and a larger department. Now Rear-Admiral Charles L Vaughan-Lee moved in and took up his post as Director of Aviation so that by the end of the month, when he officially replaced Murray Sueter, he would know his new department. Would this mean a better supply line for Samson and 3 Squadron and the other RNAS units in the Eastern Mediterranean? Only time would tell.

On 6th August Colonel Sykes returned to the Dardanelles as Colonel, 2nd Commandant, Royal Marines, and also as a Wing Captain, making him the highest-ranking RNAS officer in the Dardanelles - and by the end of the operation the most disliked by all. Sykes had promised Admiral de Robeck that he would bring back with him 60 aeroplanes, 36 pilots and 24 observers[72]. In this he failed, but he did manage to get 2 Squadron shipped out to the Dardanelles to help Samson and 3 Squadron.

While in London Sykes had talks with Murray Sueter about enlarging the air unit in the Dardanelles and Sueter promised that No 1 Squadron, under the command of Wing Commander Arthur M Longmore, would be sent out to join the fight. Longmore knew Sykes and was keen to help him build a big and effective air unit, which he wanted to be part of, so it seemed an ideal appointment. Longmore and his squadron were duly pulled out of Dunkirk and brought back to Britain to make ready to go to the Dardanelles. He was replaced at Dunkirk by Wing Commander Eugene L Gerrard and 2 Squadron. They settled in well in Dunkirk and very quickly started to take the fight to the Germans, as Samson and 3 Squadron had done. In a couple of weeks they dropped more bombs on the Germans than No 1 Squadron had done in the whole six months they had been in Dunkirk.

Longmore, however, did not want to be with Sykes 'at any price' and was not at all happy to discover that his squadron was destined for the Dardanelles. Gallipoli/Dardanelles had already developed a reputation as a dead man's posting due to the high casualty rate and he wanted to remain in Western Europe. So he contacted his uncle, a General[73] in the British Army, and got him to put pressure on his posting. The Admiralty reversed Sueter's choice and pulled 2 Squadron back out of France and returned No 1 Squadron[74]. Now Gerrard was annoyed as at long last he and his men were back in the real shooting war and feeling that they were doing their bit. His recall orders gave no hint of what their next posting would be and Gerrard and his men assumed it would be back to training duties. His frank

---

[72] Eric Ash, op. cit., page 83
[73] TNA: AIR 1/2659
[74] TNA: AIR 1/681/21/13/2209

letter to their Lordships at the Admiralty evoked their displeasure. 2 Squadron were pulled out of France on 2nd August and made ready to ship out to the Dardanelles at Dover just as 3 Squadron had done.

Sykes and Murray Sueter were also unhappy at this turn of events and did not want Gerrard in the Dardanelles. Sueter, to give him credit, was less than impressed by Longmore using family connections to get his posting changed and fired off a letter to the Admiralty[75]. Their Lordships at the Admiralty were suitably displeased with Sueter's insubordinate letter and rapped him over the knuckles for it but as the man had just lost his job he was not worried. As for Longmore, the use of a family connection was not forgotten. It was kept in a file for a board of enquiry later in the year on a different and much more serious matter. His attitude at the board was truculent and he made a number of deliberately false statements[76]. He was returned to the fleet to learn how to behave like an officer - and no family connection could save him from that.

Meanwhile, back in the Dardanelles, 3 Squadron was hard at work as usual. At 0600hrs on 6th August a group of about 150 Turkish infantry were spotted marching towards the landing zone. A Turkish aeroplane was also spotted heading for Suvla point when it was intercepted by one of 3 Squadron's aircraft and chased all the way back to its base. At 0630hrs a battery of light guns opened fire on the landing beaches until they were dived on by an aeroplane and ceased firing. At 0730hrs a 4-inch gun battery was located and an aircraft spotted a ship's guns onto the target, but the battery ceased firing before the ship could get a shot in. During a reconnaissance flight, a light field battery was spotted on the road, pulling back towards Anafarta Sagir at 0900hrs, and Turkish troops were also spotted pulling back. At 1730hrs some 2000 Infantry were spotted on the slopes of Green Hill. HMS 'Theseus' was called up by wireless but she did not acknowledge, so a message bag was dropped on the beach which was spotted being picked up.[77]

At dawn on the 7th, Bell Davies took off with Knatchbull-Hugessen as his observer heading straight for the new landing area at Suvla. They found no major attack under way and very little Turkish artillery was falling on the British beach. Bell Davies could not work out why the British forces were not advancing. They then went to look at the Turkish gun emplacements that they had found and were surprised to find they were still empty, as were the infantry trenches on Chocolate Hill. On landing Knatchbull-Hugessen rushed to the Intelligence tent and made a full report to Isaac, who duly wrote up a report and sent it to Army GHQ which was next door. Bell Davies on landing had spotted a friend of his, Jack Churchill, and on

---

[75] TNA: ADM 156/78
[76] TNA: ADM 156/79
[77] TNA: AIR 1/681/21/13/2209

approaching him he could see his friend was very angry. There was a shortage of water at Suvla and the water boats had only just left; they watched the last one leave as they talked. Bell Davies went up again in the afternoon and flew over Suvla with one of the men as an observer and yet again they could see no forward movement; the British troops were still on the beach and making no progress inland. Bell Davies then flew over the Turkish lines and found the trenches and gun emplacements still empty. He returned to Imbros and made a report which was sent up to General Hamilton, but there was no way of getting the information to the landings at Suvla and no way the information could be acted on.

3 Squadron had carried out a number of bombing patrols and attacked morning camp fires, artillery trains and supply convoys during the landings. With the help of the French, a combined attack was carried out on the Turkish airfield at Galata where five aeroplanes were spotted on the ground. On the morning of 8th August, two of the morning reconnaissance flights noted that the Turks were moving forward in large numbers; they were beginning to fill the empty trenches and were bringing forward some artillery. Yet the British troops were still very slow to advance. The advantage had been wasted. At 1000hrs a group of about 1000 Turkish infantry were spotted moving towards the landing site. At 1400hrs an even larger group of Turkish Infantry was spotted moving forward towards ANZAC and appeared to be massing ready for an assault. At 1430hrs a further group of 1500 men were spotted moving in from the north.[78] Three field guns were spotted when they were brought up and placed on the ridge between Tekke Tepe and Kavak Tepe. At 1900hrs a Turkish aeroplane was spotted and chased off by a 3 Squadron aircraft that moved in close and forced the enemy aeroplane to dive and head for its own lines yet again, dumping its bomb load on its own men.

The two SS airships were both up again on the 8th covering the ANZAC attack at Lone Pine. Wheelwright and PO Turner saw a number of attacks put in by the Turks in attempts to take the positions back from the Australians over their time on station, and the sheer loss of life was staggering. This went on day after day until 10th August when the fighting around Lone Pine finished.

On the morning of the 9th another new Royal Navy unit went into action for the first time: the 11th RNAS Maxim Squadron, under the command of Lieutenant Commander J W Stocks, which had arrived at Mudros together with No 9 RNAS Armoured Car Squadron (commanded by Lieutenant Commander A D Borton). The armoured cars were landed a week after the Maxim gun squadron but both units had arrived at the end of July, just in time for the Suvla Bay operation.

---

[78] TNA: AIR 1/681/21/13/2209

When Samson returned from leave on 9th August he went straight to the new airfield on Imbros. He found his men very down. The new aerodrome was perched on a narrow and windy isthmus and it was clear that the place was going to be the death of someone. Samson immediately started to look for a new aerodrome site and found one not too far away. What he now required was a large number of labourers to clear the rocks and scrub and make him a runway. The Army gave him some 70 Turkish prisoners and they started to clear the new airfield. At first the prisoners were under heavy guard but as they got to know each other, Samson instructed that the Turks were to be paid in cigarettes. At the end of work each day, they would go off to their prison very happy men, knowing that they would get a hot meal and be looked after. The security detail was now down to just one man and would remain at one for the rest of the campaign. It reached a point where, apart from carrying their own tools, they would also carry the guard's rifle.

One thing the ground crew were not happy about was carrying petrol in two gallon cans from Kephalo harbour up to the new airfield, something they had to do as there was a large stretch of soft sand between the harbour and the airfield that vehicles could not cross. The Army had shown they did not understand aeroplanes or the men who flew them when choosing this new site and had no idea the problems of flying. A roadway was built over the soft sand area and life did become a little better for the men of 3 Squadron. However, until the new airfield was completed later in the month, 3 Squadron still had to fly from the old one.

Bell Davies was up over ANZAC on the 10th in the first of the new 120hp Henri Farman's with Jupp as observer when they spotted a German Ettrich Taube. He came in below and behind the Taube and Jupp opened fire. After just five shots, the pilot realized he was under attack and put his aeroplane into a dive. Bell Davies followed and pulled out at 1500 feet while the German continued in his dive and managed to pull out just in time. The Australians thought the Taube had crashed as it vanished out of sight behind a large hill and they sent up a great cheer. Before long, Bell Davies would be the next to go on leave with one of the other pilots.

Between 9th May 1915 and 6th August 1915 the RNAS carried out:[79]

Spotting flights for ships and Army artillery	203
Photographic reconnaissance flights by aeroplanes	71
Bombing and/or reconnaissance flights	291
Bombs dropped: large (100lb)	120
Bombs dropped: small (20lb)	190

[79] TNA: AIR 1/681/21/13/2209

Anti-submarine patrols by SS airship	40
Fighter defence patrol	10

The 'Ben-my-Chree' had entered Kephalo bay on 5th August and she remained there until the 10th carrying out some minor repairs and coaling the ship. On the 11th she left to retrieve Lieutenant Dacre from HMS 'Roberts'. Dacre and his seaplane re-joined the ship at 0930hrs, while Flight Lieutenant Wright and his seaplane No 841 left the ship at 1015hrs and joined the 'Roberts'.

The arrival of the 'Ben-my-Chree' in the Gulf of Xeros with Short 184 seaplanes capable of carrying 14-inch torpedoes added greatly to the variety of offensive operations which the RNAS contingent could now undertake. On 12th August, at 0437hrs seaplanes 842 and 184 were swung out and placed on the water ready to put these new weapons to the test. Flight Commander Charles Edmonds, RN, was flying 842, and Flight Lieutenant Dacre was flying 184. Dacre taxied back and forth but his seaplane would not take off so it was placed back on the ship for repairs. Edmonds took off without his observer and flew with just 45 minutes of fuel to lighten his aircraft enough to carry the torpedo. He flew over the Gallipoli peninsula at low level and spotted the ship he had been briefed about in the Dardanelles, a 5000-ton transport. He came down and lined up on the merchant ship, dropping his torpedo from a range of 300 yards and an altitude of just 15 feet. It struck the ship abreast the mainmast, sending up a large amount of debris and a huge water spout, and Edmonds saw that the steamer was settling by the stern. It was subsequently discovered that the ship had been beach four days earlier after being torpedoed and shelled by the submarine HMS E14. This was the first ship to be torpedoed by an aircraft. Yet again the RNAS were showing the world what an aircraft could do and what a great weapons system it was.

The balloon ships were still busy. Tuesday 10th August saw the 'Hector' out spotting for several ships. The balloon went up at 1705hrs and came down at 1855hrs when the ship returned to Kephalo. On the 12th the 'Hector' was out at her spotting position at 1455hrs, sent up her balloon half an hour later and was up till 1740hrs. She was out again in support of Army artillery on Friday the 13th when her balloon had to come down again at 1330hrs after only 30 minutes, due to a technical problem. This was soon fixed and it went up again at 1400hrs and came down at 1715hrs. On the 14th the 'Hector' was out early and first went up to Suvla Bay between 0550hrs and 0615hrs, moving on to a new position at 1100hrs. She put the balloon up at 1130hrs but was ordered to bring it down only an hour later and return to port with best speed as the 'Manica' had been attacked by a submarine. Luckily, yet again the Germans got the depth of the ship wrong and the torpedo passed under it.

Wednesday 11th August was not a good day for Leading Mechanic Arthur George Beeton of 3 Squadron. The Turks had sent over a lone aircraft with a few bombs on board, all hand-made. Samson was in his tent when the alarm as raised and he strolled out quite nonchalantly swinging his goggles. He stopped and looked up, as one of the Turkish bombs was unbalanced and was coming down making a 'wogger-wogger' sound instead of the normal scream. Samson ordered his men to get down but when the bomb hit the ground it failed to go off. He signalled that he wanted his Nieuport started up: he was going to try to catch the Turk. He climbed in and Beeton stood in front and swung the prop. Nothing. The engine failed to start. Beeton swung the prop several more times until Samson shouted at him 'Have you doped it?' (A rotary engine required each cylinder to be primed with a drop of petrol or 'doped' from a small can be for starting.) 'No sir' replied Beeton 'I have not got my can.' Samson burst into a tirade of swearing, never once repeating the same swear word, while Beeton took off and covered the 100yds to his tent and back in very quick time. On returning to base Samson said nothing to Beeton about the incident.[80] As for the unexploded bomb, the French collected it, put a new tail on it and returned it to the Turks!

The weather was not good on Sunday 15th, but the 'Hector' was called out in the morning and cleared the harbour at 0425hrs making her way to Suvla Bay. They tried to get the balloon up at 0600hrs but it was not steady and had to come down again at 0715. They tried to raise the balloon in the afternoon but the wind was still too high, at 1828hrs they did manage to get the balloon up, but at 1900hrs the ship was attacked by a Turkish aeroplane that dropped a bomb but missed. If the crew of the 'Hector' thought Sunday was bad, it did not have a patch on Monday. Commander Rayne, the captain, had the ship on the move early for Cape Suvla and the balloon was up at 0545hrs and everything was going well and the balloon was being called on as required. At 0804hrs a shout went up from a lookout that there was a torpedo in the water heading straight for the stern of the ship. The observers in the balloon could see the submarine, which dived and passed under the ship and was spotted heading south west from the ship. They could also see the torpedo heading for the ship. The balloon came down in double-quick time but the torpedo luckily passed under the 'Hector' and the crew were greeted by two very relieved observers. However, in the excitement they had drifted a little close to the coast and came under Turkish fire, one shell passing through the ship breaking a steam pipe.

Squadron Commander Gerrard and his men were extremely happy to be heading back into a shooting war and very pleased at the prospect of working alongside Samson and 3 Squadron. They embarked for the

---

[80] Arthur Beeton, IWM Sound Archive, catalogue number 8323

Dardanelles on 15th August from Plymouth, at which point the squadron was comprised of 16 officers and 3 Warrant Officers:

Wing Commander E. L. Gerrard (C.O)

Flight Commander C. E. Robinson

Flight Commander C. M. Murphy

Flight Commander R. Smyth-Pigott

Flight Commander A. B. Gaskell

Flight Lieutenant H. A. Buss

Flight Lieutenant A. F. Bettinson

Flight Sub-Lieutenant F. Besson

Flight Sub-Lieutenant G. C. Dawson

Flight Sub-Lieutenant R. B. Munday

Flight Sub-Lieutenant L. A. Hervey

Flight Sub-Lieutenant A. C. Teesdale

Flight Sub-Lieutenant R. Y. Bush

Flight Sub-Lieutenant V. Nicholson

Flight Sub-Lieutenant N. A. Simpson

Flight Sub-Lieutenant C. E. Brisley

Warrant Officer D. Shore

Warrant Officer H. S. Gallagher

Warrant Officer A. S. Hellawell [81]

200 ground staff and the following aircraft:

6 Morane Parasols, two-seater monoplane with 80hp Rhone engine.

6 Caudrons, two-seater biplanes with 80hp Gnome engine.

6 BE2cs, two-seater biplanes with 75hp Renault engine.

4 Bristol Scouts, single-seater with 80hp Gnome engine.

2 Voisin two-seater biplanes with 140hp Canton engine, for 3 Wing.[82]

Some 30 men were transferred from No 2 Squadron to No 1 Squadron. This came about because No 1 Squadron had originally been ordered to the Dardanelles and had sent a group of 30 men ahead on 1st August to make the base ready for the Squadron's arrival. However, as we have seen, Longmore, the squadron's commander, had got his orders changed thanks to family connections[83]. Therefore when No 2 Squadron went out to the

---

[81] TNA: AIR 1/681/21/13/2209
[82] ibidem
[83] TNA: AIR 1/2659

Dardanelles instead, they absorbed No 1 Squadron's advance party into No 2 Squadron rather than send them back and handed over 30 men to No 1 Squadron. The advance party went overland to Marseilles and joined a ship of the Messageries line that took them as far as Malta where they transferred onto a destroyer, which delivered them to Imbros. As for the rest of the squadron, the bulk of the men were seasick going through the Bay of Biscay, like almost all the other members of the RNAS. The ship then stopped at Gibraltar for just a few hours before moving on to Malta, where it picked up several hundred troops who were returning to their units having spent time in hospital on the island. Most of the men had got over their sea sickness by now and enjoyed the rest of the voyage to Imbros. 2 Squadron arrived on 25th August and became operational as 2 Wing at Imbros (Kephalo Point airfield) on the 31st.

Yet again Sykes chose the site of the new airfield, the Imbros Marsh aerodrome, and yet again it was a bad position. It was situated 900 yards from Kephalo beach and to the north of the Salt Lake. It was level ground with an even surface but was liable to be too soft in wet weather. Measuring some 600 yards by 450 yards, the aerodrome was close to some high ground, which caused some very bad air currents when the wind blew in certain directions and caused a number of problems to landing aeroplanes. On most days there was a wind from the south-west at about 1,000ft above the island and, as it blew at over 100mph, this caused a number of problems at times.

Sykes now reorganised the RNAS units into something that was not naval but reflected more what he knew from the RFC:

No. 2 Wing and No. 3 Wing would act as independent units.

The Seaplane Squadron, consisting of HMS 'Ark Royal' and 'Ben-my-Chree' seaplanes. The two kite balloon ships 'Manica' and 'Hector'.

One SS Airship Section with one SS airship.[84] (Due to the poor state of the airship shed and the constant strong winds only one SS could be inflated at a time.)

It was from this point that the Squadrons now became Wings. Sykes set up his Headquarters on Imbros in the buildings he had ordered to be built while he was in England. All these changes were the direct outcome of Sykes' recommendations. In addition Sykes promised that further aeroplanes would be coming out from England and France and that trained photographers with cameras would be sent out. He also recommended a further 8 SS airships should be sent out.

---

[84] TNA: AIR 1/681/21/13/2209

On 16th August at 1500hrs Sykes went on board the 'Ben-my-Chree' to have a look at seaplane operations and stayed until the 18th. Two new pilots arrived on this day: Sub-Flight Lieutenants L C Keeble and C D Morrison. Keeble did not stay long, but after a little more training Morrison turned into a hard-working first class pilot. A limitation to using the Short seaplane more widely as a torpedo bomber was that it could only take off carrying a torpedo in perfect flying weather and calm seas. A brand new engine was required to get this war load into the air as this put a great strain on the engine, and, with the torpedo, the seaplane could only fly for a little more than 45 minutes before running out of fuel. The two attacks launched from the Ben-my-Chree were the only successes of the torpedo bombers in the Dardanelles campaign, although bombing attacks extended the tally against shipping to some extent. More than 70 bombing attacks were made during 1915, resulting in damage to two large steamers and a tug, while one lighter and six dhows were wrecked and the old Turkish battleship the 'Barbarossa' was damaged. On the 17th, a Turkish steamship was sunk by a torpedo aimed again by Edmonds. His formation mate, Flight Lieutenant Dacre, made it off the water this time and sank a Turkish tugboat:

'Got up at 0230hrs feeling very sleepy. Hands fell in at 0245hrs. Tried our engines in the sheds and looked around to see if everything was correct. I was hoisted out at 0400hrs and Edmonds just after me on a new machine, mine being the original No184. Edmonds got off quickly but I took quarter of a hour struggling to get off with my torpedo, the safety pin of which was now out. After twenty minutes I struggled the machine up to 1200ft round the Gulf, thence passing over the narrow neck of the Peninsula. It is only 3 miles across here and about 200 to 300ft height. It however looks mighty wide when you are low down over it and having your life hanging on your engine. In the semi dark several flashes from individual rifles were firing at me but no bulls were scored. Having got across the Sea of Marmara, I glided down to 330ft and eased my engine a little. At this height it is very difficult to be seen with the mountains as background and in the semi light. I passed down the centre of the straits past Gallipoli town, several small vessels and a lot of sailing ships. Six or seven miles further down I could see a hospital ship coming up and in the distance Edmonds above returning from his objective, which was several large ships in a bay about 3 miles north of the Narrows. Just then my engine started to make a terrible noise and die out so I was obliged to land. This I had to do across the wind as my height was not sufficient to turn into the wind. A heavy landing resulted but no damage. The Hospital ship was quite near and altered course towards me. I thought this must be the finish, either the numerous batteries would sink me or I should be captured and made a prisoner. I had left my usual spare cloths behind to save weight, these I carry in case of capture so that during my stay in the country at the enemy's expense I should not be in want of cloths and money. I thought this was a proper fix to be in, taxing slowly in the middle of the straits, and absolutely fed up with the engine failing me a second time. I was determined to make the best of it in consequence. Now if I dropped my torpedo it would hit the bank and wake up everything, so I thought a ruse might work. The Hospital ship was only 300yds off now so I came close up to it and waved my hand, all the wounded waved back at me and the Ship passed on up the straits. Everyone must have taken me for a friendly crafts boats were dodging round taking very little notice. I let the Hospital ship pass up and half a mile up I could see two ships in a little bay. One a large old wooden sailing ship which hardly looked sinkable and a large tug alongside a new wooden pier. I taxied up to within 500yds of it and let go my torpedo, turning around directly after up the straits. A terrific explosion followed and as I looked over my shoulder see spray descending and the tug giving a huge lurch. Then all of a sudden rifle shots pattered in the water beside me and my first idea was to get out of it being in a desperate funk. By a miracle nothing hit me and, inspired by the thought of a bullet in my back, I cranked the engine up slightly and after taxing 2 or 3 miles got off again to my great joy. Just after getting off I noticed an aerodrome right opposite the scene of the action. I pushed the machine up to 1800ft and the engine making a fearful row. Passing Gallipoli town [I] made for the narrowest part of the peninsula and when half way over worse noises occurred and a compression tap came open. I was then only able to make a long glide passing very low over the last part of land finally making with great relief the ship.'

Also on the 17th, No 3 SS Airship Squadron arrived on the transport 'Koroa' and dropped anchor off Imbros. Barges came alongside and the stores were off-loaded in the heavy sea, along with the men and balloon of No 3 SS Airship Wing. Unfortunately the balloon in its very large crate was lost over the side and had to be brought up by diver. It was salvaged the next day and joined the other airships. The weather changed on the night of the 17th. A storm came in and for the next three days there was thunder and lightning. The men of 2 Wing advance party got soaked as they tried to hang onto their poorly-erected tents while others were washed out of their tents by the river of rain water that came rushing through.

On 19th August, Samson and his observer, Captain Keith-Jopp, were carrying out a reconnaissance over Suvla when they were hit by anti-aircraft fire that hit the engine and stopped it. Samson glided the aircraft in to make a dead-stick landing. They came to a halt on the edge of the salt lake well behind the Australian lines on an upward slope which was fairly steep, so the aeroplane ran back down the hill but came to a halt undamaged. All that was required was a new magneto and they could be back in the air. But the aeroplane now came under Turkish artillery fire for some ten minutes. On re-examining the aircraft the damage was not too bad but the engine would now require a lot more work. Fortunately, at this point Samson ran into an old friend, a Major Hawker, who got him a couple of horses and they took a gentle ride back to the beach. They signalled Imbros to tell them the aeroplane would need a new engine and a bit of repair and shipped out on the mail trawler, leaving the aircraft to be picked up by a lighter later. They were halfway back to Imbros when the weather changed and it began to blow and the trawler started to ship water. The air below decks was foul and made you feel worse, so both Samson and Jopp retired to the deck and the dinghy that was lying in crutches on it. As the night went on, they became soaked to the skin and the sea state became rougher. Jopp turned from a strapping six-foot Australian into helpless invalid who had been throwing up constantly for hours (or so it seemed to Samson). On reaching Imbros, Samson leapt over the side onto the pier while poor Jopp had to be carried off the trawler and placed on the beach, all the while muttering 'never again'!

On 19th August Collet took off from 3 Wing's airfield on Imbros and had reached a height of between 150 and 185 feet when his engine failed. He turned to attempt a landing but lost control in the strong cross-winds from the cliffs and his aircraft fell vertically to the ground, bursting into flames when it hit. Between the crash site and the aerodrome was a 70-foot deep ravine which all the would-be rescuers had to scramble down and up again to get to Collet. His passenger/observer, George Lacey, sitting in the front seat of the BE2c, saw that the aeroplane was going to crash and that if he remained in his seat when they hit, the engine would shoot back and kill him. He was half out of the front seat when the impact came and he was thrown 50 yards clear but both legs were fractured.

One man was prepared for the problems of extricating Collet from his burning machine. Chief Petty Officer Michael S Keogh saw what was going to happen and grabbed a tarpaulin, which he wrapped around himself in, forced his way into the fire and got Collet out. His courage was in vain: Collet was fatally injured and died 30 minutes later. He is buried at the Lancashire Landing Cemetery in Gallipoli. Keogh was awarded the Albert Medal (2nd Class) for his attempt save Collet's life. This was the only first of a number of bad accidents all due to the very poor conditions on Imbros, particularly the miss-siting of the airfields. It was a consequence of Sykes' overweening self-confidence but lack of actual knowledge, the drive of an officer more concerned with empire building than the lives of his men.

Collet's death was a terrible blow to 3 Wing. He was one of the longest-serving squadron members and that he could be killed was quite a wake-up call, especially when death was a rare occurrence in the Wing. A number of men were affected by Collet's crash, including (not surprisingly) Samson. Worst of all was Sub-Flight Lieutenant Harold Kerby, who got a bad case of the shakes. The doctor packed him off to the 'Ark Royal' for a full rest, a bath and a few days in a clean bed. But this did not work and he was sent home. He did return to flying, though not for several months, and became an ace on the Western Front, shooting down nine aeroplanes.

Samson was now determined to get his men away from the airfield they had been using on Imbros before it could kill any more men. Sir Ian Hamilton had come out of his tent when Collet crashed to see what all the commotion was. Collet's aeroplane had missed the general's tent by only a few feet, which alarmed him as he felt his life was in danger. It was another good reason to move the airfield. Samson had some seventy Turkish prisoners working on the new airfield site that he had chosen when he returned from leave but to speed the operation up he acquired a further hundred and thirty. He also enlarged the new aerodrome so that both 2 and 3 Wings could operate in safety from the same field, a better field than the one chosen for 2 Wing by Sykes.

Even when the weather interrupted the air war, the process of supply went on, though not always smoothly. On 21st August the Merchant Fleet Auxiliary (MFA) 'Floridian' came alongside the 'Ben-my-Chree' with a load of spares and general supplies. As these were being transferred to the 'Ben-my-Chree', one of the crates from the Air Department containing urgently required seaplane spares unfortunately fell over the side into the water. As there were no divers on board, they were told to contact HMS 'Bacchante' and borrow her diving team to recover it. The diving team duly came over, retrieved the lost crate and returned to 'Bacchante' mid-morning on the 22nd. On 26th August a large number of seaplanes were grounded as the weather had not been good for flying, but Dacre and Childers managed to take off at 0550hrs in No 846, armed with a few small bombs. They returned with engine failure at 0659hrs. That evening another thunderstorm rolled in and a number of the 2 Wing men nearly lost their tents once again.

The next day, Friday the 27th, Samson rode over on his horse 'Nigger' to greet the men of 2 Wing's advance party, see how they were settling in, have a general chat and invite the men to join 3 Wing Mess. Two days later on the 29th, the SS 'Tringa' came alongside the 'Ark Royal' at 1125hrs and tied up. The remainder of 2 Wing and its aeroplanes had arrived, probably much to the relief of its advance party. The next few days was spent getting 2 Wing and its aircraft and stores ashore. While getting the aeroplanes ready for their first missions it was discovered that the fittings for the aerial cameras had been left behind in the rush to pack up and get out to the Dardanelles. Petty Officer W Pollard was sent on board the 'Ark Royal' to use the machine room to make a number of sets of camera fittings, a process that took him several days.

On 30th August Samson and Keith-Jopp excelled themselves. They were up spotting for the monitor 'M.15', which was positioned off Anzac Cove and firing at targets in Ak Bashi Liman, a range of some 16,459 metres (18,000 yards). In the harbour of Ak Bashi Liman were two small steamers, both about 200 feet long, anchored next to each other. Three or four tugs and about twenty dhows were busily bustling between the steamers and the shore unloading them. Samson then went on to report:

'I got up to 6000 feet where I could get a good view both of M15 and Ak Bashi Liman. I took care to keep about four miles away from Ak Bashi in order not to arouse their suspicions. When ready I ordered fire. The first shot fell about 800 yards short, fortunately behind the hills so that no notice was taken by the Turks. The next shot fell into the sea. We now had the range'.

A terrible panic broke out between the men on the boats and on the shore. The tugs had a number of dhows in tow which were cut loose and left to their fate while the tugs made off at their best possible speed for the Asiatic shore. The gangs on the beach, who were now very used to being attacked by Samson's men dropping bombs on them, took to their heels, chasing after the pack animals that had already broken loose and were heading for the hills. With slow but precise instructions, Jopp directed the 'M.15's fire until the eighth shot hit one of the ships. The ninth shell hit the second steamer starting a fierce fire. The 'M.15' fired on the same setting for effect. One steamer was sinking and the other was well alight as it ceased fire and Samson and his observer set off for home. As a result of this raid, big ships never came into Ak Bashi again in daylight hours.

Samson and Gerrard now sat down and divided up the jobs that had to be done between their respective squadrons. 3 Wing was to concentrate on bombing and reconnaissance of Turkish positions while 2 Wing would be mainly employed spotting for the fleet and the Army guns and also carrying out a photographic survey of the Gallipoli peninsula so that accurate up-to-date maps could be made. 3 Wing thought nothing of the over-water flights they made several times a day while 2 Wing were still finding their feet and were a little jittery about the time-over-water. Sykes and his staff, meanwhile, were not at all happy about life under canvas and moved onto the 'Ark Royal'. He was not missed: he had spent most of his time since his return from London swanning around the various Army and Naval HQs.

It was a shame he had not made good his promises about new aircraft as 3 Wing were in a fix with only some six aeroplanes operational, all of which were desperately needed a good service and most of which required fresh fabric. The Wing still managed to carry out 217 flights and spent over 400 hours in the air in August. Compare this to 'Ark Royal'. In August her seaplanes had carried out 14 spotting flights, 1 photographic reconnaissance, 2 general patrol flights and 1 experimental flight. A number of test flights were also carried out.[85]

---

[85] TNA: AIR 1/726/137/2

The 'Ark Royal's flight log for August read thus:

Machine number	Flights	Useful service	Time	Engine failures
136	4	3	2hrs 54mins	1
161	6	2	4hrs 50mins	-
162	12	10	17hrs 48mins	2
163	6	2	3hrs 55 mins	-
164	1	-	0hrs 25mins	1
922	7	1	2hrs 55mins	2
3713	4	2	2hrs 36mins	2
Totals:	**40**	**20**	**35hrs 23mins**	**8**

Sadly for the 'Ark Royal' and the 'Ben-my-Chree', experience in regard to the seaplanes showed that, despite their general usefulness and at a time when other aircraft were so few in number, there was scarcely any operation performed by them that could not have been better or more economically carried out by a land aeroplane.[86]

---

[86] TNA: AIR 1/681/21/13/2209

Chapter six
September 1915

With the appointment of Rear-Admiral Charles L Vaughan-Lee as Director of Air Services with overall responsibility for naval aviation on 1st September, 1915, Murray Sueter was made Superintendent of Aircraft Construction with full responsibility for the materiel side of all naval aircraft. At the same time he was promoted Commodore, First Class. The Royal Naval Air Service had now become a major part of the Royal Navy and as such required an Admiral in charge of the department. The job had outgrown Sueter, with units fighting on several fronts around the world, but he was not at all happy about losing his job at the top of his RNAS. As a result of this change, Sykes had now lost one of his greatest supporters and would lose his position in the RNAS in four months' time when the Navy sent him back to the Army.

The weather was not good on Wednesday 1st September and almost the whole fleet remained in harbour as a Force 6 gale battered the Dardanelles. Autumn was coming and with it a succession of storms that would hamper the air war as well as the war on the land and sea. This was also the day that the island of Tenedos was officially handed over to the French and the Royal Marines from the 'Ark Royal' returned to their ship. The fort was now occupied by a company of French Fusiliers Marins. Giving up the airfield on Tenedos was, in my opinion, the worst thing that happened to the RNAS out in Gallipoli: it led to the death of a number of pilots and observers.

The cable ship 'Levant' had now returned from a refit at Syra and had a new commander, Captain Wightman. A diary of the ship records:

'A few days of this new captain's companionship served to show us that his command of the 'Levant' was going to mean a delightful change for all of the crew on board. His cheery temperament made the lives of all who served with him more agreeable in those trying times and his boisterous laugh, annoying as it may have been in the early hours of the morning, cheered all the men and made us feel that things were not really so bad as we had been inclined to think.'

On 3rd September 'Levant' proceeded to Kephalo and made repairs there to the Imbros-Suvla and Imbros-Anzac cables which had both been damaged by a trawler running aground. September 4th saw the repair finished late in the day and 'Levant' came inside the harbour for the night as it was then too late to get to Suvla and weather was bad.

Things did not look as cheerful on land at Gallipoli, as the ground war was beginning to turn into stalemate just like the Western Front. Now the British planners looked at different ways of attacking the Turks, such as destroying the Turkish supply routes to try to starve the enemy of war materials, like ammunition from Germany. Though the Turks were losing a number of supply ships as the Russians were sinking them, some supplies were still trickling in, but once Bulgaria joined the Central Powers this trickle turned into a torrent that was funnelled by railway through to Constantinople, the main supply point. 2 and 3 Wings did not have suitable aeroplanes to attack Constantinople so a new weak spot had to be found. A large number of reconnaissance flights, both visual and photographic, were carried out to discover this.

Sir Ian Hamilton was now really beginning to feel the pressure from Whitehall and Horseguards, and especially from the press in London, to get on and get a good victory as he had promised. Several London papers had sent out reporters but their dispatches were coming back full of nothing. They were neither downbeat (nor even critical of the Army) nor upbeat; they were just mediocre because they were subject to military censorship. Faced with this, it was difficult to produce copy that was truthful and could grip the reader's imagination. Ellis Ashmead-Bartlett, who worked for the 'Daily Telegraph', covered the landing at Anzac Cove on 25th April and succeeded rather better when reporting back to antipodean readers. He had gone ashore at Anzac Cove at 2130hrs on the evening of the landing and, wearing a non-regulation green hat, was promptly arrested as a spy but was released when the boatswain who had brought him ashore testified for him. He was responsible for the first eyewitness accounts of the battle and his report of the landing was published in Australian newspapers on 8th May, before the reports of the Australian correspondent, C E W Bean. His colourful prose, unrestrained by the pursuit of accuracy which hampered Bean's dispatches, was thick with praise for the Anzacs and went down well with Australian and New Zealand audiences:

"There has been no finer feat in this war than this sudden landing in the dark and storming the heights, and, above all, holding on while the reinforcements were landing. These raw colonial troops, in these desperate hours, proved worthy to fight side by side with the heroes of Mons, the Aisne, Ypres and Neuve Chapelle."

These and other dispatches would help create the ANZAC myth.

But Ashmead-Bartlett's London dispatches were boring and, in his opinion, full of lies after they had been under the censor's pen. He was becoming highly critical in his reports of the British commander-in-chief, General Hamilton, which left him in disfavour with Sir Ian. The turning point came when instead of returning to the Dardanelles from Malta, he went to London, arriving on 6th June, to report in person to his paper on the conduct of the campaign and, for the first time in ages, to write a true report on the state of things at Gallipoli, but this naturally fell foul of the censor.

Ashmead-Bartlett now had the bit between his teeth and was not going to give in. During his time in London, he met with most of the senior political figures including the First Lord of the Admiralty and Lord Kitchener. He was building up a network of useful acquaintances to increase his options for getting the true story out in the public domain. His views and activities had not gone unnoticed in the Eastern Mediterranean. When he returned to Gallipoli, he was placed on the island of Imbros near Hamilton's headquarters where he could be kept an eye on, but he did manage to witness the new landing at Suvla during the August Offensive:

'Confusion reigned supreme. No-one seemed to know where the headquarters of the different brigades and divisions were to be found. The troops were hunting for water, the staffs were hunting for their troops, and the Turkish snipers were hunting for their prey.'

Ashmead-Bartlett had obtained a movie camera while in London with which he captured the only film footage of the battle. On 21st August he was watching from Chocolate Hill when the British IX Corps launched the final attack of the campaign, the Battle of Scimitar Hill.

When Australian journalist Keith Murdoch[87] arrived at Gallipoli in September 1915, Ashmead-Bartlett found a receptive audience for his commentary and analysis of the campaign. Murdoch travelled to London carrying a letter written on 8th September from Ashmead-Bartlett addressed to the British Prime Minister, H H Asquith. It presented his uncensored report of the situation on Gallipoli. Hamilton quickly learned about the existence of this letter (another British reporter, Henry Nevinson, has been blamed for this) which damned the campaign, describing the final offensive as:

'the most ghastly and costly fiasco in our history since the Battle of Bannockburn'.

This private letter, intended for Asquith, was intercepted in Marseilles, when Murdoch was arrested by military police and forced to hand it over. Hamilton wasted no time and ordered Ashmead-Bartlett to leave Gallipoli immediately and he, on his return to London, gave an "interview" to the 'Sunday Times' or, more exactly, an "opinion piece" presented as an interview to circumvent censorship rules. Published on 17th October, it was the first detailed account of the campaign and was widely circulated, appearing in 'The Times' and the 'Daily Mail' as well as in Australian papers.

On hearing the whole saga, Asquith demanded the letter from Hamilton but it could not be found. He agreed with Ashmead-Bartlett that he could write a private letter to his Prime Minister and that the General had no

---

[87] Father of Rupert Murdoch, the media baron of today.

right to intercept or stop that letter. Murdoch meanwhile spent some time at the Australian High Commission in London composing his own letter to his Prime Minister, Andrew Fisher, in a similar vein to the Ashmead-Bartlett letter and particularly critical of the British general and administrative staff. Due to the integrity of these two reporters, the real story of the carnage at Gallipoli was to come out and into the hands of the public. This was definitely a case of 'lions led by donkeys'. For these two reporters, this was a time when the pen was mightier than the sword. The power of the press would now bring about the end of Sir Ian Hamilton's military career, as time and time again he tried to play down what had been written about him and his campaign.

Meanwhile, back in Gallipoli, the air war continued. In the first week of September some 81 flights were carried out by the combined RNAS air group but by the end of the first week of September the weather was not good which affected their activities. The 'Ark Royal' put up six flights for a total of 7hrs 40 minutes, made up of two reconnaissance and four spotting flights, which is still not a great show. The 'Ben-my-Chree' also made six flights: two spotting, two reconnaissance and two practice flights. The 'Hector' only managed two spotting missions and was up for only up for 95 minutes in total in this first week due to the weather. 2 Wing were still finding their feet, so were carrying out a number of training flights. They made 5 visual reconnaissances and one spotting, 10 photographic and 21 training flights, a total of 25hrs 45 minutes in the air. The last of the air group, 3 Wing, carried out eight reconnaissance, 12 spotting, four bombing and two practice missions, giving them a total of 40 hours and 41minutes in the air. This meant that in this week the air group was up for over 79 hours and out of that, over 66 hours was done by the aeroplane.[88]

When 2 Wing arrived at Imbros, it had two photographers and four automatic cameras as the importance of photographic sorties had grown. By August this kind of mission had been divided into four separate types:

1. trench lines
2. photographs for the mapping section of the terrain
3. maps of gun emplacements
4. maps of forts, towns, camps and villages

Photographs continued to be taken for the map makers until December 1915 as the original maps were so inaccurate. New photographs of the Turkish trenches were taken almost every day as they changed and showed any new movements by the enemy. To give an idea of the work involved, the Anzac/Suvla front was 12 miles long and each photograph covered just 1,000yds. It required 216 photographs to cover the trench line and the rear areas including the gun positions.

---

[88] TNA: AIR 1/361/15/228/50

The light conditions over Gallipoli were very good and made objects stand out clearer there than on the Western Front. It was found the evening light provided the most extraordinary visibility and that this was the best time to locate and closely observe enemy batteries. On occasions immediately after sunset, batteries in the Krithia area could clearly be seen from 4,000ft and two miles out. For a considerable period after the first landings, the Navy required constant reconnaissance flights to be made daily:

a) Watching the shipping in the Straits.
b) Close observation of the forts and any changes in their armament.
c) Search for howitzers and guns used to fire at ships and minesweepers.
d) Close watch on the submarine nets at Nagara.

Military reconnaissance consisted of:

1) Long strategical reconnaissance flights to Malgara, Keshan, etc., and over the whole peninsula, watching for troop movements and the formation of new camps.
2) Daily dawn reconnaissance flights over known batteries, looking for any changes.
3) Road reconnaissance twice a day watching for any large movements of supplies or men.
4) Frequent flights over Ak Bashi Liman and Kilia Liman were made during the day and night looking at supplies being landed.

From time to time special reconnaissance flights were made, for example when the Army believed that a narrow-gauge railway was being built in the Keshan-Uzun Keupri area.

Commander L'Estrange Malone, captain of the 'Ben-my-Chree', and Lieutenant-Commander Archibald Cochrane, captain of submarine E7, came up with a plan to bomb the arsenal at Constantinople. The plan was simple and very daring. The E7 would pass through the Dardanelles and surface at a given time in the Sea of Marmora, while at the right time the 'Ben-my-Chree' would launch a seaplane fully bombed-up. The aircraft would fly over the Bulair Lines and then go hunting for the E7. On spotting each other, the seaplane would land alongside and the submarine would wet itself down, slide under the seaplane and fully surface. E7 would then carry the seaplane to within 30 miles of Constantinople where it would take off, bomb the arsenal and return to the submarine, refuel and return to the ship. This might sound an impossible, not to mention mad, idea but trials were actually undertaken with a seaplane to establish its centre of gravity on the submarine. It was lifted on by the deck crane of the 'Ben-my-Chree' and after balance was achieved, both the aircraft and the submarine were marked up to allow them to match up easily on the day of the operation. However, due to the sinking of the E7 on 4th September, this mission did not happen, so we will never know whether this incredible idea would have worked. It was not until 9th July 1917 that Constantinople was bombed, when the RNAS brought out from England one of its 'Bloody Pulverisers', a Handley Page O/100, which was flown by Squadron Commander K S Savory. The raid was launched from the airfield on Mudros.

On Thursday 2nd September the 'Ben-My-Chree' made a vital contribution to the war totally outside her aerial duties. She had weighed anchor at 0935hrs and was making ready to move out of the anchorage at Mudros when at 0950hrs an SOS was received from the troopship SS 'Southland' (11,899 tons). She had been torpedoed and was sinking with 1,400 men on board some 30 miles from Mudros and over 2 hours steaming from the anchorage. The German submarine UB14 had hit the 'Southland' with its last torpedo on the port side between holds 1 and 2, killing at least nine men in the initial explosion, and the ship began to settle by the head. Commander L'Estrange Malone demanded and got full steam ahead and as the 'Ben-my-Chree' passed the boom she was starting to fly to the rescue of the 'Southland'. Fly is the word – the ship was going 4 knots faster than she had ever been intended to go! Just before noon 'All Stop' was called as they were coming into the rescue zone. In the last hour the crew of the 'Ben-My Chree' had cleared the decks, all boats were swung out and manned, and all ladders, ropes and nets were hung over the side. Empty petrol cans, lifebuoys, floats and rafts were piled high on deck ready to throw into the water. The hospital ship 'Neuralia' had been the first at the scene and had made ready most of its beds on board to take the injured men but had not lowered any of its boats. Now the 'Ben-my- Chree' slipped through towards the troopship.

Unfortunately the 'Southland' was mostly manned by a scratch crew, picked up in Egypt. Many of them, stokers especially, rushed the first boats and caused havoc. Some were shot for looting, while other crewmen tried to take boats at the point of a gun and were shot. However, one crew member, 'an old sailor', showed an example of true seamanship and was badly injured while working hard to lower the boats. One of the davit ropes kept jamming in the pulley block. He tried to put it right and, as the boat was raised clear, it swung heavily outwards crushing him against the davit. He fell unconscious and was lifted into the boat by the Australian soldiers before it was lowered to the water.

Now the 'Ben-my-Chree's boats swung into action. The first, under the command of Flight Commander Edmunds, hit the water at 1215hrs followed by the second, commanded by Lieutenant Stern, at 1220hrs. Both motor launches proceeded to go alongside overcrowded rafts and boats, putting men into the empty boats they were towing. Twenty-one rafts and ship's boats were picked up by the 'Ben-my-Chree', carrying a total of 814 men, a large number of whom required some basic first aid. The ship was now full and survivors were taken to other ships that had answered the SOS and were now coming into the area of the survivors in the water. With more ships arriving, L'Estrange Malone gave the order to recover the motor boats, especially as there was the threat of a German sub in the area, and then ordered full speed. At 1442hrs she set off at full speed for Mudros, entering the harbour there at 1650hrs to a full Royal Marines band playing and all the men from the other ships cheering her. The 'Ben-my-Chree' was ordered alongside the troopship 'Transylvania' and for the next two hours transferred all the survivors she was carrying.

With most of the men off the 'Southland', Captain Kelk felt he could save his ship with the help of some volunteers. Nineteen men went down to the boilers, headed by Captain Nelson Wellington of the 21st Battalion, who received the Legion of Honour for his work this day. Lieutenant Crowther was in charge of a party of nine men, working under the direction of a ship's engineer, who started shovelling coal onto 32 fires. It took them some 90 minutes to raise the steam pressure from 70lb to 200lb. But they did it and the ship moved off slowly towards the anchorage at Mudros escorted by HMS 'Racoon'. When she reached the anchorage some stokers from other ships were put on board to take over from the Army volunteers. Not surprisingly, the soldiers were really pleased to see the sailors and gladly passed the task to them. On deck they were greeted by the captain who treated them all to a slap-up chicken dinner.[89] The 'Southland' was beached out of the way, all the equipment on board being salvaged later along with some £30,000 in the ship's safe.

On 4th September, Petty Officer Photographic Mechanic William Pollard came off the 'Ark Royal' with enough camera fittings for four aeroplanes and these were fitted later that day. The next day 2 Wing started to carry out practice photo-reconnaissance flights. The photographic unit had a makeshift dark room that was unsatisfactory in the wind as the canvas would move and let light in, so getting hold of several locals, Pollard set about designing and then building a stone dark-room. This proved to be one of the strongest buildings on the airfield and stood up to many a storm.

In late August the 'Ark Royal' had been called on by the Army to supply emergency drinking water to the ANZAC beach as they were desperately short. Again in September the Army was running out of water and, as it had a desalination plant, the 'Ark Royal' was called on once more. Small boats turned up carrying hundreds of empty fuel cans that had been used for the transport of water last time. 'Ark Royal' filled the tins, passing the full ones to the small boats and off they would go, only to return with more empty cans. This went on all day and would happen a few more times before the end of the month.

All of 'Ark Royals' seaplanes were now operating from the Ark Royal Bluff

---

[89] TNA: ADM 1/8432/263

(Aliki Bay). They were all of the same type: Short Type 166 or Short Type C seaplanes with 200hp Canton Unné engines, which was proving to be a far more reliable aircraft than any of the others so far sent to the 'Ark Royal'. These seaplanes had been designed to carry a torpedo but in fact never did, the additional power simply helping them to become reliable. 'Ark Royal' had been issued with five of these machines, Nos 161-165, and one more would join this little band in September. On 5th September Short Type C No 162 left the 'Ark Royal' and joined HMS 'Earl of Peterborough', a monitor with two 12-inch guns, and would remain with the 'Peterborough' until the end of September.

On the whole, the life of the men from the 'Ark Royal' at Ark Royal Bluff was very good and very relaxed, and they were happy. A number of visiting officers remarked that the men were distinctly cheery; they just got on with the job and there was a lack of orders being shouted. They lived in bell tents with one or two stone-built buildings constructed by the locals, one of which was a mess for the pilots and the other a signals station that was built into the sand dunes for added protection. The serviceability of the seaplanes had greatly improved in the C Type. This again cheered up the men and, in one of those circular affects you find in these circumstances, even better serviceability resulted from the more positive attitude of the mechanics. General servicing was done on the beach, which gave the men a lot of elbow room in which to work. For anything serious, the seaplane was taken back either to the 'Ark Royal', or to SS 'Penmorvah', an ex-collier. The 'Ark Royal' was a spacious ship but when the need came to work on more than two seaplanes, there was just not the room so the deck of the 'Penmorvah' was used as well.

On 6th September Sir Ian Hamilton fired his Chief Intelligence Officer, Lieutenant Colonel M C P Ward. Hamilton felt he had been given bad intelligence but this was surely a case of the bad workman blaming his tools. If he had only come out from behind his desk to look at the good intelligence supplied to his Headquarters by Lieutenant Isaac and 3 Wing, he would have found his answers and where he should have attacked. He seems simply to have been too old and set in his ways to grasp the new technology of photographic aerial intelligence, a science that could have revolutionised the campaign for him if he had only understood it and used it. Instead of claiming that he had no support from the RNAS and deriding them to the Admiralty, he should have being praising them to the heights for their help and support.

Lieutenant Harry Strain was given a change of job, leaving the 'Ark Royal' and joining Sykes in his HQ. Here he acted as the main Intelligence Officer, collecting daily reports from all the flying units, and was also supposed to act as Operations Officer for them. In this role he was supposed to identify possible targets and then distribute the missions to the various units, using copy of Isaac's photographic map to pinpoint them but all the units ignored his orders as they were contacted directly by the Navy.

It was about this time that Sykes began to fall out with the Admiralty. He was demanding the extra aeroplanes and seaplanes that he thought, wrongly, he had been promised by them. The Air Department, on the other hand, believed he already had some 89 aeroplanes and 19 seaplanes on charge. If only that had been true! From then on, Sykes launched a weekly dispatch off to the Admiralty in London on this matter, which the Admiralty, not surprisingly, took umbrage to. Admiral de Roebuck was contacted and was told to put him in his place and explain the chain of command to him. It was the beginning of the end for Sykes as far as the RNAS and the Navy were concerned.

Before that happened, Sykes was still making efforts to win himself the glory he undoubtedly believed should be his. Soon after Strain joined him, they came up with the idea of starving the Turks in the field to make them pull out of the peninsula. The plan was to take a monitor up into the Gulf of Xeros with a spotting seaplane on its deck and destroy the four flour mills in the town of Gallipoli, whose flour supplied some 77,000 loaves of bread per day for the Turkish Army. Sykes ordered a couple of reconnaissance missions and one photographic mission over the area. Once the mills were spotted, the operation was on. Admiral de Robeck agreed to the plan and Strain decided he would go as observer for the pilot, Flight Lieutenant C W Pulford. He presumably justified this on the basis that he was one of the authors of the plan but unfortunately he had no experience of spotting gunfire for a ship or of using a wireless in the air, but still he went. De Robeck, on hearing that Strain had gone as the observer, sent another seaplane up to act as the main spotter for HMS 'Raglan', a 14-inch twin-gun monitor. The new spotting seaplane arrived over the target area and then made contact with the 'Raglan'. Strain and his pilot were by now on the water and taking off just as the 'Raglan' opened fire with its first round. Strain found the spotting of ship's fire onto a target frustratingly slow and then he and his pilot had to land due to engine problems. He found out a few days later that none of the mills had been damaged or knocked out.

Both Sykes and Strain felt the operation had been bungled and they could have done better. It seems fairly certain that they were both glory hunting and had been seduced by the delusion that they and they alone would cause the Turkish Army to pull back and so win the battle for Gallipoli. They now came up with a second mission to get the mills. This was set for 2nd October and this time the 'Hector' and its monitor M.16 were used, but still the flour mills were not hit. They were bracketed but not put out of action. Sadly the reason was the inexperience of the two officers who formed the plan. If Strain had read the photographs of the mills correctly, he would have noticed a high ridge between the mills and the Gulf of Xeros where the attacks were made from. To clear the ridge, the gun fire missed the target, but those shells that were on the correct trajectory to hit the target crashed into the ridge.

The seaplanes of the 'Ark Royal' were given HMS 'Edgar' to support, so in this first week of September they took the Gunnery Officer up to show him his targets and their precise location in relation to the landmarks he could see from his ship. Short seaplane No 164 and a fresh crew were sent to Rabbit Island to support the monitor 'Roberts' on 3rd September, when seaplane No 841 returned, but poor weather put paid to several days spotting for seaplane No 3722. On 9th September 'Ben-my-Chree' launched seaplane No 846 at 1505hrs and she carried out an in-depth reconnaissance of the area from Ejelmer Bay to the Bulair Lines, three hours seven minutes from take-off to landing. They reported on transport, camps and shipping in the upper straits. As a Submarine Scout airship was finishing its work-up in this first week of September, it was clear that there was a problem with the engine noise. Because of this, not only it could be heard from miles away but also its crew could not talk to each other. Never a problem without a solution for the RNAS! A truck silencer was found that would work when fitted to the airship, rendering it inaudible at close range.

It was a good job that the 'Roberts' was operating near Rabbit Island as Samson had taken off just after lunch one day on a reconnaissance flight over the Asiatic side of the Dardanelles and suddenly realised he had lost track of time on his flight. He was running out of time and fuel to get back to his airfield. Just as his engine cut out, he managed to land on Rabbit Island. There had been no time to choose a good landing spot but he made it and he and his aeroplane were fine, so now all he had to do was wait for the 'Roberts' to come into sight and be rescued. The 'Roberts' sent out some spare fuel to him and he was able to return to Imbros, where his Wing was by now were very worried that he had gone down in the sea and were about to mount a search.

If the RNAS air raids made the Turkish Army change its pattern of operation for fear of attack, the Turkish artillery had the same effect on the Allied ships off the coast. For two days 'Levant' had been carrying out repairs to the cable off Anzac, finishing early on the morning of 9th September and, in the words of its diarist:

'cleared out before day-light to avoid the indignity of being driven out by Turkish shell fire when the enemy saw us after sunrise. It is rather amusing to watch the general exodus of ships from Anzac waters in the early hours of the morning. No ship can safely remain near the coast. We came to Kephalo and remained at anchor for the night.'

The next day they made their way to Mudros to collect food and other supplies. The 'Hector' had tried twice to carry out some spotting in the first week of September but due to the poor weather had to give it up and remain in harbour. The second time the 'Hector' launched its balloon a

Turkish gun opened fire on the ship from a range of some 12,000yds. As the exact position of the gun was not known this would turn out to be a job first of all for a visual reconnaissance mission and then possible a photographic reconnaissance.

The weather took a turn for the worse from 7th September onwards. By the 9th the winds were very strong and blowing Force 5 from the north-east and the sea state was short steep waves, which made keeping station at sea almost impossible and as for launching seaplanes, this was impossible. By Sunday 12th September the winds had reached Force 7 and nearly all ships had been driven back into a safe anchorage. The period between the 8th and Wednesday 15th September was bad for flying. 2 Wing had managed to carry out 37 missions, a total of 25 hours and 45 minutes in the air, before the weather turned bad and low cloud and dust storms made life very difficult. During the week of the storm they only managed 14 flights: six reconnaissance, two spotting, three bombing and three practice flights, a total time-in-the-air of just 12hrs 50 minutes. 3 Wing were not much better, as it was just far too dangerous when coming in to land, managing only 14hrs 30 minutes[90] in the air. The operations they managed to carry out were three reconnaissance, four spotting, one photo-reconnaissance, two bombing attacks and one practice flight. Both 2 and 3 Wing ground crews were struggling with the weather to erect two large Bessonneau hangers that had come out with Gerrard's Wing.

There were brighter moments in the storms. On 8th September Samson was delighted by the return of Flight Lieutenant Butler, who had been wounded. He now felt he had his old gang back together again. This gave 3 Wing a strength of eight pilots: Samson, Bell Davies, Thomson, Marix, Newton-Clare junior[91], Butler, Morrison and Young. One of the Greek workmen on Imbros knew the Wings were having problems due to the poor weather and took action to help improve things. On 12th September the local priest turned up at the airfield. He had come to bless the men and flying machines of 2 and 3 Wings and the balloons, as he felt they might need a little of God's help.

The tail end of the storm was still kicking up a lot of dust and making reconnaissance very difficult, a problem exacerbated by the amount of low cloud. It was due to this low cloud and dust that Newton-Clare almost came to grief. He had come down low over the ANZAC area while carrying out a reconnaissance when he was hit by AA fire and was forced to land on the Salt Lake at Suvla, banging his head badly on landing and dazing himself. As soon as his aeroplane came to rest, the Turks opened fire with their artillery which gave him quite a start, and, dizziness forgotten, he got out

---

[90] TNA: AIR 1/361/15/228/50
[91] Flight Lieutenant Walter Shackfield Newton-Clare

and ran to the safety of the Australian lines. That night he returned to his aeroplane or what was left of it and, with the aid of several strong Australians, salvaged the engine and a few instruments.

On 12th September the weather improved, whether due to divine intervention or not is impossible to say, and the 'Levant' was able to start work on repairing HMS 'Europa's cables. While at Mudros on the 13th, 'Levant' laid new cables from the shore to SS 'Aragon' and to SS 'Minnetonka'. The former was the GHQ and was rather disliked in Mudros harbour. It replaced SS 'Arcadian', well remembered for the luxury on board, contrasting with the hardships endured by the thousand acting under her orders. 'Minnetonka', the Army store's ship, provided khaki clothing for the crew of the 'Levant' so they did not look out of place when ashore.

Once the storm had passed the RNAS and the Navy could catch up on spotting and reconnaissance missions that had to be cancelled. The cruisers and destroyers had started to bombard the Turkish trenches in the early morning and late afternoon, attacking a different target each time. This kept the Turks busy repairing trenches.

The Admiral had decided that because the 'Manica' was beginning to show her age, needing a new balloon and several other repairs, she should go home for a refit. A new ship had been purchased by the Admiralty on 28th June 1915 to replace her in the Dardanelles. On 29th June this vessel was renamed HMS 'Canning' and went in for a refit at Birkenhead between June and September 1915 to turn her into a kite balloon ship. 'Canning' was the largest balloon ship to date at 5,375 tons and could carry a fully-inflated balloon in the hold, a definite improvement on her predecessors. Meanwhile, in the early hours of 13th September 'Manica' slipped her moorings and headed towards Malta and hence on to Birkenhead for a refit by Cammell, Laird & Company. Work included a replacement balloon platform, additional firepower and facilities for operating a seaplane. Flight Commander Mackworth, 'Manica's commander, reported to the Admiralty, where his expertise in kite balloon ships was now much sought after, and he was recommended for the DSO, but a requested 'summary and appreciation' of his work in the 'Manica' never reached the appropriate authority, as a result of which no further action was taken (his service record refers). He did, however, receive further advancement to the acting rank of Wing Captain in December 1917, was awarded the CBE in the following year, and served later on the Staff of the newly-established Royal Air Force, in the rank of Temporary Colonel, before becoming an Air Vice Marshal.[92]

---

[92] TNA: ADM 137/177

Two small SS (Sea Scout or Submarine Scout) non-rigid airships were now fully ready (No 3 and No 19) and by mid-September started to carry out patrols over land and sea. A third SS Airship (No 7) arrived at Imbros on 13th September and as it had a number of improvements over the other two, it was very quickly filled and got into the air. On the 15th it carried out the first night flight and it proved to be very successful at this type of work as the cooking fires showed up well and it could not be heard on the ground as it was fitted with a silencer. The bombs it carried were duly dropped but what or if they hit anything is in question. Colonel Sykes had originally proposed a force of eight 'Blimps', as they were sometimes affectionately known, but in the event, only one was put into service at a time. On a designated flying day, the airship would go up three times, each time with a different crew on board, and this way all the airship aircrew got a chance at spotting and general reconnaissance duties. The operational SS survived several bombing attacks against its shed by the Turks at Imbros until 21st October, when the SS Section was transferred to Mudros. The main reason for the move was that the prevailing winds on Imbros were not at all good for handling airships. In fact, Imbros was a bad place to base any form of aviation.

Now there was one of those 'what if' moments. On 13th September, just east of Suvla, Kemal Pasha, later known to the world as 'ATATÜRK', the founder of the modern Turkish state, just escaped being killed when his staff car was attacked by a Nieuport aircraft flown by Samson. The latter saw the car and knew it had to be someone important as there were very few cars on the road. He dived down and let go two of his three 20lb bombs but missed the vehicle, which had braked hard, allowing the occupants to get out in a great hurry and dive into a nearby culvert. Samson flew off. Twenty minutes later they decided it was safe to resume their journey, got back into their car and drove off just as Samson returned, diving at full speed, and let go his last bomb. It just missed the car but peppered it with shrapnel. Kemal Pasha survived and, as they say, the rest is history.

On 16th September with the help of the 'Hector', M.19 managed to locate a Turkish gun that had been placed in a tunnel in a hill on Abdel Rahman Bair. The ship's fire managed to collapse one of the tunnels trapping the gun and crew inside. However, the 'Hector's balloon was damaged due to the poor weather and she was sent back to Malta to make repairs to both the ship itself and the balloon in the safety of a good harbour. When she returned to Imbros a week later she was carrying a number of trucks for RNAS HQ and both Wings. On the 18th the M.19 had another go at the concealed artillery in the tunnels at Abdel Rahman Bair. She moved in close and fired at the tunnels with her one 9-inch gun and one of her shells landed on the top of the tunnels, sealing them both up.

After the attack on 30th August by monitor M.15 with Samson and Jopp acting as the spotters, the Turks had moved the unloading of supply ships to the hours of darkness. However, at first they lit the working area with flares and large fires in braziers, which could be seen by the pilots of the RNAS from several thousand feet and were often bombed as was the case on the night of 16th/17th September, when the whole Wing took part in a night attack. They started several large fires and destroyed a lot of supplies. After this date, the Turks used hand-held lanterns to light the work area at night and no heating braziers were allowed. The men just had to work harder or wrap up warm with extra clothing.

The Turkish air force had not been deterred by the raids on its airfields and had been bombing the anchorage at Kephalo and the airship shed for the last two weeks. Both Samson and Gerrard had send aeroplanes up to try to intercept the raiders but had so far failed to do so. On 16th September the Turks launched a surprise attack on the airship shed at 0745hrs using three aeroplanes. They dropped seven small bombs, the closest of which was 350 yards away from the shed, and a load of darts. No damage was done but pride was inevitably dented. The airship section proved it was business as usual when the duty airship was pulled out and the first crew went up for an hour, landing back at 1620hrs. The next flight was carried out by Lieutenant John Wheelwright as pilot and Admiral de Robeck as observer. Wheelwright took the Admiral close to the enemy positions and then flew him over his own ship.

Samson, Gerrard and Césari, the commander of MF 98 T, the French squadron on Tenedos, decided it was time to put the enemy in his place once again. Raiding RNAS airfields, or French ones, should be swiftly and firmly discouraged. They came up with a plan to destroy the Turkish airfield yet again and took off early on the 16th but the Turkish aeroplanes were not at home. A few bombs were dropped on the airfield's hangers and other buildings as a warning and they bombed targets of opportunity like several large camps and supply depots they had spotted so as not to make it a wasted trip.

The 'Levant' left Tenedos at day-break on the 16th and was off Kephalo at 0830hrs. A flag signal was made to her from the beach saying that the cables they had come to repair were now working and testing perfect and that ship should proceed to Cape Helles where another repair awaited her. The journey from Kephalo was therefore fruitless and the crew were rather annoyed that had been brought so far for nothing, though pleased to know the cables had righted themselves. The ship left immediately and arrived off Cape Tekeh after lunch and started cable work. Luckily today the beach was not being shelled and they worked in peace. Towards evening a strong wind and sea got up and they had to leave the job only half done. The 'Levant' was able to return to Helles on the 18th as the weather improved, leaving the anchorage at day-break and arriving at Cape Helles before breakfast. Now their luck broke. They found their marker buoy had disappeared so had to start the repair again from scratch. This took until about 1700hrs when they returned to Tenedos.

Due to a shortage of rifles, it was decided on 17th September to salvage a number had been lost off Walker's Ridge Pier. This work could only be carried out in the dark as it was close to the Turkish positions and was within sniper range. Mr Ward, the gunner from the 'Bacchante', was in charge and was wounded in the shoulder but the diving party managed to recover 2,892 rifles out of 3,000 that had been lost over the side and 1,800 sword bayonets. Another diving party was sent over to the ANZAC area on the evening of the 19th to dive off the pier looking for some several hundred 6-inch shells had been lost overboard by the Army on landing. After several days of searching and dragging the sea bed, no sign of the lost ammunition could be found.

General Birdwood came over to Imbros early on the 19th to meet up with General Hamilton. After the meeting in the mid-afternoon he went over to the SS airship shed and asked for a flight, which was possible as it had just landed from a patrol. They had not been up long when an artillery 'hate' was opened on the Australian lines by the Turks, starting at 1705hrs and for no good reason. Birdwood wanted a look but not in an airship, as it was too large and too slow. He was dropped off at 3 Wing. Samson was quickly put in the picture and had a Maurice Farman started and took off with the General at 1720hrs. They flew up to the ANZAC area and he had a good look at what was going on, returning at 1810hrs. Samson felt he had been neglecting No 50, his faithful old aircraft, so had it bombed up and took it up that evening to attack shipping in the Berghaz Liman area. One of 3 Wing's aeroplanes had been up earlier in the day spotting for HMS 'Humber', a 6-inch twin-gun monitor that had been called in to hit a supply dump. After a few rounds the Turks started to try to jam the wireless signal, but it did not stop the 'Humber' getting several direct hits on the dump. After dinner that night Samson and Edwards took a Maurice Farman up and attacked the shipping in the Berghaz Liman area again with four 20lb bombs. Samson had now carried out five and a half hours flying that day in four different aeroplanes. It was this sort of determination and dedication that made Samson, and 3 Wing, special.

During the storm period the 'Ben-my-Chree' had been ordered to return to Mudros to have her gun positions strengthened and improved as she was to go on a special mission for Admiral de Robeck[93] On the 16th she moved from Mudros up and into the Gulf of Xeros and several spotting operations were carried out with the monitor M.16, which had a main armament of a single 9.2-inch gun. On 18th September Flight Lieutenant Dacre and his observer Lieutenant Childers took off at 1553hrs in seaplane No 842 from

---

[93] TNA: ADM 137/177

the 'Ben-my-Chree' spotting for the M.16. Their target was the large floor mill that was producing much of the bread flour for the Turkish Army on Gallipoli that Sykes and Strain had been after. The mill was shelled for over an hour and hit several times, before they landed back at 1715hrs. On the 19th, seaplane No 842 was up at 0640hrs with the same crew and spotting yet again for monitor M.16. They very quickly found their target and destroyed it with just five rounds. The seaplane looked for some other targets but found none so returned to the ship at 0825hrs, having conclusively proved to anyone with an open mind that experienced spotters could play a vital part in warfare. How Sykes took the news is not recorded.

Samson was out on a reconnaissance flight with Isaac on the 19th when they were hit by a piece of shrapnel. On the way back the engine gave out and they were forced down into the water, where they were rescued by one of the many small ships in the area and brought back to Imbros. Samson dried himself off and after dinner went up to attack some of the camp fires at Kilia Liman. The next night Samson had yet another close shave when he was acting as observer for Bell Davies in a Henri Farman. They had found the target and bombed it but the engine started to misfire while returning to base. Davies managed to nurse the aeroplane back and they just managed to touch down before the engine finally gave out.

The week ending 21st September had been an extremely busy time for the air units as they made up for air time lost during the storm. It was during this week that 2 Wing officially became operational. The 'Ark Royal' carried out seven reconnaissance flights and four practice flights, a total of 11hrs 40 minutes in the air. This was a massive amount of time in the air for the 'Ark Royal' seaplanes, now operating from the Ark Royal Bluff. The 'Ben-my-Chree' carried out two reconnaissance flights, two spotting missions and a single bombing attack, with a total of 7hrs 22 minutes in the air. The SS airships carried out a night flight and nine other flights with a total of 6hrs 40 minutes in the air. 2 Wing carried out five reconnaissance missions, three spotting flights, four bombing attacks, four photographic missions, one anti-aeroplane patrol and nine practice flights. 3 Wing carried out more flights and time in the air than all the air units combined: six reconnaissance flights, four spotting flights, one photographic mission, 20 bombing attacks, two air patrols, and two practice flights, a total time in the air of 39hrs 45 minutes. This gave the air group a total air time of 77 hrs 48 minutes.[94] Over the week they dropped fifty-eight 20lb bombs and six 100lb bombs. During this period, the RNAS carried out 85 flights in support of the Army and the fleet, not a bad work rate for a group of men who were doing nothing! The main reason for the photographic flights was to keep the intelligence map of the Turkish trenches up to date, just in case a ground operation was planned. The Turks had been suffering a lot of

---

[94] TNA: AIR 1/361/15/228/50

heavy and accurate bombardment on their supply landing places from the big-gun monitors supported by aeroplanes and seaplanes spotting for them so they moved nearly all supply drops by ship to the night and kept them out of range of the Army's guns, but not out of range of the aeroplanes and both 2 and 3 Wing carried out harassing night attacks.[95]

Samson and Gerrard's wings had two Bessonneau hangers each and these were becoming more and more important as the winter winds blew and the fine sand and dust blew around and was sucked into the Le Rhone engines of the aeroplanes. A proper stone built mess was also slowly rising. The driving force behind it was Isaac, who wanted to be able to eat a meal in the warm and without dust. The building was quickly finished and became a very popular meeting point for all the officers. The changing seasons were affecting the senior staff officers too. General Hamilton and the main GHQ moved camp into a number of Greek-built stone buildings. It was also decided that the RNAS HQ was to be moved closer to the Wings and the new position of GHQ. This meant that the RNAS HQ was in a complete mess until the end of the month, but this did not worry any of the air unit commanders - and in fact they enjoyed the peace and quiet.

Samson seemed to collect animals: two old artillery horses, eight mules and eight donkeys, all of which were housed in very splendid stables built in a gulley to give the animals extra protection. Along with all this motley lot was Samson's own horse, Nigger, which had once belonged to the German Army before being captured near Ypres. The donkeys supplied a bit of exercise for the men - they even carried out donkey races. They were also used as a means of transport to GHQ, that is, if they would work. There were times when the animal would take off like a racehorse and other times when it would just stand and 'not answer its helm or telegraphs'. But all the men enjoyed having the animals around. They found they could get a little bit of peace and just chill out for a few minutes.

Another favoured animal on the island was the humble duck. There were two or three large flocks and these became an important source of fresh meat. A number of officers from the fleet had been coming ashore to shoot them but Samson felt he had to protect 'his' ducks and an armed guard was placed on the pier to stop any officer coming ashore with shooting in mind. He put it around that some of the aeroplanes had been damaged by wild shooting and therefore it was now banned. He also issued a standing order that all game shot was for the pot and from August till the end of the year they bagged 105 head, including a number of rabbits and hares. Césari, on Tenedos with his French squadron, was very well-provisioned with food and wine and Samson and his officers would go and eat with the French

---

[95] TNA: ADM 137/177

when they could. No doubt about it, it was just so much better than their own food!

On Wednesday 22nd September the Turks carried out an air attack on the ANZAC position targeting the fresh water tanks, the only source of fresh water in the position for all the ANZAC troops. After this attack it was decided to camouflage the tanks with brushwood. The same day three Turkish aeroplanes attacked the airfield at Imbros. Some six bombs were dropped and all exploded but did no damage at all. These attacks continued. On 27th September Petty Officer Pollard was placed in the sick bay, which was nothing more than a converted aeroplane crate, on a bed that was a stretcher mounted on a couple of trestles. He was abruptly woken from his sleep by the whistle of a bomb coming down. The next thing he knew there were two explosions and his bed collapsed. This was the only damage caused by the Turkish air attack that day, except possibly a little to Pollard's dignity as he required a change of bedding!

Both Samson and Gerrard were worried about the quality of the observers that they were being sent from England and decided to run a course on observing. It was open to anyone from any of the Wings or artillery units and covered wireless operation, Aldiss lamp Morse and photographic interpretation, which would help them identify targets on the ground. A target raft was built for HMS 'Abercrombie' that was going to be used by the students for spotting practice and guiding the gun onto target. Samson also put the minds of his men to overcoming the problem of a single-seat aeroplane being used for photographic reconnaissance missions. What was required was a camera fitted with a rapid-change glass negative box, but all that were available were being sent to the Western Front. Petty Officer Pollard and some of the other photographic men had been working on an automatic glass slide changer for single-seat aeroplanes and, with the help of Bateman and some of the other engineering staff, came up with a system that worked. The first unit was fitted to an aeroplane of 3 Wing and the second was fitted to one of 'Ark Royal's seaplanes. Both units worked very well, and several more were built and fitted to other aeroplanes.

The weather was not good at all for the airships but several night flights were carried out, and on the 23rd when the moon was very bright SS-7 guided HMS 'Venerable' and HMS 'Talbot's gunfire onto a Turkish camp. While this could be seen in the moonlight, the explosions of the shells could not be spotted, and it was proposed that further experiments would be carried out on a darker night. Bombing missions were also carried out in the dark but the results could not been seen until daylight came. The wind was causing so much damage to the airship shed that spare parts had to be taken from one of the other kits just to repair the shed on Imbros. On the 25th, the SS-7 went up again at 2030hrs, cruised up to Suvla Bay after dark and started spotting again for the same ships, HMS 'Venerable' and HMS 'Talbot'. They were some 4,000ft up when the wireless decided to break down so the bombardment had to stop as they could not use the Aldiss lamp as it would give their position away to the AA guns. For the next two days, the Turks attacked the airship shed on Imbros. Fortunately, the closest they got with their bombs was within 175 yards.

Short seaplane No 164, which had been on Rabbit Island with HMS 'Edgar', had to be collected on 27th September and returned to the 'Ark Royal' as it had had major fabric damage done to it by the blast from the main armament. This was a constant problem with seaplanes carried on the monitors. Once the repairs to the fabric had been made, the aircraft flew back to Rabbit Island. The 'Hector', meanwhile, had returned from Malta but due to the weather remained in harbour.

The 'Ben-my-Chree' pulled out and moved up and into the Gulf of Xeros on the 27th so that an in-depth reconnaissance could be carried out from Teifur Keui to Kavak, especially of the railway lines. The seaplanes also carried bombs so when they came across a target of opportunity they could have a go. At 0802hrs and 0809hrs seaplanes No 3721 and 3722 were placed in the water and took off to carry out a bombing attack. At 0838hrs a Turkish aeroplane was spotted and the ship opened fire on it with its AA guns. The aircraft turned and flew away in the direction of Bulair and the airfield at Galata. The weather conditions were beginning to deteriorate so no further shoots could be carried out by monitor M.16 till the end of the month.

A new battery of 6-inch guns arrived at Helles for the Army and had to be ranged onto various targets, a job given to 2 Wing so they could gain some very valuable spotting practice. The SS 'Henry James' had also turned up at long last with all of 2 Wing's vehicles and other large bulky supplies and stores, plus two new pilots for 3 Wing, Lieutenant Gilbert F Smylie and Lieutenant Nicholson. Both men would turn out to be very good pilots and fitted in well with life in 3 Wing. All the spare men from both Wings and the 'Ark Royal' got stuck in top the job of unloading the ship and getting it all ashore. The 'Henry James' was also carrying one seaplane for the 'Ark Royal' and three Henry Farman aeroplanes for 3 Wing.

2 Wing carried out an in-depth reconnaissance of the Helles area, looking for any changes in gun positions or additions to the trench line both photographically and visually. 3 Wing carried out the same task over the ANZAC area of operations, between the other missions, including a number of deep-penetration bombing missions on supply depots and reserve area camps of the Turks. Reports from prisoners and other intelligence sources show that these attacks were causing a lot of damage, especially when they used the 100lb bomb. It was now very clear to Samson that an aeroplane that could lift four 100lb bombs was urgently required so that a larger punch could be delivered on the enemy. This he conveyed to the Air Department at the Admiralty in one of his reports.

The number of Turkish air attacks on Imbros had been increasing, striking 2 and 3 Wings areas, GHQ and RNAS HQ, and the airship shed. Samson increased the number of fighter patrols but this did not help. On the morning of 28th September one man was killed and another wounded in a Turkish air attack on 3 Wing. The dead man was Officer's Steward 1st Class W Garwood, Samson's batman, who had looked after Samson for a number of years from peacetime to war. This called for a spectacular retaliation. That afternoon Samson led ten aeroplanes from 3 Wing and MF 98 T to attack the Turkish airfields at Galata and Chanak. Galata was attacked with some fifteen 20lb bombs, all dropped on the tented encampment of the airfield. Chanak airfield was hit with four 100lb bombs and four 20lb bombs while the town of Chanak was also attacked with one 100lb bomb and four 20lb bombs. The 100-pounder hit a large house and badly damaged it.

During September, Samson carried out a number of experiments with machine-guns fitted to aeroplanes. He had given up his faithful No 50 as it had become too slow and too old and his main mount from now on was one of the new 80hp Nieuport Scouts, which had a top speed of 110mph and a maximum ceiling of 17,552ft. He had a Lewis gun fitted to this, the gun slotting into the upper wing at an angle of 45 degrees giving him the ability to attack enemy aeroplanes from below. Samson also wanted to fit Lewis guns to all pusher aeroplanes and carried out a number of experiments with these. After a bombing attack he would dive down on the target and the observer would open fire with the machine-gun, a manoeuvre that proved to be very effective. The one problem with the Nieuport was that the Le Rhone rotary engine attracted dust like bees to a honey pot, a really bad habit in this particular part of the world. One day the engine packed up on Bell Davies' Nieuport and he ended up in the water five miles short of Imbros. A trawler stopped and picked him up but his aircraft sank under tow. The loss of an aeroplane in the sea due to engine failure was becoming a regular thing.

With the advent of cooler weather the number of flies had gone down and due to this the sickness rate had decreased and on the whole the men were in very good spirits. Some projects that had been moving along at a snail's pace now picked up, one of which was the narrow-gauge railway. Samson wanted this constructed to link the airfields to the main pier. The first part of the railway was laid on the Ark Royal Bluff, running from the edge of the sea to the inland Salt Lake and allowing the seaplanes to be moved back in stormy conditions. The line was then extended from Ark Royal Bluff to 2 and 3 Wings' airfields while the last bit was down to the pier. This helped with the supply of petrol and many other things coming ashore. As they had no engine, the wagons were pulled by the mules but this was a great time saver and the men liked it.

The working-up had gone well for 2 Wing and they had just about found their feet. Now they were in a position to take over all the reconnaissance work for the Helles area and in a few more weeks they would be able to take over the ANZAC cover as well. This would leave Samson and 3 Wing free to carry out bombing attacks both locally and deep into enemy territory and to undertake deep reconnaissance of the Turkish lines of communications. Samson and Sykes both received a copy of Murray Sueter's telegram on 27th September, reporting that six Bristol Scout machines were being fitted with machine-guns and were due to leave Grain Island in ten days. These would be the first real fighter aircraft in the Dardanelles.

Sykes decided that he needed a senior Transport Officer so Lieutenant Marsden was sent to Mudros to fill the post. Part of his job was to secure passages back to England, as well as local transport to Alexandria. Sykes had also decided that he would open a central repair workshop for the aeroplanes. To staff it he took men from both squadrons, a move that did not go down at all well with both Wing Commanders nor with the men themselves. They would report in each morning and then drift back to their own workshops. In the end no aeroplanes were ever repaired in the central workshop.

A Turkish prisoner was sent over to Imbros with information that might be of use to the RNAS Wings. Isaac had a long chat with the man, who, it turned out, knew the location of Liman von Sanders HQ. He pinpointed the target on a map and gave it to Samson. The next thing Isaac knew was that six aeroplanes leapt into the air, all groaning under the weight of bombs they were carrying. The HQ was found and all the bombs were dropped on the tented encampment. After that von Sanders had to move his HQ on a regular basis as Samson kept finding it and delivering a devastating bombing attack on the tented village. Some of the operations against this target were combined attacks with either the French MF 98 T or 2 Wing or with both units coming along to add extra weight.

The month of September had been eventful and brought changes to all units in the area. For the crew of the 'Levant', Suvla Bay appeared at the beginning of September as the most delightful and peaceful anchorage they could possibly have and Captain Wightman discussed it as a possible base for the ship where they could rest after work at Anzac or Helles and enjoy the bathing free from shellfire. But by the end of the month this plan was definitely abandoned and they no longer looked upon Suvla as the delightful haven they at first thought it. Ships were shelled there more than anywhere else except Anzac and only a fool of a captain would anchor there in the daytime. Much as they disliked Mudros, the crew agreed that it was the only place in these waters where we they could drop anchor with a feeling that it would not be hurriedly hove up in the night and they could sleep peacefully in their bunks.

Commander Charles Rumney Samson on his horse, 'Nigger', in front of the inn in Tenedos village.

Flight Commander C H Collet in a DFW Mars, c1914

Flight Commanders Marix (left) and Thompson on Tenedos, Gallipoli, July 1915

Squadron Commander R Bell Davies

HMS Ark Royal

Ark Royal and Short seaplane Type 166 with Union flag national insignia

Deck view of crane at work with Sopwith Schneider seaplane, Ark Royal

Short Type 184 torpedo bomber seaplane

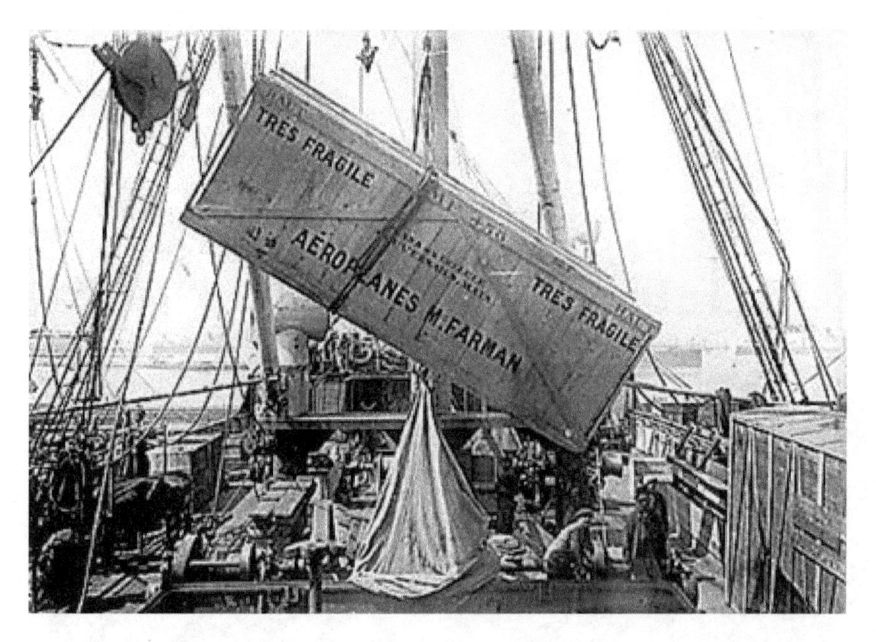

Unloading a Maurice Farman aeroplane. The aircraft might be 'Tres Fragile' but the crates were strong enough to be adapted to living quarters!

Unloading aeroplanes at Tenedos.

Taking aircraft up to the airfield from the beach on Tenedos.

Reggie Marix with his Farman

Samson with his Nieuport.

Samson enjoying a quiet moment.

Building gun pits for anti-aircraft guns. The Turkish prisoners of war willingly undertook jobs on the airfield, where they had food, shelter and relative safety.

HMS Manica with her balloon emerging from the hold

HMS Hector. Note bulge of balloon in forward hold.

Balloon aloft, showing observers' basket

HMS Ben-my-Chree, showing the large hangar-space aft

Short Type 184 alongside Ben-my-Chree. Roundel and tri-coloured tail insignia are clearly visible.

No 856, Type 860, taxiing away from Ben-my-Chree

Sir Ian Hamilton's HQ on Imbros

3 Wing's airfield on Imbros

2 Wing's airfield on Imbros

An unfortunate pilot falls victim to Imbros' crosswinds

An Avro 504B sent to No. 3 Wing at Imbros in late August 1915

Henri Farman F27, No. 3 Wing, Imbros

Maurice Farman No 33

A Voisin at rest

3 Squadron aircraft with one of their home-made bombs

Samson about to take off with the first 500lb bomb

Samson in his Nieuport

Chapter seven
October to December 1915

The first week of October had been a very busy time for the seaplanes of the 'Ark Royal'. They carried out five spotting missions, three photographic reconnaissances and five visual reconnaissances, in which they carried bombs ready for targets of opportunity, and all this work was carried out by just three seaplanes, which were in the air for a total of 12hrs 48 minutes. There was still one seaplane with the 'Roberts' at Rabbit Island and the other seaplane, No 164, was still being repaired, having been caught by the blast of the 'Roberts' main armament, which had stripped off a lot of the fabric. This had all now been replaced but still the aircraft was not flying right. A new seaplane had arrived, Short No 166, and was being erected; it would soon take its place in the Ark Royal Flight.

Co-operation between the two Wings was leading to increased efficiency in the use of the land aircraft. Samson and Gerrard together had come up with a standing patrol list which was very good for training flights. In the morning, patrols would be flown over the Straits, the immediate fronts of Suvla, Anzac and Helles, along the roads between Bulair and Boghali, and up the Asiatic shore up to Chanak. Photographic flights were better carried out in the early afternoon[96] so afternoons would be dedicated to spotting missions for the monitors and other ships unless a special target came up.

This co-operation extended to exchange of expertise. 2 Wing were due to carry out a large number of spotting flights this week but only eight were carried out and then all but one of these flights failed due to wireless problems. They were having a number of problems tuning in their wireless sets. In the end Gerrard asked Samson for help which he was only too pleased to give and lent 2 Wing his wireless expert, who in fact had come from the Royal Navy wireless section. Autumn was now here and its effects were being felt by the flyers. During this first week of October, the Wing carried out eight reconnaissance flights, and seven photographic flights over Suvla and Helles, but the results were not very good due to the weather conditions. Nevertheless, the Wing still managed to log 47hrs 16minutes in the air on 25 service flights and 22 wireless testing flights. One aeroplane was lost this week when a pilot suffered total engine failure on landing and crashed landed. Luckily the pilot was okay if a little shaken. The dust and sand was constantly causing problems. It got into your clothing, food, machine-guns, wireless sets and engines and this all resulted in a lot of extra servicing.[97] Another Bessonneau hanger was up and being used to service the aeroplanes in to keep out this invasive dust that made life so unpleasant.

---

[96] TNA: AIR 1/2284/209/75/11
[97] TNA: ADM 137/177

3 Wing were also having a busy time, spending some 56hrs 35 minutes in the air this week. They carried out 10 spotting flights, five reconnaissance flights, five photographic reconnaissance flights and also ten air patrols, as the Turkish air force was making a real nuisance of itself. They managed to chase off a number of Turkish aeroplanes but one or two got through and attacked the airship shed. The photographic reconnaissance patrols were from Suvla to ANZAC and the main task was to update the intelligence map. The Wing also carried out 28 bomb attacks on various targets, using a total of twelve 100lb bombs and forty-nine 20lb bombs, in all 2,180 pounds or just sixty pounds short of an imperial ton. One of Samson's pilots, Newton-Clare junior, had a close run thing. Late in the day on his way back from bombing Galata his engine stopped and he made a good landing on the Salt Lake under the Turkish guns. He managed to fix the fault and took off just as the first light was in the sky, heading back to Imbros where they all given him up for lost. It was a great relief that he made it back.

On 3rd October one of the Wing was up spotting for Monitor M.15; their target was the flour mills in the town of Gallipoli. They changed target after a few rounds had hit the ridge line behind the flour mills as it was clear they would do a lot of damage to the ridge but none to the flour mills. Now they focussed on shipping. With their second shot they hit a large tug that must have been loaded with ammunition as the explosion was very big. They also sank two small supply ships and a dhow.

The 'Hector', now fully repaired after the storm in which she was damaged, had sailed from Mudros back up to the anchorage at Kephalo, where HMS 'Canning' arrived on 2nd October. She was to relieve HMS 'Manica' which had already left for England and a major refit. But the two balloon ships would not carry out much spotting as due to the very poor weather they were unable to fly their balloons.

The bad weather that was hampering the balloon ships was also making cable work harder. The 'Levant' was having greater trouble repairing the broken cables due to the weather de-generating. On 2nd October she left Tenedos at 1100hrs for Kephalo, having received instructions to repair the Suvla cable there, and broken the previous night by a trawler. The damaged cable was quickly repaired and the ship remained outside Kephalo for the night. By 7th October the weather was too bad for cable work to continue and it was felt that 'Levant' should return to Mudros and seek shelter.

The 'Ben-my-Chree' was still in Mudros harbour carrying out a number of minor repairs and a general servicing of tired equipment, so it carried out no flying during this first week of October but the airships had a busy week and were up ten times. They now had two main patrol areas: one was from Rabbit Island to Mitylene and the other was Imbros, Lemnos and Strati. These were mainly anti-U-Boat patrols as this was the main danger to the fleet. They were in the air for 39hrs 51 minutes and during these flights they carried out a number of very successful wireless tests. Yet again they were having to repair the airship shed as the wind was tearing the canvas covering into bits and generally weakening the structure.

The unloading of the SS 'Henry James' was finished by 5th October. It had taken far longer than expected due to the poor weather, but 2 Wing had all its equipment now and some new desperately-needed aeroplanes had arrived for 3 Wing. Both the main GHQ and RNAS HQ had finished their moves to their new positions on the western side of 'K' beach where they were protected from the prevailing northerly winds by a hill. They also had better roads and water supply on that side of the harbour. The new course for the observers was going well and a number of the men showed real promise. Even some of the old hands showed a marked improvement in their signalling.

The weather now took another turn for the worse and a fierce storm blew up on the night of 6th-7th October. The men of 2 and 3 Wing spent the night trying to save their aeroplanes, tents and Bessonneau hangers, which they managed to do. The front lines on both sides took a lot of damage and a substantial amount of stores were lost along with a number of small boats. Of the six Turkish aircraft at Galata airfield, only one was left undamaged but it crashed on take-off the next day. It was not until the end of the month that replacement aircraft arrived, this time by rail.

A second seaplane was detached from the 'Ark Royal' to go and join the monitor HMS 'Raglan' and the cruiser HMS 'Theseus', whose mission was to bombard Gallipoli and try to hit the flour mills yet again. By Rabbit Island, HMS 'Roberts' was still using a spotter seaplane in its attacks on the Asiatic Turkish gun batteries. The 'Ark Royal's seaplanes also carried out two spotting missions for HMS 'Edgar', one reconnaissance mission over the Narrows and two photographic reconnaissances flights. The 'Ben-my-Chree' was still in Mudros having repairs carried out but had detached a seaplane to Mitylene.

General Hamilton wrote in his diary on 7th October:

'Wasted energy brooding over addled eggs of the past. Are the high gods bringing our new Iliad to grief in a spirit of wanton mischief? At whose door will history leave the blame for the helpless, hopeless fix we are left in – rotting with disease and told to take it easy?'

While it seems incongruous for him to compare himself, a peacetime soldier totally out of his depth, with the experienced warlords of Ancient Greece, he was rightly becoming very worried about his position as commander of the Gallipoli force as more and more disaffected senior officers such as General Stopford were beginning to contribute to the overall air of gloom in GHQ. The prospect of evacuation was raised on 11th October but Hamilton firmly resisted the suggestion, fearing the damage to both his and British prestige, but it was becoming very clear that his days were numbered.

The stormy autumn weather greatly affected flying this week. 2 Wing managed to carry out 25hrs 9 minutes' worth of flying, most of this test-flying of the new aeroplanes. Twenty-four test flights were carried out in all, plus four photographic reconnaissance, nine reconnaissance and seven spotting flights. Some 15 flights had to be cancelled due to the low cloud and poor weather, but the men of 2 Wing grew in confidence every day as they got used to the flying conditions out in the Dardanelles. On 12th October the Wing suffered its first loss when an aeroplane, BE2c No 1126, crashed soon after take-off. The aircraft did a circuit and all seemed well but as it turned into the wind, it was caught in a strong gust which threw the aeroplane onto the ground near the salt lake. The pilot was seriously injured but the observer, CPO Wallace McLellan, was killed. Due to the hilly nature of Imbros, very strong eddies and crosswinds occur on the island in certain wind conditions and make take-off and landing very difficult. The nature of the terrain and the hills is such that the airfield should never have been built there, and several more men would lose their lives because of this very basic mistake.

The more-experienced 3 Wing managed to carry out 36 flights and were in the air for 53hrs 20 minutes overall this week. They carried out eight spotting flights for the Navy, nine bombing attacks on various tented camps, 12 reconnaissance flights, three photographic reconnaissance flights but four flights were called off due to poor weather and one due to engine failure. The most successful bombing raid was carried out on 6th October when the town of Chanack was attacked. Some twelve 20lb bombs were dropped, with at least one bomb destroying a storage building in the fort. Two of the reconnaissance flights were long-range and covered the towns of Keshan and Malgara, both north of the Gulf of Xeros. They brought back important information on fresh troop formations camping in the area.[98] Operations for the two RNAS wings would be hampered by the sinking of the collier 'Barnsfield' with 1,200 gallons of aviation fuel and other supplies on board between Malta and Imbros.

The SS airships carried out seven anti-U-Boat patrols and five training flights for new pilots during the week. A couple of air tests were also carried out on wireless communications. The airship shed was showing signs of falling apart and it was being considered if it might not be better to build a permanent shed. However, as it was felt that Imbros was definitely not a good home for aviation, a scouting party was sent out to the other islands to find a new home for the airships.

---

[98] TNA: ADM 137/177

On 9th October an urgent call from GHQ reached the 'Levant': all cables to Helles were broken and communications were completely cut. The ship left in a great hurry at about 0230hrs and arrived at 0900hrs. On-going ashore, they found that four cables were cut and one was faulty, all damaged by a lighter that had washed ashore during the night. One cable was repaired and two new ends were laid ready for diverting and repairing two more cables the next day. Fortunately for the 'Levant's crew, Helles was fairly quiet: only a few shells were fired at the beach and camp. A naval steam boat was assigned to help in the repair of the cables and they obtained some interesting curios from its cox'n. They were still trying to repair the damage off Cape Helles on the 11th. A Turkish aeroplane flew over the ship in the direction of Imbros that morning but was driven back by anti-aircraft guns on shore. Captain Wightman grabbed a rifle and also had several shots at the enemy aeroplane himself, quite convinced he could bring it down!

On 11th October, Bulgaria entered the First World War. Secretly courted by both sides during the conflict as a potential ally in the tumultuous Balkan region, Bulgaria eventually decided in favour of the Central Powers. In his statement of 11th October, its Prime Minster Vasil Radoslavov argued that confronting the Allied powers - Britain, France and Russia - alongside Germany, Austria-Hungary and the Ottoman Empire was desirable not only for economic reasons, as the latter two countries were Bulgaria's chief trading partners, but also as a way for the country to defend itself against the aggression of Serbia, the Russian ally and major power in the Balkans that Radoslavov considered to be his country's 'greatest foe'. This would bring a number of problems for Samson as an increase in supplies and heavy guns would now start to arrive by railway, and new and replacement aeroplanes would begin to arrive for the Turks.

The 'Ark Royal's seaplanes did no flying from 12th-19th October due to the poor weather; they could not get off the beach at Ark Royal Bluff, as the beach was now known. Rumours were beginning to grow that the 'Ark Royal' was going to up-anchor and go to new hunting grounds as Gallipoli was now a stalemate and she was not required any more, especially as winter was coming and the weather was going to get a lot worse.

The 'Ben-my-Chree' had been out of action since 30th September, tied up alongside the repair ship 'Reliance', but on 14th October her repairs were finished and she was ready for action. One of the major bits of work was a boiler-clean as she had been working flat out and operating at full speed for most of the time she had been in theatre and her boilers had become furred up. The opportunity was taken to mount anti-aircraft guns on the hangar roof. Seaplane No 842 was transferred to HMS 'Euryalus' while the ship was laid up. Fifty 20lb and twenty 100lb bombs went with the seaplane, enough to have their own private war! No 842, its crew and support staff returned to the ship on 10th October. On the 15th, a new Short arrived for the 'Ben-my-Chree', No 850, but the hangar was absolutely full and so it was put on the beach with 'Ark Royal's seaplanes. Here it would be fully assembled and tested, and, once ready it would be swopped with No 842, which was getting on a bit. Officially the 'Ben-my-Chree' now had six seaplanes: four Shorts, Nos 842, 846, 849 and 850, and two Schneiders, Nos 3721 and 3722. The ship would now join a small naval force that was going to sail up the Gulf of Xeros and bombard the Bulgarian port of Dédé Agatch. This consisted of two elderly cruisers, 'Theseus' and 'Doris', three Monitors, M.19, M.29 and M.31,[99] and 14 support ships like destroyers and trawlers. The French also sent a similar force of two cruisers 'Kléber' and the 'Askold' and eight other ships.

Late in the evening of 16th October a cable arrived for General Hamilton marked 'Secret and Personal'. He had gone to bed as he was feeling unwell but was woken up and given the code books and the cable. The message was from Lord Kitchener, informing him of a second cable that would be arriving soon. From the tone of Kitchener's cable it was clear that he was being recalled to London. The messenger from the signals section asked if he wanted to be woken when the next cable arrived but Hamilton knew what it would say and decided to wait until morning. With the Dardanelles expedition stalled, Hamilton was dismissed as commander and recalled to London on October 16th, effectively ending his military career. On the 17th, he left Imbros never to return. He was replaced by Lieutenant General Sir Charles Monro. Now with a new Army commander in theatre, Samson was hopeful that the RNAS might just get a little acknowledgement of all their hard work.

The 'Hector' was ordered to move over to Rabbit Island and see if they could help with the spotting for the 'Roberts', and HMS 'Canning' now came up from Mudros and joined the fleet. Autumn and winter brought relief from the heat but also led to gales, blizzards and flooding, resulting in men drowning and freezing to death, while thousands suffered frostbite. Between 13th-19th October, 2 Wing carried out 27 flights, though not all the flights were successful and they had to return to base without completing their mission. They did manage to complete two reconnaissance flights, two photographic reconnaissance flights and six spotting flights. The airship managed to carry out five short flights but due to the poor weather and the state of the sea, it was becoming very difficult to carry out anti-submarine flights so this job was passed to the RNAS Wings. 3 Wing carried out 22 flights and they too suffered due to the poor weather, but they did manage to carry out two reconnaissance flights, three photographic flights, three spotting flights, four pamphlet dropping missions and seven bombing attacks. One aeroplane was lost when it suffered engine failure over Suvla and had to make a forced landing on the

---

[99] TNA: ADM 137/177

Salt Lake. The crew were fine and managed to get to the Australian lines with Turkish artillery following them. They went back that evening and managed to salvage the engine and some other bits but the next day the Turks set about destroying the aeroplane and used about 300 artillery rounds in the process. It was at this time that Samson lost his best friend when Flight Lieutenant Reggie Marix was recalled to England. Samson found this very hard to take as more and more of his close friends were leaving the squadron and in their place he was getting men with less than ten hours flying time.[100]

On 17th October two new observers, Lieutenants Noel H Boles and Annesley, plus three pilots, Flight Commander Hans O Busk, and Flight Lieutenants Charles A Maitland-Heriot and Isaac H W (Jack) Barnato, arrived at the Wing. Boles was a Lieutenant in the Dorsetshire Regiment before volunteering as an observer. He would be killed in January 1916 and is buried in the Lancashire Landing Cemetery on Gallipoli. On the 19th, a Voisin of 2 Wing flown by Maitland-Heriot with CPO Bill Pollard as observer took 72 photographs while on a standard photographic reconnaissance. Sykes insisted that the new pilots and observers should be tested in their use of the wireless and the Aldiss lamp, they all passed but were found to be a little slow.

Winter was coming to Gallipoli. The weather took a real turn for the worse from the 20th when a northerly gale came sweeping in and forced many of the ships to move to the south side of the islands to get some protection. The rain was torrential and a number of the trenches filled with water. Up till now water had not caused any difficulties but now problems like trench foot started to appear amongst the men. On the 22nd the wind increased in strength. In the morning it whipped up sand and dust storms both on Gallipoli and Imbros while in the afternoon the rain started and became almost tropical in the force with which it came down. The SS 'Belmont' and SS 'Swanley' arrived with new stores of fuel and bombs and many other requirements, including the winter flying gear that Samson asked for back in August, but the weather was so bad that they could not be unloaded. Everything and everyone had to sit and wait. The storm lasted until 25th October when flying started again.

Lieutenant George Davidson, 89th Field Ambulance, RAMC, 29th Division, wrote in his diary on 24th October:

'The above weather forecast was wonderfully accurate, the cold snap ran from the 19th to 24th Yesterday opened rough, wet and cold, but later in the day the wind fell to an absolute calm and the temperature rose. Today is ideal, not a breath of wind, a few fleecy clouds, and delightfully warm. Geese are flying south in thousands. Where do they all come from? The

---

[100] TNA: ADM 137/177

lakes of Norway and Sweden, Finland and Northern Russia, or where? Their destination is no doubt that delectable country for the winter, Africa'.

It was these geese that the officers of 3 Wing went after with two Paradox shotguns. Some were very good shots and the daily shoot ensured that fresh meat was found for the table in all messes.

The situation at Gallipoli was complicated by the entry of Bulgaria into the war on the side of the Central Powers. In early October the British and French opened a second Mediterranean front at Salonika, removing three divisions from Gallipoli and reducing the flow of reinforcements. A land route between Germany and the Ottoman Empire through Bulgaria was now opened, enabling Germany to supply heavy artillery to devastate the Allied trench network, especially on the confined front at Anzac, as well as modern aircraft and experienced crews. Kitchener demanded an early report from Monro once he had had a chance for a good look around.

General Monro arrived at Imbros on 28th October and set to straight away. The staff at GHQ found their new commander very decisive and personable with a very professional approach, but he was a hard man who did not like incompetence or inefficiency. He did however have a very open mind and grasped new technologies like photographic intelligence gathering and just how useful an air arm was. General Hamilton had started with a force of 200,000 and had had a large number of reinforcements, but the Army Monro was taking over only had a strength of 114,000 men. He also found that while the British and French units were capable of holding ground but not attacking, the ANZACs were still in the mood for a good scrap. This was not what Kitchener wanted to hear. Hamilton had not suggested in any of his reports that his force was spent, a shell of its former self, but in his report Monro suggested they pull out. Along with his report went a number of reports from the Corps commanders including General Birdwood, all of whom except for Birdwood wanted to pull what out was left of their men. He was promoted to the permanent rank of lieutenant-general on 28th October and given command of the newly-formed Dardanelles Army.

The Dardanelles Army was created as a result of the reorganization of headquarters when a second Mediterranean front opened at Salonika. Prior to this, all British and Dominion units in the Mediterranean came under GHQ of the Mediterranean Expeditionary Force (MEF). When it was formed in late 1915, it comprised the three army corps of the British Army operating on Gallipoli, the British VIII Corps and IX Corps as well as the Australian and New Zealand Army Corps and the Canadian 1st Newfoundland Regiment. It was created to manage operations at Gallipoli while the Salonika Army managed operations at Salonika, both armies coming under the command of the MEF, which was also responsible for the defence of Egypt. The Dardanelles Army was short-lived as, by the time of its creation, offensive operations at Gallipoli had ceased and plans for the evacuation were being made in spite of the fact that before General Hamilton left his command, he argued that a proposed evacuation of the peninsula would cost up to 50 per cent casualties.

Kitchener was doing his very best to keep the Dardanelles/Gallipoli campaign alive and returned to a plan that Captain Keyes had come up with: the resumption of the naval attack to force the channel to Constantinople. Vice Admiral de Robeck refused to risk his fleet again, and in this he was supported by the Admiralty. General Monro had had enough and went off to Cairo to talk to General Sir John Maxwell, commander of British forces in Egypt. Kitchener then relieved Monro of his command and put him in command of the Salonika operation instead, while Birdwood was placed in command of Gallipoli. Thus it was that for most of its existence, the Dardanelles Army was commanded by Lieutenant General William Birdwood. Kitchener felt that the only thing left to him was to go out to Gallipoli and take a good look for himself. The men on Gallipoli did not give a flying fig for all these political wrangling's. They just wanted out of the mess that this war had become.

Between 19th and 26th October very little flying took place due to the weather and in fact it could only take place on three days[101]. The 'Ark Royal' managed to carry out one successful spotting mission for HMS 'Edgar' and HMS 'Grafton' and a reconnaissance of the shipping in the Narrows. One seaplane was still with the monitor 'Roberts' by Rabbit Island. An 'Ark Royal' seaplane carried out a special mission: an attack on the anti-submarine net across the Narrows at Nagara. A 100lb bomb was fitted with a parachute, the bomb was dropped just north of the net and the parachute opened and drifted down and onto the target. Unfortunately the seaplane could not hang around any longer to check on the result as the anti-aircraft fire was getting very close and was proving to be very accurate. Meanwhile the RNAS survey team on the 'Ark Royal' had been trying to find a new airfield for the Wings to operate from and a new site for the Airship Section to build a new shed.

The 'Ben-my-Chree' carried out attacks on Bulgarian targets on the 21st, 25th and 26th October. On the 21st, Flight Lieutenant Dacre and his observer, Lieutenant Childers, managed to take off at 1244hrs but quickly found they were flying into a gale. They returned to the ship at 1255hrs, having lost their wingtip floats but still managed to put the seaplane down, fold the wings and taxi it to the side of the ship. The cruisers and monitors bombarded the port and town of Dedé Agatch - a very one-sided attack as the port had no defences. The port, railway and barracks were all badly damaged and one train hit exploded with a great cloud, being shot up into

---

[101] TNA: ADM 137/177

the sky and lighting up the docks. The 'Ben-my-Chree' and the rest of the fleet then ran for shelter and came back on station on the 25th. A photographic flight was launched at 1425hrs to record the damage, flown in seaplane No 849 by Lieutenant Edmonds with Childers as observer. While they took their pictures, Lieutenants Banks-Price and Wright took off at 1444hrs flying their Schneiders armed with incendiary and 20lb bombs and attacked the railway. The following day, 26th October, Dacre and Childers took off in seaplane No 846 at 0846hrs to carry out a spotting mission for the ships. As they flew over Dedé Agatch at just 600 feet, they could see that the town was still burning and the marshalling yards were a mess, with wagons overturned all over the place. They flew on just below the clouds and picked out their target: the railway junction at Bodoma. They got the monitors on target very quickly and then set about destroying the railway. Unfortunately their engine started to run rough and they had to return to the ship, landing back with a dead engine at 1030hrs but their place was taken by Edmonds and Childers who took off in seaplane No 842 at 1200hrs and returned at 1336hrs, having finished the destruction of the rail junction. These reconnaissance flights were the first in this area of Balkans.[102]

The weather had been so bad that both 'Hector' and the 'Canning' ran for shelter in Mudros harbour and stayed there for the whole week. The SS airship had to be deflated due to the storm, but the airship shed sustained a lot of damage as a large amount of the canvas was torn off the shed sides, requiring major repairs. 2 Wing managed to carry out 29 flights, with a total flying time of 31hrs 10 minutes, the bulk of which was done on the 25th when every aeroplane in the Wing was put into the air. Five spotting flights were carried out, and three photographic reconnaissance flights and two tactical reconnaissance flights were made. Anti-submarine patrols were also carried out, but a number of missions were called off due to low cloud and/or very poor visibility. Lieutenants Munday and Sassoon of 2 Wing were on their way back, having carried out a photographic reconnaissance mission, when their engine failed and they were forced to ditch in the sea. Both men were picked up a little damp but with no serious injuries and their aeroplane, a BE2c, was taken in tow and brought back to the beach in front of the airfield. The aircraft remained afloat for some five hours but the 40 photographic plates were damaged by the sea water and could not be developed. 3 Wing only managed 13 flights and were in the air for 14hrs 34 minutes. Again all their flights were carried out on the 25th, starting with two long-range reconnaissance missions, one spotting flight and three bombing attacks. These were all carried out, but the six other flights that went out could not complete their bombing or reconnaissance missions due to low cloud and mist. They still let go their bombs on what they thought was a target. In all, Samson's men dropped seventeen 20lb

---

[102] TNA: ADM 137/177

bombs and six 100lb bombs on this one day, their main targets being tented encampments.[103] One of Samson's standing morning patrols over the Narrows spotted a second anti-submarine net had been put in place.

Besides the weather, there were other hazards facing the RNAS aircrew, some for which no amount of training could prepare them. On 30th October an aeroplane of 2 Wing was coming into land when its occupants were faced by an oncoming rampaging donkey that had escaped and become spooked. By standing hard on the rudder pedal the pilot managed to miss the animal but the aircraft rolled over and had to be written off. The donkey survived.

The weather greatly improved between 26th October and 3rd November and every aeroplane and pilot was put up in the air. In total 113 flying hours was completed. The 'Ark Royal' carried out three spotting missions for HMS 'Edgar' and the seaplane with the 'Roberts' carried out several spotting missions for the monitor.

With the start of a new month, the weather picked up and a lot of flying was carried out in this first week of November but there were also developments on the ground. On 1st November a metrological officer arrived to join the RNAS units' HQ. Two men were assigned to help put up his tent and help in general in laying out his equipment. The same day two men volunteered to become full-time observers and were placed on the observer course run by HQ. Also on 1st November it was decided to pull the RNAS Armoured Car machine gunners out of the line and to send these men over to join 3 Wing. Bell Davies in particular felt these were veterans of battle and should be kept as a single unit. They set to and, using scrap bits of wood and packing cases, built themselves a waterproof barracks, which was a lot better than their hole in the ground. Having finished the barracks they now dug a new well for the airfield to improve the supply of fresh water. All in all, a useful unit to have around!

But now disaster had to strike. On 2nd November a fire broke out in one of 3 Wing's repair workshops and very quickly got out of control. It burned for some two and half hours, due to the fact that the workshop was inside an aeroplane packing case, and a number of spares and other equipment were lost. The fire was started by accident. When Leading Mechanic Arthur Beeton was cleaning the valves of a Nieuport's engine, a small ball-bearing dropped out. He passed it to crew chief Sam Leigh, who had never seen anything like it before and dropped it in a basin of petrol that was used to clean larger engine parts. Then he struck a match and the next thing they knew was a great 'whumph' as the petrol caught alight - and the fire was off and there was no stopping it. They tried to put it out by shovelling sand

---

[103] TNA: ADM 137/177

into the basin but this simply caused the fire to cascade over the side and across the floor. The men had to evacuate the workshop quickly as flames were closing the way out. Once outside they saw that the workshop lorry had also caught fire but this was only a small conflagration and they managed to put it out.

This must have seemed a golden opportunity to Sykes to score a victory over his infuriating subordinate. He carried out a formal review of what happened and laid the blame at Commander Samson's door for allowing this accident to occur. He then held an informal court of enquiry about the fire and eventually the whole incident found its way back to London. A few weeks later a letter from the Admiralty arrived for Samson, stating that he had incurred their Lordships' displeasure. Samson went to see his senior officer, Vice Admiral John de Robeck, as he wanted to complain about the charge. Why should he be blamed for an accident he could neither foresee nor prevent and at which he was not even present? Sykes making trouble locally was one thing but this was taking things too far. De Robeck promptly put it into perspective, telling Samson:

'Not to worry he had incurred their Lordships displeasure 3 times and once their severe displeasure and yet he still managed to become an Admiral.'

Sykes had in fact shot himself in the foot by his behaviour. The Navy now felt that he had overstepped the mark and most of the senior officers would have nothing to do with the man. When he left in January, the Navy were only too pleased to see the back of him.

Back to flying. On 1st November at 2330hrs the 'Ark Royal' up-anchored and set sail for Port Lero for special duties. The 'Ben-my-Chree' was still working off Bulgaria and the port of Dedé Agatch. Four photographic reconnaissance flights had been carried out and each time the seaplanes carried a few small bombs for any tempting targets that presented themselves. Several bombing attacks were also carried out specifically on the port itself. The weather was still far too hazy for the balloon ships to operate so both HMS 'Canning' and HMS 'Hector' remained in Mudros. 2 Wing carried out 33 missions and 22 test flights during this week, made up of 16 reconnaissance missions, four photographic reconnaissance flights and five spotting flights, the remainder being standing patrols over Helles and the Narrows. This made a total flying time of 60hrs 32 minutes. During this period 3 Wing successfully carried out 29 flights, five of which were test flights, over 40hrs 35 minutes of flying. This was made up of eight spotting flights, eight reconnaissance flights (three of which were long-range), and three bombing attacks. Bombs were also carried on five of the reconnaissance missions and dropped on targets of opportunity. Intelligence gathered from captured Turkish soldiers clearly showed the bombing of camps was having a real effect on their morale. The SS airship had been deflated and would now stay that way until after the Section moved to Lemnos. In preparation for this, all the canvas that remained had now been removed from the airship shed and parts of it were being moved to Lemnos.[104]

There were now changes and manoeuvres amongst the senior officers. On 3rd November, General Monro departed on a visit to Egypt to discuss the impact of an evacuation, leaving Birdwood in temporary command. He would never return. On 4th November Admiral de Robeck received a personal signal from Arthur Balfour, now First Lord of the Admiralty, suggesting that he take some leave as he had been in action for such a long period of time and that he should hand over to an officer who was prepared, if directed, to take the fleet up the Dardanelles and re-open the naval conflict. De Robeck smelt a rat, that rat being Captain Keyes, as this was his plan to 'Damn the torpedoes and full steam ahead!' To Keyes they were old ships so they did not matter. To de Robeck it was another hopeless attack that would lose valuable trained naval personnel along with any ships that came to grief. The Turkish defences had not lessened and he knew about the extra submarine net now in place since late October. It was time to call a halt to such mad plans.

Kitchener left London for the Dardanelles on the 4th, but not before sending General Birdwood a telegram imploring him to:

'Re-consider and hang on in Gallipoli, as I consider evacuation a frightful disaster which should be avoided at all costs'.

Kitchener regarded the Keyes' plan as the only way for his Dardanelles operation to be saved and was due to meet the captain at Marseilles on his way out but they missed each other. Keyes then went to Mudros to meet with Kitchener, but by then the latter had seen the battlefield and was now totally convinced that withdrawal was the only option open to them.

Kitchener had landed on 9th November at Imbros. After consulting with the commanders of VIII Corps at Helles, IX Corps at Suvla, and the ANZAC Corps, Kitchener then went on a tour of the trenches and other areas on the 13th. He also met with Samson and some other airmen over dinner. Having visited the trench lines, Kitchener then went to the rest area on Imbros. He went down Rest Gully to 2nd Australian Division and there saw the YMCA canteen - a splendid Sydney concern, which did manage to do something for the men here and at Imbros despite great difficulties:

"Hello! - YMCA!' he said. Then, turning to a man, "What can you get in there?' he asked. 'Nuts!' said the man promptly. `Oh yes, but I mean, generally - what have they got in there?' 'Nothing!' said the man.

Kitchener now agreed with Monro and passed his recommendation to the British Cabinet, who confirmed the decision to evacuate in early December.

---

[104] TNA: ADM 137/177

On 5th November the Admiralty sent a telegram to de Robeck saying:

'Desirable to bomb railway bridge over Maritza River near Usum Kopru'.

Bombing this bridge was very important as it carried the main railway line from Berlin, which brought in lots of supplies. Samson and Gerrard were informed of this, but Sykes had to interfere: he felt the 'Ben-my-Chree' seaplanes were closer so better suited to the job of bombing the bridges. These were set on stone pillars while their upper works were made from steel girders. The eastern bridge had six closely-spaced stone piers while the other had just two.[105] As it would be a 400-mile return flight mainly over sea and enemy held territory, both Wings set about altering some of their aeroplanes and fitting them with extra fuel tanks, Samson felt they needed to carry six hours' worth of fuel just to be on the safe side in case of head winds.

With improved weather the number of flying hours increased to 151½hrs during the period 2nd to 9th November. The daily reports from the meteorologist were proving to be very useful, but not all the time, as weather will be weather. The observer classes were still being run every afternoon. The 'Ark Royal' was now on detached duties off Mitylene and Salonika but no reports had been sent back Sykes at HQ, and no reports of flying hours had come from the detached seaplane with the 'Roberts' off Rabbit Island. The 'Ben-my-Chree' had been operating in the Gulf of Xeros and attacking targets in Bulgaria. Her seaplanes had also carried out a number (3-4) of reconnaissance flights over the bridges at Usum Kopru, the port of Dedé Agatch and the railway linking the two targets. There had also been four bombing missions but bombs were carried on all reconnaissance flights as well for targets of opportunity. Both the 'Hector' and the 'Canning' were still in Mudros harbour as the weather was unsuitable for them to operate. 2 Wing had carried out 52 missions and 34 test or practice flights, with a total time in the air of 93hrs 8 minutes. There were 26 short-range reconnaissance missions, seven spotting flights, four photographic reconnaissance flights, four bombing missions and the rest were standing patrols over Helles and the Narrows looking for submarines and enemy aeroplanes. A special photographic flight was made over the nets at Nagara, the aeroplane suffering a number of hits from AA fire for its pains. 3 Wing carried out 27 missions and two test flights, total air time 56hrs 22 minutes. Nine long-distance reconnaissance flights, two bombing attacks and 3 photographic reconnaissance flights were made, and 12 spotting missions were carried out. All the bombing missions were long-range on the railway bridges at Usum Kopru. The SS airship was now all packed up and ready to move to its new home on Lemnos, the advance

---

[105] TNA: ADM 137/177

party having already left for Mudros to get things ready for the main party.[106]

The flour mills in the town of Gallipoli had been attacked every few days throughout October by aeroplane or by warship with a spotting aeroplane, but without any success. On 8th November monitor M.16 attacked the flour mills with a spotting aeroplane from 2 Wing yet again, but this time they hit the mill with four rounds and did considerable damage to the building and machinery inside. When the first two rounds hit they had to stop firing as the spotter aeroplane could no longer see the target as a great cloud of flour had erupted out of the building.

Also on 8th November Samson and Bell Davies set off in a Maurice Farman aeroplane carrying two 112lb and two 20lb bombs to try to destroy the railway bridge. The flight went well and when they arrived over the target, they dropped to 800ft and were met by a fusillade of small-arms fire. Their two bombs exploded, missing the bridge but damaging the railway line. The two seaplanes sent by the 'Ben-my-Chree' managed to cut the railway line but they too missed the bridge. On the way back to Imbros, Samson and Bell Davies carried out a long-range reconnaissance and found the following:

'To the south of the railway bridges there is a road bridge which looks to have been strongly built.
At Uzum Keupri the whole town is surrounded by encampments. It is impossible to estimate the number of men they could contain.
At Kara Bunar camp possibly containing 5000 men.
At Kurtbili camp probably containing 5000 men, ten stables each 150ft long and large stacks of hay.
Kayajikeui a small camp of 20 tents.
At Saraili large camp capable of containing 10,000 men to 15,000 men.
Chaflikeui camp for about 1500 men.'

They then went on to write about the vast amount of cultivation that the soldiers were doing and the large herds of sheep, goats and cattle. They also noted the large amounts of bullock carts and the animals at several points. It is fascinating to see the amount of useful detail that could be brought in in just one reconnaissance report.

3 Wing carried out further attacks on the bridges on the 10th, 13th and 16th with no luck. They managed to cut the railway line each time and this led to a dramatic increase in anti-aircraft fire, forcing the aeroplanes and seaplanes to bomb from several thousand feet. The attack on the 10th was made by Bell Davies and Captain Walser in very severe weather conditions. For most of the flight they could not climb above 1,500ft due to storm

---

[106] TNA: ADM 137/177

clouds but flying below the cloud meant they had to fly through heavy rain from time to time. Later the same day Flight Lieutenant Thomson and Captain Jopp attacked the large camp at Kara Bunar. On arriving over the camp, they could see little movement so they circled it. Once enough movement was spotted they came down to 1,700ft and let go all their bombs. During the day, 2 Wing sent five aeroplanes out to attack the bridges at Usum Kopru; they got close but did not hit the bridges. Flight Commander Busk with Lieutenant William Samson, now recovered from his injuries, as observer, were ordered to attack the bridges at Usum Kopru. They took off late in the day, hoping for a break in the weather but it did not happen, forcing them to take off into a rain storm. They climbed to 2,000ft and pushed on to their target, arriving in heavy rain. Cutting their engine, they dived on the bridge, only to be met by new AA guns and heavy machine-gun and rifle fire. After all that trouble, the bombs exploded about 30ft from the bridge. On their way back they were caught in a storm cloud and had no idea which way was up or down. Busk let the aeroplane fall on its own only to discover on exiting the cloud that they were upside down and very close to the water! He quickly sorted the aircraft out and continued with the return flight.

The weather once again was not good between 9th-16th November and flying was confined to just two days, total time in the air being 96½hrs. The hut built for RNAS HQ was now finished and the winter huts for the NCOs and men would be finished in the next few days and not a moment too soon! Winter was here with all the problems that brought for flying. Both the 'Ark Royal' and the 'Ben-my-Chree' were still away on detached duty and no reports came in from them at that time. The 'Canning' and 'Hector' were still holed up in Mudros harbour due to the weather. The Airship Section had now finished its move and building had started on a new shed for the airship.[107] Only the landplanes were reporting any action. 2 Wing carried out 35 successful missions and 12 test or practice flights with a total of 57hrs 14 minutes in the air. Reconnaissance flights were made, two photographic reconnaissance missions were carried out, three long-range bombing attacks were carried with 3 Wing while one long-range reconnaissance mission and one long-range night bombing raid were also carried out. On 13th November Lieutenant Commander Smyth-Pigott of 2 Wing carried out a night attack on the bridges. At the time this was the longest night flight of the war and I believe it was not bettered. He took off at 1800hrs with two 112lb bombs and two 20lb bombs, and at first could not find the bridges so flew north over them. Turning south he picked up the river in the moonlight and followed it to the target. On reaching the bridge he cut his engine, dived down onto his target and – missed! He was devastated. He landed back at Imbros at 2200hrs with a total time in the air of four hours 15 minutes and was met by the doctor, who administered

---

[107] TNA: ADM 137/177

some very welcome medicinal brandy to help beat the cold. 3 Wing carried out 17 missions and two test or practice flights, making a total time in the air of 39hrs 16 minutes. Four short-range reconnaissance flights, one spotting flight and 11 long-range reconnaissance missions were made but, following standard practice, bombs were carried on all of these and any targets of opportunity were hit. All objectives were in the area of Ferijik-Kuleli Burgas-Kavak. Some of the camps attacked seemed to be empty as no signs of life could be seen. Very few trains were seen during the attacks on the railway, either by day or night.

On 19th November Squadron-Commander Richard Bell Davies and Flight Sub-Lieutenant Gilbert Smylie were part of a five-aeroplane attack on Ferrijik Junction. Smylie's machine was hit and brought down by very heavy ground fire. The pilot planed down over the station, releasing all his bombs except one, which failed to release from a very low altitude. He continued his descent towards a dried-out marsh only a mile and a half from Ferrijik Junction, and enemy troops could be seen gathering. On landing he saw the one hung-up unexploded bomb so he set fire to his machine, knowing that the bomb would ensure its destruction. He then decided to make his way towards Turkish territory. At this moment he saw Bell Davies descending, and, fearing that he would come down near the burning machine and thus be caught up in the explosion, Smylie ran back towards his aircraft and started to shoot at the bomb with his pistol at short range. Luckily he hit it with his third shot. Bell Davies landed a safe distance from the burning machine and to his great relief found only one crew member of the aeroplane and not the two he thought might be there. The Nieuport he was flying was once a two-seater but the forward seat had been removed and the hole covered over. He stood up and, holding the stick to one side, Smylie dived into the cockpit and crawled over the rudder pedals and under the instrument panel and managed to squeeze himself into the very small space. Bell Davies spotted a group of enemy soldiers approaching so pointed his aeroplane down a dried-up watercourse to take off. They had a good run and climbed into the air with no difficulty. The others flying on the raid had returned and the worst was thought to have happened when Bell Davies landed alone. Some of the other pilots gathered around to find out what had happened when they heard shouting coming from the front of the aeroplane. It took two hours, and a lot of grumbling on his part, to get Smylie out of his diminutive hiding place!

The weather did not improve at all between 16th and 23rd November. Flying was restricted due to some very low cloud and strong winds and in fact could only take place on three days during this week, but the landplanes still managed 48hrs 14 minutes in the air. The 'Ark Royal' and 'Ben-my-Chree' were still away on detachment and no reports on their flying were sent in while the 'Hector' and the 'Canning' were still tied up in Mudros. 2 Wing carried out 28 missions and nine test or practice flights, making a total time in the air of 19hrs 35 minutes. They carried out nine reconnaissance missions, six spotting missions, three photographic reconnaissance missions, and all but one of the rest of their missions were made up of standard morning and evening patrols. The one exception was a long-distance reconnaissance flight in which the aeroplane also carried four bombs - standard now for all long-range trips - two 112lb bombs and two 20lb bombs. 3 Wing carried out 15 missions and four test or practice flights, with a total air time of 28hrs 18 minutes. Six long-range reconnaissance missions were also carried out, three of which carried bombs for targets of opportunity on the way home. In addition there were two long-range bombing raids against the railway bridges at Kuleli Burgas,[108] two spotting missions and three photographic reconnaissance operations.

On 22nd November, Kitchener sent a telegram to the War Committee back in London recommending a partial evacuation. While evacuating Anzac and Suvla, he wanted to retain Helles to assist the Royal Navy in any future operations as there was a fear that a U-Boat base might be established in the Straits with access to dockyard facilities back at Constantinople. The General Staff had come to the same conclusion at the same time. Meanwhile Admiral de Robeck was ordered to take some home leave, and on 25th November he left the fleet in the hands of Rear Admiral Wemyss and headed home, making it very clear that he would be back.

The weather now became so bad that almost no flying was done during the period of 25th November to 2nd December. The meteorological officer measured the wind speed at a steady 60mph with even stronger gusts. The only flying done was by 2 and 3 Wing and they only managed a grand total of 39hrs 47 minutes. On 26th November Flight Sub-Lieutenant J H Rose of 3 Wing and his observer, 2nd Lieutenant W H Bastow, were returning from a patrol and just coming into land when their aeroplane was caught in a gust of wind and tipped over just before the wheels came down on the ground. The aeroplane flipped over nose to tail several times, disintegrating as it did so. Both men were killed.

The storm proper started on the 27th with thunderstorms and torrential rain. This changed the next day to a northward direction when the first of the winter snow arrived, with very hard frosts at night. This caused extreme hardship for both British and Turkish forces in their trenches. The worst effects were at Suvla. The river beds in all the ravines and gullies there that drained the high ground above Anafarta village into the sea became rushing torrents, in places many feet deep. In the trenches near the river bed the water rose three feet in as many minute. Some men were drowned and over 12,000 were evacuated from Suvla, 2,700 from Anzac and 1,200 from Helles, many suffering from frostbite. The Turkish forces

---

[108] TNA: ADM 137/177

suffered just as badly if not worse: many of their dead were washed down and into the British positions.

On 28th November, the wind speed at 2,000ft was found to be 110mph and this was accompanied by low cloud, rain, sleet and snow. The storm caused both Wings considerable worries, the biggest being that the wind would pick up the Bessonneau hangars and carry them away. A number of tears in the canvas, due to the wind pressure, had started to show so they tried to erect a windbreak to protect them from the north-easterly gale. The storm blew down a large number of tents and the men had to find shelter where they could. Most of the small lighter craft were destroyed, putting the unloading of supplies and stores at risk. On Imbros, a large number of streams and a dried-up river bed sprang into life and swept away men and their equipment. The donkeys, mules and horses belonging to 3 Wing had to be rescued as their gully became a river. 2 Wing's airfield had now turned into a sticky mess making landings and take-offs very dangerous, so both wings were using the 3 Wing airfield.

The 'Ark Royal' and the 'Ben-my-Chree' were still away on detached duties so no reports arrived at RNAS HQ. The 'Hector' and 'Canning' were both still confined to Mudros harbour because of the weather. 2 Wing manged to carry out 27 flights: 19 operational sorties and eight test or training flights, making a total flying time of just 28hrs 22 minutes. They carried out four reconnaissance flights and one long-distance reconnaissance, on all of which bombs were carried. Two spotting flights were managed before the weather closed in and the rest of the sorties were standing morning patrols and patrols over the Narrows and anti-submarine patrols. 3 Wing only managed just ten flights: one photographic reconnaissance, three reconnaissance flights, one spotting flight, four bombing raids and just one night flight. A report from Naval Intelligence had found that 3 Wing's long-range bombing attacks on the Turkish strategical reserve in the Usum Kopru and Keshan areas had proven to be very successful and caused a large number of casualties.[109] The Airship Section were now fully employed in building a stronger shed for the airship and making the site capable of taking the larger Coastal Airship, which was due to arrive in the new year.

In late November a Turkish crew in a German Albatros C.I shot down a French aircraft over Gaba Tepe. The French had split their escadrille into two flights of five aeroplanes and they too were working very hard supporting the French ships and Army, but also carried out a number of combined bombing operations with 2 and 3 Wing. The first flight carried out 300 flying hours while the second flight carried out 339 flying hours in November. They too suffered in the great storm.

---

[109] TNA: AIR 1/2284/209/75/11

Two Austro-Hungarian artillery units, the 36. Haubitzbatterie and 9. Motor-Mörser Batterie arrived at the end of November, providing a substantial increase in heavy artillery for the Turks. These guns would be a first class pain to the British troops. The k.u.k 24 cm Motor-Mörser-Batterie 9 was the first heavy battery to arrive in Turkey. It was loaded on barges at Vienna on 15th October and moved down the Danube with four officers and 80 men, arriving at Uzunköprü on the Turkish-Bulgarian border on 22nd October where it got immediate orders to join the 5th Army at Gallipoli. Commander 2nd Lieutenant Höpflinger and automobile officer 2nd Lieutenant Filipp then went to Istanbul to visit Enver Pasha and the Sultan to be given their orders while the battery, with four guns and seven vehicles under command of Lieutenant Sitta and Lieutenant Lindner, got ready to move to Gallipoli. The rest of the battery under command of Captain Barber and Lieutenant Jeschek with 183 men arrived in Turkey on November 15th and began the march to Gallipoli four days later. The ammunition and supply train was made up of 120 bullock wagons and it took three days and a 170 km walk for the battery to arrive at its allotted position, which was very well hidden. On November 27th the battery opened fire. The British trenches and positions on Mestan Tepe and Pinar Tepe were the first to be hit and the next day the battery fired on the well-fortified Bloody Ridge.

In the morning of 1st December, 3 Wing managed to put up two flights. Flight Lieutenant Vernon and Captain Jopp took off at 1010hrs and landed back at 1220hrs, just 2hrs 10 minutes later. Their target was Ferejik railway junction, where they hit the line with one of their bombs from 2,000ft. Samson took off at 1110hrs, carried out a patrol over Helles and then flew up to Nagara Point. A Turkish seaplane attacked 2 Wing at lunchtime that day so in the afternoon Gerrard replied in kind by sending over two aeroplanes and bombing the seaplane base at Kusa Burnu. The first up was Flight Sub-Lieutenant Besson at 1530hrs, who landed back at 1610hrs. The second was Flight Sub-Lieutenant Simpson, who took off at 1540hrs. His engine started to run rough on reaching Naidos so he dropped his bombs from 8,500ft. He then spotted a hostile aeroplane on his starboard bow that opened fire on him from the rear cockpit with a machine-gun. Simpson managed to get on his tail and opened fire with his Lewis gun, which jammed after just 20 rounds. Just at this moment his engine also failed and he lost 1,500ft. His engine now restarted but was still very sick so he turned for home and luckily made it.

On 2nd December, a 3 Wing aeroplane piloted by Flight Commander Busk with Captain Jopp as observer was up spotting for HMS 'Earl of Peterborough' when they broke off and dived on an enemy aircraft, a Taube, that was lining up to bomb the 'Peterborough'. Busk had closed to within 50 yards when Jopp opened fire with his Lewis gun. The enemy aeroplane returned fire then dived, pulling out at 1,000ft to find Busk still on his tail. He dived for the ground and levelled out at 200ft, but by now

Busk and Jopp were taking a serious amount of accurate ground fire, which discouraged them from following it further. The two 3 Wing men returned to base with a few holes in their aircraft. The same day Samson took off at 0959hrs in chase of what was thought to be a hostile aeroplane, and, with the sun in his eyes, he slowly closed on his target. It turned out to be French.

Although Admiral de Robeck was on leave in London, he attended a meeting of the War Council on 2nd December that led to the government deciding that time was up for Gallipoli.

On 3rd December, Major-General Arthur Lynden-Bell, General Monro's Chief of Staff, to whom all this naval theorising by the likes of Keyes was nothing more than a nuisance, wrote:

'The Navy are giving us a great deal of trouble - I say the Navy but it is really Roger Keyes - by continually trying to urge us to help them in putting forward their pet scheme of forcing the Narrows. This we absolutely decline to do as we cannot see how the operation could possibly succeed, and if it did succeed it would not help the military situation at all. This has been pointed out frequently to the Vice-Admiral and to Keyes, but they still persist, and their last effort has been to wire to the Admiralty and urge that we should make a land attack on Achi Baba. To this we have replied that the operation is quite beyond our powers and would require at least 100,000 men.'

This whole lingering distraction to the process of planning the inevitable evacuation was described by Lyndon-Bell as 'The swan song of the lunatics!' It is a view which is very difficult to argue with.

On 4th December, one of Samson's new pilots greatly impressed the Australians and enhanced 3 Wing's reputation for very accurate bombing. Flight Sub-Lieutenant Vernon and Midshipman Sissmore were supposed to be on a spotting mission for monitor M.29, but the target was obscured and the cloud base was in places below 1,000ft. As they had some bombs on board, they went looking for a target and spotted some Turkish troops in a gully close to ANZAC. They let go their bombs with more excitement than planning and one bomb sailed over the edge of the gully towards the Australian frontline and exploded. They could not see the result but headed back to Imbros expecting the worse. On landing Vernon reported to Samson, explaining that he might have killed some Australians, but just at that moment Samson was called to the telephone. There he was greeted by a very happy Australian demanding that they carry out the bombing of the Turkish trench again as a lot of Turks were killed. He did not reply - he could not admit to a fluke - but was extremely relieved that no Australians were killed.

The weather was not improving. The problem now was that the cloud cover was 10/10s with a maximum ceiling of just 1,000ft, meaning that all aeroplanes would sustain damage from ground fire. It would remain like that until about 8th December. Although the 'Ark Royal' was still on detached duty at Salonika, it had managed to put a flying report for the period 9th-23rd November on a passing trawler. They had logged 31½ hours of flying and carried out a number of anti-submarine patrols off Salonika. In addition they carried out an intense photographic reconnaissance of the Salonika area. One of 'Ark Royal's seaplanes was still with the 'Roberts' at Rabbit Island, and the 'Ben-my-Chree' was still also on detached duties. The low cloud made the deployment of the two balloon ships impracticable so they both stayed on in Mudros harbour. The men of the Airship Section were making significant progress with their building work. They had now managed to clear most of the ground of scrub and had laid the first large concrete slab for one of the new sheds. During the week 2nd to 8th December, 2 Wing managed, despite the low cloud, to carry out 24 successful operations in 53hrs 36 minutes flying time. There were eight reconnaissance flights, six spotting operations, four bombing attacks and three anti-submarine patrols plus three attacks on enemy seaplanes. In the same period 3 Wing carried out 15 operations in 41hrs 50 minutes in the air. Five long-distance reconnaissance flights took place, all aeroplanes on these flights carrying bombs and attacking targets of opportunity, plus four local bombing attacks on Turkish gun positions and four spotting flights, though one of these was the one cut short by Busk and Jopp. No photographic reconnaissance flights could take place as it was just far too dangerous. The low-flying slow moving aircraft made unmissable targets and would be shot out of the sky.

The British government, having prevaricated for several weeks, finally sanctioned an evacuation of Gallipoli on 7th December. Unfortunately by this time the weather was very bad and a heavy blizzard had set in, making such an operation hazardous. General Hamilton had felt that the casualty figure during the evacuation could be as high as 70%. Some officers believed this was a great overestimation and that, as long as good discipline could be maintained, then there should be no problem. A plan for evacuation was put in place by General White, the Chief of Staff. He decided to slowly withdraw men and equipment over a period of days and only at night, whilst giving the Turks the impression that everything was normal, yet he also wanted all flying and bombing to stop as this greatly annoyed the Turk. But as Samson pointed out, if he and the two Wings suddenly stopped flying and bombing, this would convince the Turk that something was up. A solution was reached: they increased their bombing but stopped doing photographic work, so still flew the same number of sorties.

One major problem facing General White and the planners was that the storm had sunk or badly damaged a large number of small lighters so necessary to ferry men out to the larger ships, which would slow the evacuation. Therefore it was decided that Suvla and ANZAC would be evacuated first and Helles would follow later, possibly in the New Year once the first body of men was out of the way. The number of men left until the last night would be governed by the number of lighters available to pull them off the beaches. The plan was that over ten nights from 10th/11th to 19th/20th of December 1915, 85,000 troops would be quietly and efficiently evacuated from the Anzac beaches and the Suvla Bay area. All went like clockwork unlike so much else in Gallipoli. The last man left the beach at 0530hrs on 20th December. Even the weather was on their side and helped mask the withdrawal.

In the lead up to the actual evacuations, a number of tactics were employed to mask what was happening. These included:
Silent stunts periods where there was no shooting or activity from the Anzac lines.
'Smoking fatigues': groups of men standing and talking in areas known to be under observation by Turkish artillery.
Drip rifles were used to ensure that a sporadic rate of fire was maintained after the last man had left. Two small tins were placed one above the other, the top one full of water and the bottom one, with the trigger string attached to it, empty. At the last minute, small holes would be punched in the upper tin, water would trickle into the lower one, and the rifle would fire as soon as the lower tin had become sufficiently heavy to activate it as a weight. These were placed at intervals along the trenches and would fire every now and then. The drip rifle was invented by Lance Corporal W C Scurry of the 7th Battalion, AIF, with assistance from his mate, Private A H Lawrence. For the part he played in making the evacuation a success, Scurry was mentioned in dispatches, awarded the Distinguished Conduct Medal, and promoted to sergeant.
Another similar device ran a string holding back the trigger of a rifle through a candle, which slowly burnt down, severed the string, and released the trigger.
On 17th December a game of cricket was played as a diversionary tactic during preparations for the evacuation. It was held on the only piece of flat ground, the site now known as 'Shell Green', but had to be abandoned after Turkish shells landed close by.

All movement from the beaches was restricted to the hours of darkness, apart from the sick or wounded that would normally be taken off in daylight. During the night, stores were removed from the beach and not replaced, along with unwanted equipment, again making it look as though they were getting ready for the winter. The men would cover their boots with rags or old socks to muffle the sound of them going down to the beach and the same was done with the mules and horses.

Between 8th-14th December the two RNAS aeroplane Wings clocked up 107 hours in the air, though a large proportion of the flights could not be carried out successfully due the low cloud and misty conditions. The 'Ark Royal' was still on detached duty off Salonika and was working well. The 'Ben-my-Chree' was ordered to return to Imbros as she was to act as one of the reserve ships if things went wrong and the men had to be taken off in a hurry. 2 Wing carried out 60 operational flights, very few of which were completed successfully, and six test flights. The successful missions were six reconnaissance flights, five spotting flights, three bombing raids, and two flights to observe the effects of the bombardment of the Turkish positions and ships in and around the Olive Grove. Five patrols were sent in search of submarines and enemy aeroplanes. One Turkish aircraft was attacked and chased back over its own lines. Two machines were lost during this week, both due to engine failure. The first crashed landed into the lagoon and was destroyed, but the crew were safe and the engine and some instruments were salvaged. The second crashed into the sea near one of the monitors and the aeroplane was towed back to Imbros. Once again, the engine was salvaged and the crew were unhurt and flew again. 2 Wing also carried out an attack on the nets across the narrows at Nagara on 8th December. Four BE2c took off at 0700hrs with a two-minute gap between each aircraft. The first aeroplane over the target was flown by Lieutenant Commander Smyth-Pigott, who dropped his bombs from 1,700ft about 100yds north of the net. Flight Sub-Lieutenant C E Brisley was the next over the nets and dropped his bombs about 250 yards above the nets. Next was Flight Sub-Lieutenant R Y Bush, who could not drop his bombs as he could not see the nets due to the very low cloud, so returned to base. His aeroplane was refuelled and was taken up by Flight Sub-Lieutenant M A Simpson who found the target and dropped his bombs 200 yards north of the net. All the bombs were fitted with parachutes, all of which worked, and a time fuse. It was to explode as it drifted down in or near the net and damage it. Captain Charles E Robinson, RMLI, took-off at 0710hrs and did not return from the mission. He was not seen again. 3 Wing received its last batch of new pilots: Lieutenants Black, Cecil H Brinsmead and P E H Wakeley. It carried out 25 missions and five test flights during the week, with a total flying time of 39 hours and 48 minutes: seven reconnaissance flights, three long-range reconnaissance flights with bombs carried, five bombing raids and two anti-submarine hunts. The 'Hector' remain in Mudros while on 10th December 'Canning' moved up to Imbros and carried out three balloon assents. The Airship Section were still working on their new airship shed.

Originally the generals had decided to keep everything very quiet during the evacuation but as Samson had pointed out, it would look very suspicious if he and his men were not up patrolling every day or dropping the morning bombs on the breakfast camp fire. The other thing that Samson, Gerrard and Césari could and did do was to put up an umbrella of air cover over the Anzac/Suvla Bay area so that the Turks would not know what was going on. The weather was still bad between 14th and 21st December but the large amount of low cloud suited the men of the RNAS, as this meant they could dominate the area. During this week, 2 Wing were in the air for 56hrs 20 minutes and carried out 31 successful operations: eight reconnaissance missions, eight spotting missions for various monitors, 12 patrols and three bombing raids. Most of the reconnaissance flights carried bombs as usual and were used on any target of opportunity that presented itself. 3 Wing were in the air for 49hrs 40 minutes in the same period of time and carried out 30 operational flights: five reconnaissance missions, three spotting missions, three bombing raids on the Turkish airfield and 19 patrols. Again, most of the patrols carried bombs. The 'Ben-my-Chree' returned on the 18th and over the next three days carried out anti-submarine patrols. The French made numerous patrols and nuisance raids over the Turkish lines, all just to keep the enemy's head down and in his trench.

On 19th December, the last full day at Anzac and Suvla Bay, there were only a few thousand men manning the trenches so every aeroplane and pilot that could fly did fly. 2 Wing carried out eight patrols, most of them were between 90 minutes and two hours long. 3 Wing carried out seven patrols, all over two hours in length except for Bell Davies, who chased off a Turkish Taube. The two RNAS wings alone were in the air for a combined time of 27hrs 35 minutes and were joined by the French, who in the air for about eight hours. One thing that was beginning to worry Samson about 3 Wing was the growing number of accidents that were happening, silly little things like the 20lb bomb that came loose from the bomb rack as he took off on 16th December. It exploded under him, throwing his aircraft into the air and tearing off most of the fabric, but he just managed to keep control. He got rid of the other bombs and banged the aeroplane down whereupon it disintegrated around him. He and his men had been at war for very nearly 16 months with no real leave or a break. They were all sick and all very tired. 2 Wing had only been on operational duties for five months but they too were showing signs of fatigue. And when this takes hold, accidents and mistakes will happen.

It was at this point that Samson had been sent out from England a new 500lb bomb, the largest built so far. It was the largest dropped to date by any allied aeroplane, a giant to be treated with real respect. This was not the time for errors. Samson would not let any other pilot take up this monster of a bomb; he would go up alone and would use one of the large Henri Farnham aircraft. He took his time making sure the engine was running smoothly, then revved it up and shot off down the runway, soaring into the air like a bird. Without a murmur from his aeroplane, he headed up towards Anzac looking for a suitable target. He found a large building that had smoke coming from its chimneys and let go the bomb, but due to the low cloud he could not see the result. He returned after the war and discovered that he had not just hit the building but had completely destroyed it.

Ironically, in spite of fears that there would be a very high casualty rate, the evacuation became the most successful operation of the whole campaign. How secrecy was kept was a mystery to all, as the fact had been known amongst the men for some time yet it is almost certain the enemy never had an inkling of what the next move was going to be. On the last night anything of any use, like ammunition, was thrown into the sea, set on fire or set as a booby trap for the Turks when they came over. Calm weather was all that was required for the last night of the withdrawal, as there were still 5,000 men who had manned Anzac trenches to be taken off.

During the entire evacuation, the troops were very disciplined and organised and they were generally glad to be leaving. However, all of them felt bad about leaving their dead comrades behind. There are many stories of Anzac soldiers visiting and tending the graves of their mates in the days leading up to the evacuation. At 0530hrs on 20th December the last men left Anzac Cove and Suvla Bay and not one man was lost in the operation. As the last boats pulled away, timed explosions went off destroying tunnels, mines and setting fires that destroyed stores that were left on the beach. After a short rest on Lemnos Island, all the men were taken to Mudros and Imbros where they were sorted and placed into troopships. From there they were transported to Egypt, where their great "adventure" had begun. They were very different men, though. In Egypt, the AIF regrouped and reorganised and then started to train, preparing itself for an even greater challenge - the Western Front.

On the 20th, both Wings carried out several reconnaissance flights. 2 Wing carried out visual reconnaissance flights over Helles and Suvla while 3 Wing carried out photographic reconnaissance flights over Suvla and Anzac. Many of the pictures were obscured by the smoke that drifted from the burning food stacks. 3 Wing also carried out three standing patrols and Samson gave chase to an enemy aeroplane but could not catch it. The men were becoming quite excited as rumours went round that they all going home, but not before Christmas, as both Wings had bought a number of turkey chicks that were being fed on a mixture of bully beef and soaked biscuits to help fatten them up for the big day.

In spite of the evacuations, the amount of flying did not go down between 22nd December and 1st January but in fact increased. During this period 2 Wing were in the air for 50hrs 20 minutes and carried out 35 successful flights. Three photographic reconnaissance flights were made, during which they exposed over 100 glass plates, and 12 reconnaissance flights, 16 spotting missions and two patrols were carried out. All flights were armed with bombs. They also made two bombing raids.

Christmas Day was sunny and warm, a pleasant change from the recent weather. It turned out to be a very busy day for both Wings. 2 Wing carried out nine flights, three were photographic reconnaissance, where again over 100 glass plates were exposed, and the rest were patrols but all were armed with bombs. Their unseasonal activities were copied by the Turks. The men of 2 Wing were disturbed when an enemy aeroplane came over and bombed their airfield. One of the bombs landed near Fred Knowles, one of the ground crew, but failed to explode. It sent him into shock, so his comrades fed him his daily ration of rum and put him to bed. He woke up two days later and returned to duty none the worse for the experience.

On Christmas Day Samson was given orders that he and his unit were to pack up and go home. Their work in the Dardanelles was finished and they were to hand over all spares and equipment to 2 Wing. This was the best Christmas present the Navy could have given Samson and his men, who were by now desperate for a rest. All of 3 Wing flights that day were either bombing raids or armed patrols. At 1700hrs the Wing had a game of football: officers verses the men. It very quickly became clear that they were all very unfit and the football match turned into a game of tag, as each man could only managed ten minutes before requiring a rest. That evening the whole Wing sat down to a real turkey dinner. In 3 Wing's last flying period they carried out 28 missions and were in the air for 39hrs 35 minutes. They carried out seven reconnaissance flights, three photographic flights, one spotting mission, 13 patrols and four bombing raids. Their friends from Tenedos were leaving Gallipoli too. Just after Christmas Captaine Césari came over to Imbros to see Samson and to say goodbye as he was ordered to take his unit home.

On 28th December Flight Commander Busk and Captain Edwards carried out a very important reconnaissance flight. Unfortunately for Captain A Walser, who had just boarded a ship that was going to take him for a spot of medical leave in Egypt, Commander Sykes had particularly wanted him to undertake this and called him back do it. By the time Walser got off the ship and back to the airfield, the flight had already gone ahead with Busk and Edwards. Returning to the port, he found his leave ship had left and he now had to wait for a few days for the next one!

Busk and Edwards took off at 1510hrs and headed up to the Narrows, where they were passed, at a higher altitude, by a Taube. As it flew over, the crew threw a bomb at Busk, but missed. This called for an armed response! As they were closing on the enemy aeroplane, a second one shot out of the clouds in front of them but spotting Busk on the charge, it peeled away and dived back into the cloud heading for the ground. Busk and Edwards managed to catch the other aircraft and gave it several long bursts before their gun jammed. They carried out the rest of the reconnaissance and returned to base landing at 1715hrs. Edwards then went off to catch the leave ship that was taking him to Egypt and a rest.

Commander Samson's last flight was on 28th December. He took off at 1515hrs and chased an enemy aeroplane but could not catch him, landing back at Imbros at 1545hrs. He would not fly with 3 Squadron or 3 Wing again. The Eastchurch Squadron, 3 Squadron, 3 Wing – call it what you like, it was Samson's Squadron and now it was breaking up for good. It had set a brilliant example of what a fighting squadron could be. Three days later Gerrard gave the officers of 3 Wing a farewell dinner. On 1st January 1916 Commander Samson, Commander Bell Davies and Flight Lieutenant Thomson were piped off the island by their men and then rowed out to their waiting ship by the officers of his Wing. Extraordinary honours for extraordinary men and thoroughly deserved.

Conclusion

It is customary in Britain to hold some sort of enquiry when a military enterprise ends in a fiasco so it was no surprise to anyone when in due course the details of the ill-fated Dardanelles/Gallipoli Campaign were subject to scrutiny. The double name is because the Royal Navy in their documents call the area 'the Dardanelles', while the Army refers to the area as 'Gallipoli'.

The initial idea had seemed sensible enough at the time it was agreed upon to those in charge of the war. When the Turkish Empire had entered the war on the side of the Central Powers in November 1914 and went on the offensive against the Russians, launching an attack through the Caucasus on Christmas Day that year, Russia's Tsar Nicholas II had appealed to Britain, asking for help. The British response was a plan to use the Royal Navy to take control of the Dardanelles Straits from where they could attack and capture Constantinople, the Turkish capital, allowing them to link up with their Russian allies and knock Turkey out of the war. Sir Winston Churchill, First Lord of the Admiralty, was confident that the Navy, acting alone, could succeed in in this but when on 19th February a flotilla of British and French ships pounded the outer forts of the Dardanelles and a month later attempted to penetrate the Straits, the offensive failed, with the loss of six ships, three sunk and three damaged. A land force would be needed after all.

If the Secretary for War, Lord Kitchener, had been worthy of his post, he would have had a proper respect for his enemy. However, although he had promised General Sir Ian Hamilton and Churchill that the Turks would be easily defeated, they were not the pushover the British had hoped for. Led by Mustafa Kemal Atatürk, they had had time to prepare the ground. They built new trenches, dug in artillery and machine-guns and turned the beaches into killing grounds. A force of British, French and ANZAC (Australian and New Zealand Army Corps) troops landed on the Gallipoli peninsula on 25th April 1915. As the first foot touched the beach they came under a withering fire that cut the leading men down. Under constant attack, they took cover and dug in as best as they could among the rocks and the steep cliffs, always overlooked by the Turk.

Now this in itself was not necessarily fatal to the whole mission but unfortunately error followed crucial error with few bright points amongst the gloom. It was Kitchener's choice, and his mistake, to put Hamilton in overall command of the army in Gallipoli, a parade ground soldier with no proper battle experience. This elderly novice was sent to run a campaign with inaccurate maps, no intelligence on the Turkish forces and very inexperienced troops, to name but a few of the things that were wrong with the Army. He was also sadly not a man to welcome the new technology that was being offered him that could have helped him at least make a reasonable fist of the whole thing. He was not alone. There were those amongst his senior officers who also preferred to ignore vital help they were offered that might, in fact, have turned Gallipoli into a success instead of an ignominious defeat.

If the Army was slow to embrace modern methods, the Royal Navy was not. And this invaluable assistance was offered to Hamilton and his fellow officers by units of the Royal Navy - new units with new ways of doing things, suitable for a twentieth century war. The inventiveness of the Navy was seemingly endless, from relatively simple things like the beetle, an armoured landing craft for infantry and stores, to the balloon ships HMS 'Manica', 'Hector' and 'Canning', conceived and delivered in only a few weeks to overcome the problem of not being able to raise a spotting balloon for artillery or naval warships on shore. It was the Navy that introduced the cable laying ships 'Levant' and 'Levant II' to provide telephonic communications between the Army units and between ships and shore. Among the British land forces, only the Australians had wireless but the Navy not only provided wireless, they also provided the operators. This was a means of communication that assisted the all-important spotting for the artillery and naval guns. And then there were the new Submarine or Sea Scout airships, another quick-fire answer to an urgent problem. Innovation, constant innovation, to meet the everyday challenges of warfare.

But for sheer versatility, nothing compares to the aircraft squadrons of the RNAS in the Eastern Mediterranean. At first it was thought that the 'Ark Royal', the first purpose-built aircraft carrier with its complement of seaplanes, would answer reconnaissance and bombing needs but the ship proved to be disappointing in her performance. The 'Ben-My-Chree', a new seaplane carrier that was sent out to support her, was much more successful, perhaps as much due to the tough and charismatic personality of her captain, Commander Cecil L'Estrange Malone, as to a modified design and the types of aircraft she carried.

However, undoubtedly the cream of the crop were the naval land aircraft squadrons. Time and time again 2 Wing under Wing Commander Eugene Gerrard and 3 Wing under Wing Commander Charles Samson outperformed the seaplanes in every task they undertook. 3 Wing, known as 3 Squadron when they first came to the eastern Mediterranean, were the most experienced and decorated flying unit in the British armed forces. Their exploits on land and in the air in France and Belgium had already made them legends: the 'Motor Bandits'. Their work now in Gallipoli was just as inventive, just as dedicated and just as spectacular.

They produced maps of the battlefield from photographs taken at first by a hand-held camera belonging to one of the squadron's officers, Lieutenant

Butler. These made it possible for land, sea and air forces to all know they were looking at (and aiming at) the same places. The photographs they took of trench lines, gun emplacements, forts, towns, camps and villages gave invaluable information of where the enemy was, in what force, and what he was doing. Thousands of photographs were taken and the results rushed to HQ when something particularly notable was seen by 3 Wing's intelligence staff. What a shame it was that so few senior officers were prepared to take them seriously and to work on the basis of the information they provided, until at last in some cases it was almost pushed in their faces. General Hamilton claimed that aerial reconnaissance was no good and that he never saw any of it, though he did have the grace to admit (in his book written post-war) to seeing some pictures. General Birdwood in particular praised the work of the RNAS aerial reconnaissance flights as did Admiral de Robeck. For a number of officers it must have come as a shock just what you could see from the air. If only this work had been properly examined and recognised as vital, the whole course of the ground campaign could have been different, but ignorance and prejudice were dominant at HQ.

3 Wing started spotting for ships using the system they developed in France. At first this was rough but it soon became very accurate and some ships were very good at it. Between 18th February and 31st December 1915, 338 spotting flights were carried out by British aeroplanes and a further 10 were carried out by MT 98 T, the French escadrille, for British ships. If their success was not all that was hoped, a large part was due to the armament of the older battleships which could not elevate high enough to allow a shell to fall into a fort or deep gully and mostly used solid shot, fairly useless against stone forts and the earthen revetments of a gun-pit. It was not until the monitors arrived with their smaller calibre guns but large amount of high-explosive rounds that things did improve in the destruction of targets.

The RNAS did everything in their power to help and work in complete harmony with the Royal Navy, but the task was more difficult with the Army. When it came to spotting for the Army, the artillery had a number of problems working with the aircraft. Most important, they had no experience in wireless spotting with aeroplanes and they had no wireless signalling unit, so no way of signalling to aircraft. Wireless stations were opened by the RNAS at Helles, Anzac and Suvla and these posts were manned by Navy wireless operators, which greatly improved the Army spotting flights, but the whole process from message to guns to firing to spotting to reporting again took a very long time so the Army tended to use the balloons for their spotting as they used telephones via the warships. However Samson and his pilots frequently risked their lives landing on the deadly airstrip at Helles to personally rush vital intelligence to HQ.

One of the biggest successes of the air wings and the balloons were that they forced the enemy to change the way he worked on the battlefield, bringing up supplies and in the rear. As soon as the kite balloon went up, the Turkish gunners ceased fire and went into hiding. The same became true when the Turkish forces heard an aeroplane. Instantly there was the anticipation of a well-aimed bomb coming down on a convoy, a camp or a campfire. Guns were ordered to cease fire when an aeroplane could be heard or seen in the area. After the war, Major Osman Zati Bey stated that British aeroplanes always found their guns and very quickly at that, so they had to keep moving them. Work was done at night to avoid attacks, then work was done at night without lights to avoid attacks. It was standing orders for all Samson's pilots to carry bombs on all flights to drop on targets of opportunity if they had no specific target for them and it was this constant fear of attack that inhibited the Turkish Army's movements.

3 Wing did not rest upon its laurels in this respect. At first the bombs scared both the men and pack animals but they got used to it, so Samson and his men started to switch their engines off and silently glide down and drop their bombs and this worked for a while. In the end one of Samson's men came up with the idea of putting whistles on the bombs, so a loud screaming sound could be heard as the bomb fell. The scrub that covered the landscape was one thing the men of 3 Wing wanted to get rid of so they had a go at building their own incendiary bomb. This was, as Samson put it the 'father of all Bombs'. They used a 26-gallon petrol tank filled with a mixture of paraffin and petrol as the main body and fashioned a streamlined tail from sheet metal. The head was also streamlined and was fitted with the fuse, which was made from a Verey light pistol with a cartridge in it, and (as an extra) a 20lb bomb was rigged to it. It did explode but the 20lb bomb dispersed the fire too much and put a lot of the flames out. Of the nearly twenty-six and a half tons of bombs dropped by the RNAS over Gallipoli, four tons was dropped by Samson alone.

Now we come to some of the great 'what ifs' in history. If General Birdwood had taken notice of the information brought to him by Samson and his men that there were no Turkish troops in the trenches in front of him and ordered his men to advance, would Australia now celebrate Gallipoli as a magnificent triumph of their inexperienced troops instead of a hellish bloodbath in flyblown trenches? Lieutenant-General Sir Frederick Stopford was given similar information and also did not act on it. Could Gallipoli have been a success if these men had trusted their intelligence providers? And could some of the awful massacres have been prevented if they had listened to the warnings of men who had seen the enemy preparations awaiting their troops?

As we know, they did not act on what they heard and did not trust air intelligence until it was too late to make a difference. Nevertheless, the RNAS Wings gave the Army one last invaluable gift – total air supremacy over the battlefield during the evacuation. It was a first for aviation and ensured that no further lives were lost in this mismanaged campaign. The Generals showed their appreciation of this amazing feat and all the others that preceded it by using the excuse of a lack of aerial intelligence and no aerial support as one of the reasons for their failure during the investigation into the failure of the Dardanelles! Yet reams of intelligence reports still exist in surviving naval documents - why did the Generals not get a copy? The RNAS produced over 7,000 prints: did none of the Generals see any of these or were they all items of the imagination?

The result of this was that the RNAS was written out of the official history. Even today many modern military historians write the RNAS out of the Dardanelles; you would think, reading their books, that there never was an air war. Write the RNAS out and you also write out the men. Men like the personnel of 3 Wing, who under their charismatic leader Commander Samson had been fighting on the front line without a break since August 1914. Yet in spite of the endless action and debilitating fatigue, they still achieved results on a truly amazing scale and the credit for this must largely go to their leader.

Charles Rumney Samson was an intelligent and able man of incredible personal stamina and outstanding courage, a naval officer who took the war to the enemy in any and every way he could think of. He showed by his own actions how war could be fought in the air (and at times on land too!) His example fired the officers and men under his command to their own feats of excellence. His record was second to none, his legacy was his men and his fate was to be forgotten by history while lesser men got the glory. May this book restore something of what history and his country owe him.

Appendix 1

Transcription from AIR 1/361/15/228/50: reports on RNAS, Eastern Med., Jan-May 1915

No. 3 Wing
R.N.A.S.
Imbros Island

Sir

I have the honour to forward the following description of portable buildings.

Each squadron should be provided with these buildings, which have otherwise to be erected.

The following buildings are required

1. Carpenters work shop
2. Engineers work shop
3. General store
4. Office
5. Acetylene welding shop
6. Armourers shop

The following are the type required

Wood sides, made in sections joined together by bolts. The sides are supported by wooden posts. The roof is made of thick canvas tarpaulin and secures to the sides by means of lacings. There are also straps to secure the roof to the supporting beam on the inner side.

The first 3 buildings are of the same size ie. 20 feet long 15 feet wide. 9 feet high with a roof pitched 3 ft above the side level in the centre.

The office and the Armourers shop are 15 feet long 10 feet wide and 9 feet high. The Acetylene welding shop is the same size.

The provision of these buildings will facilitate the work of a squadron tremendously as these stores take a long time to build and sometimes cannot be built for lack of material.

The method I suggest of errecting *[sic]* these buildings is the method I now carry out viz sink the building by digging 3 foot deep pit.

This minimises risk of a fire spreading and also gives a certain ammount *[sic]* of protection against weather and bombs. The side sections of the buildings should be small enough to be transported in motor lorries.

The sections should be strongly made.

The office should be fitted with colapsible *[sic]* shelves, which would fit into places provided for them on the walls.

The office furniture should consist of
Desk with drawers
Two tables for clerks
2 Safes. (1 large 1 small).
3 chairs
1 stove.

Additional buildings for a wing.
Are
A Additional office
B Map room   20 feet long.   10 feet wide.   9 feet high.
C Additional store

                I have the honour to be sir
                    your obedient servant
                      C R Samson
                          Commander RN

11th ??? 1915

Appendix two:

Extracts from 3 Wing Standing Orders, December 1915:

No. 3 Wing
R.N.A.S.

Sir,

I have the honour to present a few extracts from my "Standing Orders", which I think may be of some use. A few of my orders are of course local ones.

I have the honour to be Sir,
Your obedient Servant,
C. R. Samson.
Commander R.N.

Dec. 4th. 1915.

1) Pilots always to be armed with a revolver or pistol; to carry binoculars; some safety device, either waistcoat, patent life belt or petrol can.
2) Observers always to carry rifle; proper charts for journey (in addition to small scale chart of whole peninsula); binoculars; life saving device or petrol can; watch, if not fitted to the Aeroplane.
3) Pilot is always to examine his control before starting; always to taxi at slow speed; always to lock his control (in Aeroplanes fitted with Samson locking gear) before leaving his seat on completion of flight.
4) Pilot is always to see that he has ample fuel for the flight contemplated.
5) If on arriving near the enemy's lines; the original flight ordered cannot be carried out, the pilot is always to attempt some other flight, i.e:-

    reconnaissance of Anzac, Suvla, transport on roads, or shipping in straits.

    Remember:- anything seen from the air may be of value, and save a flight being wasted.
6) At all times the pilot should carry out independent observations and note down what he sees (noting the times.) Nail a pad of paper on the instrument board for this purpose.
    Particular attention being paid to shipping in the straits.

7) Pilots and observers are to familiarize themselves with the photographs of Turkish Men-of-War described in "The World's Fighting Ships." This book is in the office.
8) On the return from a flight pilot and observer to immediately report to me, or in my absence, to the senior officer present. The observer is to telephone the important part of his report to Hd Qrs and then make out his report. The report is to be made out <u>immediately</u> after the return from a flight.
9) The pilot is immediately to inform the senior ERA & the carpenter of any defects in the engine or aeroplane. He is also to report this to me.
10) In reporting shipping in the Straits, report as follows:
    1. Position of ship
    2. Whether at anchor or underweigh
    3. Nature of ship
        a. If a man of war, - length, number of funnels, number of masts, guns [if seen], name if recognised from photograph.
        b. If a merchant ship: - length, number of funnels, number of masts, general shape.
        c. If the ship is underweigh, note if she is moving
        d. If she is moving: - to where she is heading and what she appears to be doing (see may be patrolling or towing lighters etc).
11) Always make certain of things. Many a backward glance on the return journey will fix the ships destination.
12) Don't exaggerate the size of ships. Practise estimating the size of ships by using the rules in the memo published by me.
13) Don't make wild statements like:-

'Kilia Liman, large number of sailing ships', report as follows:-
'Kilia Liman 11.5 a.m. alongside centre pier, One Dhow about 60ft long. At ancho in bay N.Side. 6 Dhows about 60 ft long.'

A small accurate report is worth pages of rhetoric giving no real information.

14) If the position of a gun cannot be accurately fixed; report:- gun, position could not be fixed accurately but close to 13629.
15) If an enemy aeroplane is sighted, attack it, reporting you are doing so if spotting.
16) Remember in a 'pusher biplane' with a machine gun, you should be a winner everytime [sic], if he stops to fight. Observer must keep cool, and remember to take careful aim and always to open fire with a <u>few</u> shots at long range (adjusting his sight.) Then reserve your fire until within 400 or 500 yards.

17) Always let the pilot know when you are getting close to the end of your belt.
18) Don't open fire until you are certain it is a German. You must not open fire until you have seen the <u>markings</u>.
19) In bomb dropping, always note the effect of the bomb. Good targets for bombs are (1) Camps, (2) Shipping, (3) Stores, (4) Piers, (5) Transport columns.

   Make use of the Sun and wind when arriving to attack and when escaping.
20) Report everything you see however trivial it may appear to you.
21) Always everynow [sic] and then take a look round for Taubes; don't forget to look behind.
22) Never approach your own Aerodrome at a high altitude.
23) The Pilot is always to keep a look out for friendly aeroplanes, and to observe the rule of the road.
24) If another aeroplane is seen about to start from your Aerodrome, don't land until it has started.
25) Don't try and do what is termed by some people as 'Stunt Flying.' This is not wanted for War, and is not conduct required of an officer.
26) Don't dispise [sic] Anti-Aircraft Guns. Remember all the time to give them as little chance as possible compatible with doing your job. i.2. [sic] don't remain flying at the same height, or keeping for long periods on the same course.
27) H. Farman. 130 H.P. Canton Unne: Engine to be throttled to 1250 as soon as you have left the ground and climbed to 300ft; Machine not to be climbed with engine at more than this speed, unless very urgent. Engine to be kept well throttled down all the time after the requisite height is obtained. Pilots are to look at their oil gauges frequently.
28) H. Farman 110 H.P. Renault.

   To be climbed well throttled down after first 300ft.

   These engines suddenly drop revolutions, appearing to be about to stop. Juggling with the throttle will make them pick up again. About every 15 minutes let the engine run at full power for one minute.
29) If the engine fails when out of reach of land: attempt to alight as close to the nearest ship as possible. A Torpedo boat Destroyer for preference.

   Pay attention to the following points when alighting on the water in a land aeroplane.

   1) Always land head to wind.

2) Always alight as slowly as possible.
3) Always get the tail in first.
4) Let go your safety belt before alighting.
5) Release your bombs <u>before</u> alighting and see that you drop them well clear of any ship.

30) If you alight at Suvla or Helles (alight if possible on places marked on chart in Wing Commander's Office.) Remember fire will be opened on the Aeroplane <u>immediately</u>. Leave the neighbourhood of the Aeroplane at once, and wait until the fire ceases. Then remove the instruments and wireless gear. Immediately after landing, the observer is to telephone or signal to Wing Headquarters stating the damage if known, and the safety or otherwise of the crew.

31) M. Farman Aeroplanes: If the engine stops, the observer is to at once look at the main petrol tap. As this sometimes shuts due to vibration.

32) Proceedure [*sic*] to be followed when forced to alight in Hostile territory.
   a) Always land as far away from villages, roads, bodies of troops, camps etc., and on as good a piece of ground as you can find.
   b) Burn the Aeroplane <u>immediately</u>.
   c) Destroy all letters (private and otherwise) charts codes etc.
   d) If another Aeroplane is sighted do not let it alight, unless the <u>ground</u> is good and no enemy are close.
   e) If the ground is good and the coast is clear stand <u>MOTIONLESS</u> to the East of the best landing ground, and at the windward end. Immediately the Aeroplane alights, run after it, turn it, and get in. Don't waste time. It there are two occupants and only one can be taken, the pilot is to be taken.
   f) If the ground is bad or the enemy approaching, stand in a conspicuous position and wave your arms, holding your cap scarf or coat to render them more visible. The Aeroplane will then not alight, but will stay in the neighbourhood as long as possible in case a chance of rescue occurs.
   g) If you have any bombs or grenades in the Aeroplane, and you have time, place them clear of the Aeroplane, unwind the fans, and hope they will detonate on being handled.

Commodore Murray Sueter added a note to the cover of the Admiralty folder this is stored in:

> 'Please note last para   Spirit of Drake the Pirate isn't it?
> MFS 2/1/16'

Appendix three

Ranks of officers in the RNAS in the Dardanelles, 1915

In this book Royal Navy and Royal Marine officers are usually given their naval ranks but there were two separate systems in operation in the RNAS. Officers who had joined the RNAS for flying duties directly from the Royal Navy had RN ranks as well as RNAS ranks. The two were completely separate for seniority and promotion purposes.

Officers who joined for flying duties pre-war from the RFC pool of officers, like Marix, had only RNAS ranks, as did officers who joined the RNAS directly as pilots at the beginning of the war. Those officers who joined the RNAS in a non-flying role kept their RN rank if from the Navy or were RNVR officers if they joined the RNAS direct, like Felix Samson. The following table is a list of selected officers in the RNAS in the Dardanelles to show how this worked.

Name	RNAS rank/seniority	RN rank/seniority
Bell Davies, R	Squadron Commander, 01.07.14	Lieutenant, 30.06.08
Butler, Charles H	Flight Lieutenant, 11.09.14	None
Clark-Hall, Robert H	Squadron Commander, 01.07.14	Lieutenant Commander, 15.10.11
Collet, Charles H	Flight Lieutenant, 01.07.14	Lieutenant, RMA, 01.07.06 Captain, RMA, 23.02.15
Gerrard, Eugene L	Squadron Commander, 01.07.14	Brevet Major, RMLI, 03.01.14
Marix, Reginald L G	Flight Lieutenant, 01.07.14	None
Newton-Clare, Edward	Flight Lieutenant, 01.07.14	None
Osmond, Edward	Flight Lieutenant, 01.07.14	Lieutenant, 30.08.11
Peirse, Richard E C	Flight Lieutenant, 01.07.14	None
Samson, Charles R	Wing Commander, 01.07.14	Acting Commander, 01.01.13
Samson, Felix R	None	Lieutenant, RNVR, 11.08.14
Samson, William L	None	Lieutenant, RNVR, 21.08.14
Wedgwood, Josiah C	None	Lieutenant Commander, RNVR, 15.09.14

Bibliography

Published sources consulted include:

Ash, Eric. *Sir Frederick Sykes and the Air Revolution, 1912-1918*. London: Frank Cass, 1999.

Ashmead-Bartlett, E. *The Uncensored Dardanelles*. London: Forgotten Books, 2012.

Aspinall-Oglander, C F. *Military Operations Gallipoli, vol 1 & 2*. Faber, 1929. Reprint: Nashville: The Battery Press, 1992.

Asquith, H H. *Letters to Venetia Stanley. Selected and edited by Michael & Eleanor Brock*. Oxford: Oxford University Press, 1985.

Bell Davies, Richard. *Sailor in the Air: the memoirs of Vice Admiral Richard Bell Davies*. London: Peter Davies, 1967.

Broadbent, Harvey. *Defending Gallipoli: the Turkish story*. Carlton, Victoria, Australia: Melbourne University Press, 2015.

Burns, Ian M. *Ben-My-Chree*. Leicester: Colin Huston, 2008.

Bush, Eric. *Gallipoli*. London: Allen & Unwin, 1975.

Cassar, George H. *The French and the Dardanelles*. London: Allen & Unwin, 1971.

Chasseaud, Peter, & Doyle, Peter. *Grasping Gallipoli*. Staplehurst, UK: Spellmount, 2005.

Creighton, Rev O. *With the Twenty-Ninth Division in Gallipoli*. Uckfield, UK: Naval & Military Press, 2004.

Dolan, Hugh. *36 Days*. Sidney, Australia: Pan Macmillan, 2010.

Dolan, Hugh. *Gallipoli Air War*. Sidney, Australia: Pan Macmillan, 2013.

Erickson, Edward J. *Ordered to Die: A History of the Ottoman Army in the First World War*. Westport, USA: Greenwood Press, 2001.

Gray, Edwyn A. *The U-Boat War 1914-1918*. 1994

Hamilton, Sir Ian. *Gallipoli War Diary, vol 1 & 2*. Jefferson Publication, 2015.

Hickey, Michael. *Gallipoli*. London: John Murray, 1995.

HMSO. *Lord Kitchener and Winston Churchill: The Dardanelles Part I 1914-15: The First Report of the Dardanelles Commission*. London: The Stationery Office, 2000.

HMSO. *Defeat at Gallipoli: The Dardanelles Part II 1915-16: The Second Report of the Dardanelles Commission*. London: The Stationery Office, 2000.

James, Robert Rhodes. *Gallipoli*. London: B T Batsford Ltd, 1965.

Jones, H A. *The War in the Air, Vol II*. 1928

Journal: Vol 38/2; Vol 44/4; Vol 45/4; Vol 47/1; 47/3; 47/4. Cross & Cockade International.

Keyes, Sir Roger. *The Naval Memoirs*. London: Thornton Butterworth, 1934.
King, Brad. *Royal Naval Air Service 1912-1918*. Crowborough, UK: Hikoki Publications, 1997.
Layman, R D. *Naval Aviation in the First World War*. London: Caxton Editions, 2002.
Lea, John. *Reggie, The Life of Air Vice-Marshal R L G Marix CB DSO*. Durham: Pentland Press, 1994.
Lewis, Bruce. *A Few of the First*. London: Leo Cooper, 1997.
Magnus, Philip. *Kitchener*. London: John Murray, 1958.
Moorehead, Alan. *Gallipoli*. London: Hamish Hamilton, 1956.
Mowthorpe, Ces. *Battlebags: British Airships of the First World War*, Stroud: Wrens Park Publishing, 1995.
Nalder, R F H. *The Royal Corps of Signals*.
Nevinson, Henry W. *The Dardanelles Campaign*. London: Nisbet & Co, 1918.
Newman, Steve. *Gallipoli Then and Now*. London: After the Battle, 2000.
Oliver, John. *Samson and the Dunkirk Circus*. Amazon, 2017
Plummer, Steve. J. *A Man of Invention*. Cloth Wrap Publishing, Amazon, 2010.
Robbins, G J & Rosher, Harold. *In the Royal Naval Air Service*. London: Chatto & Windus, 1916.
Samson, Charles Rumney. *Flights and Fights*. Reprint: Nashville: The Battery Press, 1991.
Sturtivant, Ray & Page, Gordon. *Royal Naval Aircraft Serials and Units 1911-1919*. Tonbridge, UK: Air Britain, 1992.
The Tenedos Times, Monthly Journal of the Mediterranean Destroyer Flotilla. London: George Allen & Unwin, 1917.
Wedgwood, Josiah C. *Memoirs of a Fighting Life*. London: Hutchinson, 1941.
Wedgwood Benn, Captain William. *In the Side Shows*. Nabu Public Domain Reprints, 2010.
Wester-Wemyss, Lord. *The Navy in the Dardanelles Campaign*. Uckfield, UK: Naval & Military Press, 2010.

Websites consulted include:

www.atlantic-cable.com/CableStories/Spalding: A L Spalding's diary, 1915
www.naval-history.net: Log book home page, HMS 'Ark Royal'
www.naval-history.net: Log book home page, HMS 'Vengeance'

Archives consulted include:

The Churchill Archives, Churchill College, Cambridge, CB3 0DS

The Imperial War Museum, Lambeth Road, London SE1 6HZ

The National Archives, Kew, Richmond, Surrey, TW9 4DUTW9 4DUw

    (The following files were particularly useful:)

ADM 1/8418/99	ADM 1/8432/263
ADM 53/44047	ADM 116/1352
ADM 137/177	ADM 137/1089
ADM 156/78	ADM 156/79
AIR 1/11/15/1/44	AIR 1/115/15/39/60
AIR 1/148/15/83/2	AIR 1/184/15/222/2
AIR 1/188/15/226/5	AIR 1/2099/207/20/7
AIR 1/2099/207/20/9	AIR 1/2119/207/72/2
AIR 1/2284/209/75/11	AIR 1/2301/212/7
AIR 1/2659	AIR 1/361/15/228/50
AIR 1/479/15/312/239	AIR 1/669/17/122/788
AIR 1/672/17/134/20	AIR 1/681/21/13/2209
AIR 1/682/21/13/2226	AIR 1/695/21/20/20
AIR 1/7/6/172	AIR 1/724/76/6
AIR 1/726/137/2	AIR 10/1109

Index

2 Squadron RNAS,, 72, 120, 126. *see also 2 Wing RNAS*

3 Squadron RNAS, 2-6, 8, 12, 14, 16, 19, 21-2, 25, 28-9, 31, 33-4, 37-8, 40, 43-4, 47, 51-2, 54-6, 59, 62, 64, 66-7, 71-4, 80-2, 84-6, 88-90, 92, 95, 97-101, 103-8, 110-2, 115-6, 120-23, 125, 182, 184. *also 3 Wing RNAS*

3 Squadron RNAS Armoured Car Section, 63

4 Squadron RNAS Armoured Car Section, 63

2 Wing RNAS, 127, 129, 131-2, 137, 140, 144, 149, 152-5, 157-8, 160-1, 164-6, 168-71, 173-4, 176, 178-81, 184. *see also 2 Squadron RNAS*

3 Wing RNAS, 3, 108, 126-7, 130-2, 137, 141, 144, 148-9, 151-4, 156-8, 160, 162, 164-6, 168-70, 172-6, 178-82, 184-8, 190. *see also 3 Squadron RNAS*

aerial photography, 4, 31, 34, 45, 53, 56, 79. *See also photographic reconnaissance*

airfields, Turkish:
 Canakkale (Chanak), 40, 102, 108, 153
  (Anglo-French bombing raid on, 102)
 Galata, 122, 153
  (Anglo-French bombing raid on, 122)

armoured car sections, 17, 25, 49, 55, 58, 63, 74

Beeton, Leading Mechanic Arthur G, 17, 32, 62, 125, 165

Bell Davies, Squadron Commander Richard, 3, 10-2, 14-7, 22, 28, 41, 51-2, 64, 69, 78, 106-8, 110-3, 115, 117, 121, 123, 144, 149, 153, 165, 169, 171, 179, 182, 194-5
 wins VC, 3, 171

Bill Samson, see Samson, William

Birdwood, Lieutenant General William R, GOC ANZAC Corps, 34, 50, 72-3, 103, 148, 162-3, 167, 185-6

bombing, *passim*

bombing raids, 33, 44, 80, 152, 158, 168, 170

Busk, Flight Commander Hans O, 161, 170, 174, 176, 181

Butler, Flight Lieutenant Charles H, 15, 28, 31, 37, 44, 50, 52, 59, 67, 85, 97-8, 106, 144, 185, 194

Cape Helles landing strip, 54, 61, 64, 69, 85, 91, 93, 185, 193

Césari, Capitaine Antoine, 20, 56, 66-7, 69, 105, 147, 150, 178, 181

Churchill, Winston S, First Lord of the Admiralty, 1, 43, 76-7, 96, 183, 195, 197

Clark-Hall, Commander Robert H, 6-7, 14, 19, 22, 25-6, 28, 47, 53, 80, 98, 114, 194

Collet, Captain Charles H, 10, 12, 14-5, 28, 33, 38-41, 51, 71, 92, 107, 115, 130-1, 194

de Robeck, Vice-Admiral Sir John, 18-9, 24, 29, 34, 36, 68, 75, 78, 87, 90, 94, 99, 103, 106-8, 110, 115, 120, 142, 147-8, 163, 166-8, 172, 175, 185

Felix Samson, *see Samson, Felix*

French squadron, *see L'escadrille MF 98 T*

Gerrard, Wing Commander Eugene L, 120-1, 125-6, 132, 144, 147, 150-1, 155, 168, 174, 178, 182, 184, 194

Hamilton, General Sir Ian S, 34, 39, 42, 45-6, 49, 51-2, 54, 58, 64, 73, 85-6, 97-8, 101, 103, 108, 111, 115-7, 119, 122, 131, 135-6, 141, 148, 150, 157, 160, 162-3, 176, 183-5, 195

HMS 'Ark Royal', seaplane carrier, 2, 5-8, 12-4, 18-22, 24-9, 33, 35, 38, 40-1, 47, 52-4, 62-3, 65, 67-8, 70-2, 74-

5, 79-80, 83, 87, 90, 93, 95-6, 98, 103, 105-7, 109, 111-3, 115, 127, 130-4, 137, 140-1, 143, 149, 152, 155, 157, 159, 163, 165-6, 168, 170-1, 173, 176, 178, 184

HMS 'Ben-my-Chree', seaplane carrier, 3-4, 80, 83, 89, 95, 107, 113, 124, 127, 131, 133, 137-9, 143, 148-9, 152, 156-7, 159, 163, 166, 168-71, 173, 176, 178-9

HMS 'Hector', kite balloon ship, 83-4, 95, 101, 103-6, 109, 113, 119, 124-5, 127, 137, 142-3, 146, 152, 156, 160, 164, 166, 168, 170-1, 173, 178, 184

HMS 'Manica', kite balloon ship, 3, 5, 33-7, 41, 44, 47-8, 52-5, 59, 62, 65, 67, 74, 80, 83, 95, 101-3, 114, 119, 124, 127, 145, 156, 184

Hogg, Major R E T, 37, 50-1, 72, 88, 92

Hunter-Weston, Major-General Aylmer, 4, 37, 44, 45, 48-9, 54, 58, 63-4, 84-5

Imbros, island and airfield, 3, 18-9, 34, 66, 72, 74-5, 79, 81, 84, 87, 92-4, 96, 103, 107-12, 114-5, 122-3, 127, 129-31, 134, 136-7, 143-4, 146, 148-9, 151, 153-4, 156, 158-62, 167, 169-70, 173, 175, 178, 180-2, 188

intelligence and intelligence reports, 4, 14, 34, 38, 40, 43-4, 51, 62-4, 67, 72-4, 90, 98, 102-3, 106-7, 112, 117, 141, 149, 152, 156, 162, 183, 185-7

intelligence distribution system, 3 Squadron/Wing, 34, 38, 39, 58, 64

Isaac, Lieutenant Bernard, intelligence officer, 3 Squadron/Wing, 25, 29, 33-4, 37-40, 43-4, 52, 58, 61, 64, 67, 71-2, 103, 106, 108, 121, 141-2, 149-50, 154, 161

Jopp, *see Keith-Jopp*

Keith-Jopp, 90, 100, 129-32, 146, 170, 174, 17

Kephalo Point airfield, Imbros, 107, 127 *See also Imbros*

Kilner, Captain Cecil F, 6-7, 13, 26, 28, 47, 53, 62-3, 68, 71, 74-5, 79, 109

Kitchener, Lord K of Khartoum, Secretary of State for War, 1, 34, 39, 42, 76-7, 97, 116, 119, 136, 160, 162-3, 167, 172, 183, 195-6

kite balloon sections, 35, 46, 119

L'escadrille MF 98 T, 9, 31, 55-6, 66, 89, 92, 99, 105-6, 110, 147, 150

L'Estrange Malone, Commander Cecil J, 80, 83, 89, 101, 103, 113, 138-40, 184

Longmore, Wing Commander Arthur M, 2, 120-1, 126

Mackworth, Flight Commander John D, 35-7, 41, 145

Marix, 9, 12, 14, 25, 28, 44, 50-2, 61, 64, 71, 91, 100, 106-8, 110, 117, 144, 161, 194, 196

night bombing, 99, 170

Osmond, Lieutenant Edward, 12, 15, 28, 40, 50, 52, 60, 72, 99-100, 194

Peirse, Flight Lieutenant Richard E, 28, 33, 38, 40, 51, 70, 100, 194

photographic map, 34, 37, 40, 142

photographic reconnaissance, 4, 31, 39-40, 50, 62, 71, 92, 106, 132, 144, 149, 151, 155-6, 158, 160-1, 164, 166, 168, 170, 172-3, 176, 180-1

reconnaissance and reconnaissance flights, *passim*

Samson, Commander Charles Rumney, *passim*

Samson, Lieutenant Felix, 100, 107, 194

Samson, Lieutenant William, 12, 52, 94, 100, 170, 194

Sea Scout airships, *see SS airships*

Sissmore, Midshipman John E, 50, 113, 175

Spalding, Alfred L, 60-1, 63, 78, 196

spotting, *passim*

spotting, method used by 3 Squadron, 32-3

SS airships, 3, 72, 85, 114, 118, 122, 127, 143, 146, 149, 158, 184

SS3, 114, 118, 146

SS7, 146

SS19, 114, 118, 146

SS 'Levant I', cable ship, 84, 184

SS 'Levant II', cable ship, 54-6, 58, 60, 62-3, 66-7, 70, 78, 84, 92, 106, 134, 143, 145, 147, 154, 156, 159, 184

SS 'River Clyde', 49, 50-2

Standing Orders, 3 Squadron/Wing, 186, 190-3

Submarine Scout (SS) airship, *see SS airship*

Sueter, Commodore Murray, 2, 59, 78-9, 89, 93, 95-7, 110, 120-1, 134, 154, 193

Sykes, Brevet Lieutenant Colonel Frederick, 94-5, 103, 105-8, 110, 120-1, 127, 130-2, 134, 141-2, 146, 149, 154, 161, 166, 168, 181, 195

telephone communications, 37, 48, 54, 56, 58, 61, 64-5, 67, 71, 175, 191, 193

Tenedos, island and airfield, 3-4, 6-8, 10, 18-25, 28-34, 37-41, 43, 46, 51-2, 54, 56-8, 61-2, 64, 66-7, 70, 79, 81-2, 84, 86-7, 89, 91-3, 97, 99-100, 102, 104-7, 109-10, 112, 134, 147, 150, 156, 181, 196

Thomson, Flight Lieutenant G L, 12, 28, 31, 51, 67, 98, 106, 144, 170, 182

torpedo operations, seaplanes, 3, 80, 83, 89, 101, 124, 128-9

trench maps, 106

Warner, Lieutenant R, RM, 39-40, 92, 97

Wedgwood, Lieutenant Commander Josiah C, 17, 49, 55, 58, 63, 194, 196

Williamson, Flight Commander Hugh A, 6, 8, 13

W/T or wireless, 26, 29, 33, 35, 37, 41-2, 47-8, 50, 58-9, 64-5, 72, 83, 88, 97, 102, 106, 113-4, 118, 121, 142, 148, 151, 155, 157-8, 161, 184-5, 193

CPSIA information can be obtained
at www.ICGtesting.com
Printed in the USA
LVHW051005270519
619122LV00031B/683/P